AVADE®

WORKPLACE VIOLENCE PREVENTION

Healthcare Advanced Student Guide

Education, Prevention & Mitigation for Violence in the Workplace

D1369809

David Fowler

Founder and Author of
AVADE® Workplace Violence Training Programs

Healthcare Advanced Student Guide

Education, Prevention & Mitigation for Violence in the Workplace

ISBN: 978-198166574-7

Disclaimer

The author and the publisher, Personal Safety Training, Inc., do not dictate policies or procedures for the use of any violence prevention, self-defense, or any physical intervention authorized for use by a department/agency or private individual. The suggestions/options disseminated in this book are simply that, suggestions or options. Each individual, department, or agency is responsible for developing their own "policies and procedures" regarding the use of violence prevention, self-defense, and physical intervention for their personnel and for themselves. Although every effort has been made for this book to be complete and accurate, it is impossible to predict, discuss or plan for every circumstance or situation which might arise in the course of defending yourself during any contact with a violent or aggressive person(s) or during a crime.

Every reader must always take into consideration his/her experience, physical abilities, professional responsibilities, agency and department procedures, and local, state, and federal legal requirements. With this in mind, each reader must evaluate the recommendations and techniques contained in this book and decide for himself (herself) which should be used and under what circumstances. Each reader assumes the risk of loss, injury, and damages associated with this book and the use of the information obtained in it. The author and publisher, Personal Safety Training, Inc., cannot guarantee or warrant the legal, medical, tactical, or technical suggestions/options in this book. **ANY IMPLIED WARRANTIES ARE EXPRESSLY DISAVOWED.**

Personal Safety Training Inc. Telephone: (208) 691-7481
www.AVADEtraining.com www.PersonalSafetyTraining.com

Also, by David Fowler
Violence In The Workplace, Violence In the Workplace II, Violence In the Workplace III,
Be Safe Not Sorry, To Serve and Protect, SURVIVE an Active Shooter

ACKNOWLEDGEMENTS

I would like to thank the many teachers, instructors, mentors, and friends that have helped make this program a reality. Without your help, inspiration, and invaluable knowledge, this wouldn't have been possible.
To all of you, I am eternally grateful.

I would also like to thank the thousands of individuals that I have worked with whose direct and indirect contribution to this program has made it possible for me to do what I feel on purpose to do.

Special thanks to the following individuals for their support and technical advice: Jason Blessinger, Carter Fowler, Genelle Fowler, Patrick Gibney, Brian Goodwin, Jamie Lang, and Eduardo Montez.

I would also like to thank my family for their support; I love you all so much!

David Fowler
Founder, AVADE® Personal Safety Training & Workplace Violence Prevention Programs
President, Personal Safety Training, Inc.

ii

CONTENTS

xii

Introduction to Violence in the Workplace

Incidents of Workplace Violence happen every second, minute, and hour of each day in the United States. OSHA and the CDC have declared that workplace violence is now an epidemic in some industries. Hospitals, government, law enforcement, and corporate security continue to tighten down, but there are steps YOU can take, as an individual, to protect yourself from violence while on the job.

AVADE® Workplace Violence Prevention Training and **education** designed for agencies to **prevent** and **mitigate** the risk of violence to individuals in **Healthcare** and **Corporate** workplace environments.

The **AVADE® WPV Prevention** training program meets the requirements of State and Federal guidelines, as well as OSHA's General Duty Clause, to provide employees with a workplace free from recognized hazards likely to cause death or serious physical harm.

*AVADE® Training also meets Healthcare's Joint Commission Regulatory Compliance/Standard for maintaining a Workplace Violence Prevention Training program.

An employer's overall plan should include administrative, behavioral, and environmental strategies to prevent and mitigate the risk of workplace violence.
The AVADE® training course provides this level of education and will also empower you to:

- Identify, prevent, and respond to workplace violence by using universal precautions against violence by applying the principles of the AVADE® Workplace Violence Prevention training.
- Learn the characteristics of aggressive and violent individuals, patients, guests, and visitors in the workplace environment.
- Enhance your safety by utilizing verbal and physical maneuvers to diffuse and avoid violent and aggressive behavior.
- Learn the predicting factors of aggression and violence in the workplace and how they are related to the components of assault, and how to respond accordingly.
- Learn strategies to avoid physical harm by applying the principles of time and distance.

The **AVADE® Workplace Violence Prevention Training Program** was researched and developed to be the most complete and effective workplace violence prevention training program. The **AVADE® WPV Prevention Training Program** is tailored specifically to the unique needs and dynamics of the healthcare and corporate environments.

Have YOU Experienced or Been a Victim of Workplace Violence?

Have you ever...

- Been Verbally Harassed?
- Been Intimidated by Someone?
- Been Threatened by Someone?
- Received Obscene Phone Calls / Cyber Comm?
- Had Your Property Damage?
- Been Robbed (Robbery)?
- Been Involved in a Bomb Threat Situation?
- Had Someone Verbally Assault You?
- Witnessed a Completed or Attempted Suicide?
- Been Stalked by Someone?
- Had a Road Rage Situation?
- Experienced Gang Violence?
- Been Physically Assaulted?
    - Pushed, Shoved, Grabbed, Kicked, or Slapped
    - Been the Target of Edged Weapon or Guns
    - Been the Target of Sexual Assault/Harassment
- Been Taken Hostage/Kidnapped?
- Been Threatened/Attacked with a Weapon?
- Been Involved in a Terrorism Incident?

If you answered YES to any of the above questions, then you have witnessed or experienced workplace violence.

Barriers to Reporting Incidents of WPV[1]

- A culture that considers workplace violence part of the job - **"it's just part of the job."**
- **Fear** of being accused of **inadequate performance** or of **being blamed** for the incident, and **fear of retaliation** by the offender and or the employer/supervisor.
- Lack of awareness of the **reporting system**.
- A **belief** that **reporting will not change** the current systems or decrease the potential for future incidents of violence (**complacency**).
- A **belief** that the incident was **not serious enough to report**. Unintentional violence, e.g., incidents involving Alzheimer's patients, Behavioral Health, on/off Meds, etc.
- **Lack of manager and employer support** and training **related to reporting** and managing workplace violence.
- A lack of agreement on **definitions of violence**, e.g., does it include verbal harassment?

    Removing these barriers requires a multifront strategy and the buy-in from staff and their employer.

---

[1] https://www.nursingworld.org/~495349/globalassets/docs/ana/ethics/endabuse-issue-brief-final.pdf

Workplace Violence Defined

Workplace Violence: <u>Any act of aggression</u>, verbal assault, physical assault, or threatening behavior that occurs in the workplace environment and causes physical or emotional harm to guests, patients, staff, or visitors.

The National Institute for Occupational Safety and Health Administration (NIOSH) and the Occupational Safety and Health Administration (OSHA) defines workplace violence as any physical assault, threatening behavior, or verbal abuse occurring in the workplace. Violence includes overt and covert behaviors ranging in aggressiveness from verbal harassment to murder.

The Myths of Workplace Violence

There are several dangerous myths about workplace violence. Knowing the truth will help you to be better prepared if you ever face an incident of workplace violence.

1. **It won't happen here!**
2. **There is nothing we can do about it.**
3. **Management and the Agency just don't care.**

Myth #1: That would never happen where I work.
Workplace violence can happen at any place of employment, with social services and healthcare being the highest in non-fatal assaults against employees.

Myth #2: There's nothing you can do about it. People just snap. You can't predict it.
This is, perhaps, the most dangerous myth about workplace violence. In virtually every case, there were signs that the violent person was escalating and about to perpetrate a crime. The only caveat to this is that we don't always have the opportunity to see the signs. A person may just walk into your place of business and go off. This is more prevalent in healthcare, law enforcement, and security industries as their work is based on emergent needs. Prevention is the key to creating a safe and friendly environment for guests and visitors, as well as a safer workplace for staff. It IS possible to prevent and reduce the effects of violence. The most important step is to establish a comprehensive program in the workplace dedicated to education, preventing and mitigating violence, tracking incidents, and providing support for those affected.

Myth #3: My employer doesn't care.
Employers do understand the risks and do care. Many employers are adopting policies and procedures for preventing workplace violence. Aside from the human cost, workplace violence costs businesses a lot of money and productivity.

The Cost of Workplace Violence

ESTIMATED COSTS

The costs to US businesses is estimated at more than **$120 billion dollars per year.**

NON-FATAL ASSAULTS

Non-fatal workplace assaults equal **876,000 lost workdays per year. Millions** in lost wages yearly.

JURY AWARDS

The average jury award where the **employer failed** to take proactive, preventive measures under **OSHA guidelines** equals **$3.1 million per person/incident.**

Currently, there is no federal standard that requires workplace violence protections. However, The **Occupational Safety and Health Act of 1970** (OSH Act)1 mandates that, in addition to compliance with hazard-specific standards, all employers have a general duty to **provide their employees with a workplace free from recognized hazards** likely to cause.

OSHA will rely on Section 5a-1 of the OSH Act, the "**General Duty Clause,**" for enforcement authority. Failure to implement these guidelines is not in itself a violation of the General Duty Clause; however, employers can be cited for violating the General Duty Clause if there is a recognized hazard of workplace violence in their establishments, and they do nothing to prevent or abate it. These standards address employee safety and security risks.

In September of 2011, OSHA announced a new directive targeting workplace violence prevention. In this directive, OSHA is actively investigating and citing employers for failure to keep their workplace safe from threats and incidents of workplace violence. Some states have sought legislative solutions, including mandatory establishment of a comprehensive prevention program for employers and employees.

As a participant going through AVADE® Workplace Violence Prevention Training. Ask your employer if they have adopted policies and procedures and response training for preventing workplace violence. If not, request to have AVADE® procedures and policy implementation. At the very least, integrate these safety habits. Ultimately, your personal safety is YOUR responsibility, however your employer may simply not know what's available for you and your co-workers. www.avadetraining.com

Crime and Violence in Society

Crime and violence in our society impact businesses and workplaces on a scale that may not be measurable by statistical data. Violence in the workplace is commonly understood as any physical assault, emotional or verbal abuse, or threatening, harassing, or coercive behavior in the work setting that causes physical or emotional harm.

Violence Statistics

2020 Major Cities' Reported Crimes[2]

- 2020 was the first year in over a century that the crime rate rose by 13% in one year
- Los Angeles police reported 322 homicides, up 30% from 2019
- New York City police reported 437 homicides, up 40% from 2019
- Chicago police reported more than 750 murders, up 50% from 2019
- Murder rates from 2019 to 2020 were up 36.7% across 57 major cities

2020 Unprecedented Murder Spike in Major Cities[3]

- Seattle saw the largest spike with a 74.1% increase in homicide rates from 2019
- Murders were up in 51 out of 57 major US cities
- New York mayor told NPR: "it's certainly related to the fact that the criminal justice system is on pause [due to COVID-19 restrictions], and that's causing a lot of problems."

2020 Crime Statistics[4]

- January to June 2020: Aggravated assault offenses were up 4.6% from 2019
- 63 of the 66 largest police jurisdictions saw increases in at least one category of violent crimes in 2020 (including homicide, rape, robbery, or aggravated assault)[5]
- May to June 2020, homicides in 20 major US cities increased by 37%, led by Chicago, Philadelphia, and Milwaukee[6]
- Aggravated assaults were up by 35%

2   https://www.npr.org/2021/01/06/953254623/massive-1-year-rise-in-homicide-rates-collided-with-the-pandemic-in-2020
3   https://www.statista.com/chart/23905/change-in-homicides-in-us-cities/
4   https://www.fbi.gov/news/pressrel/press-releases/overview-of-preliminary-uniform-crime-report-january-june-2020
5   https://www.cnn.com/2021/04/03/us/us-crime-rate-rise-2020/index.html
6   https://www.cnn.com/2020/08/16/us/violent-crime-soars-confidence-in-police-takes-hit/index.html

Potential Reasons for 2020 Crime Spike[7]

- After the George Floyd incident in May 2020, confidence in police decreased for Americans.

- Law enforcement experts: diminished public confidence in the police and increased rates of violent crime in American cities go hand in hand.

- The crime increases in the spring and summer of 2020 coincided with:

  - Fewer pandemic-related shutdowns

  - Mass unemployment due to the pandemic

  - Protests condemning police violence against minorities

  - Summer when crime normally increases.[8]

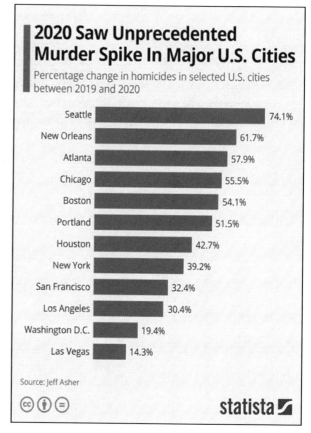

2020 Saw Unprecedented Murder Spike In Major U.S. Cities

Percentage change in homicides in selected U.S. cities between 2019 and 2020

Seattle	74.1%
New Orleans	61.7%
Atlanta	57.9%
Chicago	55.5%
Boston	54.1%
Portland	51.5%
Houston	42.7%
New York	39.2%
San Francisco	32.4%
Los Angeles	30.4%
Washington D.C.	19.4%
Las Vegas	14.3%

Source: Jeff Asher

statista

2021 Crime Statistics & Potential Causes[9]

- Crime surge of 33% from 2019 to 2020 remained increasing into the first quarter of 2021

- Homicides in Chicago were up 33% in the first three months of 2021 compared to 2020, while shootings are up nearly 40% for the same period year-over-year.

- Experts noted a "perfect storm" of factors for rising crime rates:
  - Economic collapse, pandemic lockdowns ending, de-policing in major cities after protests that called for the abolition of police departments, shifts in police resources from neighborhoods to downtown areas because of said protests, and the release of criminal defendants pretrial or before sentences were completed to reduce risk of Covid-19 spread in jails.

- 2020 was the deadliest gun violence year on record. Comparatively, 2021 is set to be even deadlier.

- Jan.- May 2021, gun violence killed 8,100 people in the US. 54 lives were lost each day.

---

[7] https://www.cnn.com/2020/08/16/us/violent-crime-soars-confidence-in-police-takes-hit/index.html
[8] https://www.cnn.com/2020/08/16/us/nyc-chicago-gun-violence/index.html
[9] https://www.cnn.com/2021/04/03/us/us-crime-rate-rise-2020/index.html

Healthcare Workplace Violence Statistics

- Healthcare workers are more likely to be victimized by workplace violence than any other industry.[10]

- Healthcare leads all other sectors in incidents of non-fatal assaults. Nearly 4-5x greater than all other sectors.

- Healthcare workers are more likely to be attacked than prison guards or police officers.

- Nurses are most at risk, with female nurses being the most vulnerable.

- Acts of workplace violence (WPV) can cause physical and/or psychological harm to emergency nurses.

- WPV can lead to job dissatisfaction, emotional exhaustion, burnout, secondary traumatic stress, PTSD, absenteeism, and intentions to leave the job or nursing profession, all of which have potential impacts on patient care.

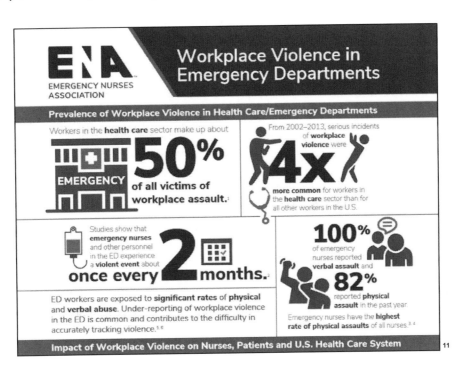

Workplace violence can be devastating to deal with. If you have suffered from a violent incident, you may need to seek some type of assistance (Employee Assistance Program). Learning the **AVADE® techniques** in the training course and in this student guide, and integrating them into your life and habits, will help ensure that you know what to look for. This will reduce the chances of YOU becoming a victim of workplace violence.

---

10 https://www.bls.gov/iif/oshwc/cfoi/workplace-violence-healthcare-2018.htm
11 https://dailynurse.com/workplace-violence-in-the-ed-nurses-physicians-launch-new-campaign/

AVADE® WPV Safety Principles

The AVADE® philosophy incorporates learning new habits, skills, and actions that employers and employees can use to enhance their de-escalation skills, personal safety, and their ability to defend themselves or others from dangerous situations, crime, and violence.

AVADE® training programs are based on the Workplace Violence Safety Principles:

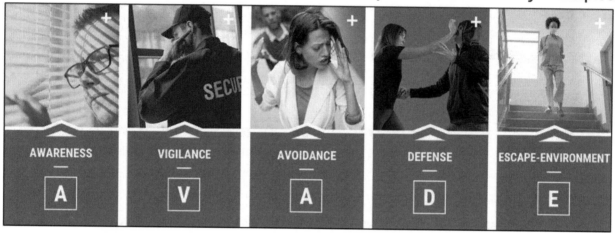

AWARENESS	VIGILANCE	AVOIDANCE	DEFENSE	ESCAPE-ENVIRONMENT
A	V	A	D	E

AVADE® has been taught in private corporations, healthcare agencies, schools, community programs, and civic institutions for many years. The founder of the AVADE® Training programs, David Fowler, has over thirty years of experience and has made personal safety training his life's work. He has an extensive background in training, martial science, use-of-force, and all functions of security management and operations. He is also the author of *Be Safe Not Sorry: The Art and Science of Keeping You and Your Family Safe from Crime and Violence*, available on amazon.com and at his websites:

www.personalsafetytraining.com and **www.avadetraining.com**

"The overall vision and philosophy of the AVADE® Training program is the moral essence of life itself: to live a safe and positive life with peace, security, harmony and freedom of choice." "Creating a Culture of Safety in the Workplace and the Life-Place."

AVADE® System Exercise

_____

_____

_____

_____

_____

_____

_____

_____

_____

AVADE® Workplace Violence Prevention is Evidence-Based Training

AVADE® WPV Prevention Training is based on research from OSHA, FBI, ASIS, IAHSS, CDC, NIOSH, TJC, SHRM, BLS, State WPV Laws, Department of Labor & Industries, the Dept. of Justice, and more...

- **OSHA – Occupational Safety and Health** Administration Safety & Health Topics – WPV **http://www.osha.gov/SLTC/workplaceviolence/**

- **OSHA – Occupational Safety and Health Administration** Guidelines for Preventing Workplace Violence for Health Care & Social Service Workers **(OSHA 3148-01R 2004) http://www.osha.gov/Publications/osha3148.pdf**

- **What is Workplace Violence - OSHA Fact Sheet** **http://www.osha.gov/OshDoc/data_General_Facts/factsheet-workplace-violence.pdf**

- **FBI – Federal Bureau of Investigation** Workplace Violence Issues in Response **https://www.fbi.gov/stats-services/publications/workplace-violence**

- **FBI:** Workplace Violence Prevention Readiness and Response **https://leb.fbi.gov/2011/january/workplace-violence-prevention-readiness-and-response**

- **ANA – American Nurses Association** Workplace Violence in the Healthcare Settings **http://nursingworld.org/workplaceviolence**

- **Workplace Violence in Healthcare Recognized, but not Regulated** **http://www.nursingworld.org/MainMenuCategories/ANAMarketplace/ANAPeriodicals/OJIN/TableofContents/Volume92004/No3Sept04/ViolenceinHealthCare.aspx**

- **ENA (Emergency Nurses Association) Emergency Department Violence Surveillance Study https://www.ena.org/practice-research/research/Documents/ENAEDVSReportNovember2011.pdf**

- **CDC – Centers for Disease Control and Prevention** Occupational Violence **http://www.cdc.gov/niosh/topics/violence/**

- **NIOSH – National Institute for Occupational Safety and Health** Workplace Violence Prevention Strategies & Research **http://www.cdc.gov/niosh/docs/2006-144/pdfs/2006-144.pdf**

- **Bureau of Labor Statistics (BLS)** U.S. Department of Labor, Bureau of Labor Statistics *Census of Fatal Occupational Injuries* **http://www.bls.gov/iif/oshwc/cfoi/cftb0286.pdf**

- **IAHSS (International Association for Healthcare Security & Safety)** **http://www.iahss.org/?page=guidelines**

- **U.S. Department of Labor, Bureau of Labor Statistics** Survey of Occupational Injuries and Illnesses **http://www.bls.gov/news.release/osh2.nr0.htm**

- **WISHA Regional Directive Department of Labor and Industries** Violence in the Workplace **http://www.lni.wa.gov/Safety/Rules/Policies/PDFs/WRD505.pdf**

- **Washington Department of Labor and Industries** Workplace Violence: Awareness and Prevention for Employers and Employees **http://www.lni.wa.gov/IPUB/417-140-000.pdf**

- **U.S. Department of Justice, Bureau of Justice Statistics** Criminal Victimization, 2014 **http://www.bjs.gov/content/pub/pdf/cv14.pdf**

- **State Healthcare Laws and Guidelines for Preventing Workplace Violence:** CA - **http://codes.findlaw.com/ca/health-and-safety-code/hsc-sect-1257-8.html** WA - **http://www.lni.wa.gov/Safety/Topics/AtoZ/WPV/RCW49-19.asp** OR - **http://www.orosha.org/resource-newsletter/2015/08/Feat02.html**

- **WISHA Regional Directive Department of Labor and Industries Violence in the** Workplacehttp://www.lni.wa.gov/Safety/Rules/Policies/PDFs/WRD505.pdf

- **The Joint Commission:** Sentinel Event Alert Issue, Preventing Violence in the healthcare setting. **http://www.jointcommission.org/sentinel_event_alert_issue_45_preventing_violence_in_ the_health_care_setting_/**

- **SHRM – Society for Human Resources Management:** Violence Prevention Programs **http://www.shrm.org/hrdisciplines/orgempdev/articles/pages/violence-prevention- programs.aspx**

A comprehensive look at the **AVADE® Training's** research can be found in the bibliography at the back of this student guide.

The AVADE® Workplace Violence Prevention system is designed to give you the training and education you'll need in the prevention and mitigation of violence in the workplace. Agencies must also consider and implement the appropriate administrative, behavioral, and environmental categories for developing protocols and procedures for their workplace violence prevention plan.

AVADE® Workplace Violence Prevention Modules and Objectives

AVADE® Training is a modular-based training program that can be taught in:
E-Learning - Employee orientation - 2-hour sessions – 4-hour sessions – 8-hour sessions – 2-day and 3-day sessions - Or presented during safety or departmental meetings throughout a 12-month period. - Or modular training combining classroom, self-defense, and defensive control tactics—4-8+ hrs.

AVADE® WPV Prevention Level I Modules & Objectives

AVADE® principles and learning objectives are integrated throughout the administrative, behavioral, and environmental components of an effective workplace violence prevention plan.

1. **Awareness:** How to increase your overall **awareness** of worker risks of violence (i.e., your vulnerability in the workplace) and provide **strategies** to **prevent** and **mitigate** these risks.

2. **Vigilance:** The **characteristics** of violence and the **predicting factors** related to violence.

3. **Avoidance:** How incidents of workplace violence are **reduced** and **eliminated** through **administrative, behavioral,** and **environmental** protocols and procedures.

4. **Interpersonal Communications:** The **assault cycle** and how to develop skills to **de-escalate** the different types of aggressive behaviors; these are important factors in mitigating workplace violence.

5. **Defense of Self and Others:** How to **mitigate liability risk** through proper **documentation** and how reasonable **use of force** can be used to defend oneself or others.

6. **Stress Management:** Methods of **team debriefing, post-incident response**, and **techniques** for dealing with daily stressors.

7. **Time & Distance:** Understand the **reactionary response** to a physical or weapon **assault situation.**

8. **Escape Planning:** Pre-plan **escape routes** from all environments, as well as learning **physical maneuvers** and **positioning** to prevent isolation and assaultive situations.

9. **Environmental Factors:** Understand appropriate **safety techniques** and **departmental systems** and procedures for the **different areas** of the workplace.

10. **Emergency Codes and Procedures:** Provide and **increase awareness** of the agency's **protocols and procedures** for responding to an emergent situation.

The AVADE® Training Program is Incorporated into Three Training Levels:

Level I – Education, Prevention and Mitigation for Violence in the Workplace
Level II – Self-Defense Tactics and Techniques
Level III – Defensive Control Tactics and Techniques

AVADE® Level I Education, Prevention, and Mitigation of WPV

- Awareness
- Vigilance
- Avoidance
- Interpersonal Communication
- Defense of Self and Others
- Stress Management
- Time & Distance
- Escape Planning
- Environmental Factors
- Emergency Codes and Procedures

AVADE® Level II Self-Defense Tactics

- The Goal of Self-Defense
- Fundamentals of Self-Defense
- Defensive Blocking Techniques
- PDT's (Personal Defensive Techniques)
- Defense from Physical Assaults (Frontal)
- Defense from Physical Assaults (Rear)
- Elements of Reporting Self-Defense and Use-of-Force

AVADE® Level III Defensive Control Tactics

- Introduction to Defensive Control
- Fundamentals of Defensive Control
- Contact and Cover Positioning
- Escort Strategies and Techniques
- Control and Decentralization Techniques
- Healthcare Restraint Techniques
- Elements of Reporting Self-Defense and Use-of-Force

The AVADE® Level II and III training is designed for agencies to mitigate the potential of injury and liability risk when using lawful defenses or controlling an aggressive individual.

The tactics and techniques in this training curriculum are for incidents where the aggressor is physically combative, resistive, and unarmed.

The **AVADE® Workplace Violence Prevention** Training program will teach you how to recognize emerging situations, how to deal with someone (de-escalation) before they become violent, how to survive and escape a violent attack, and much, much more. Read carefully. Integrate the lessons you learn here. Unfortunately, one day you may be responsible for saving your own life—and the lives of your co-workers.

AVADE® Level I Education, Prevention and Mitigation of WPV (All Staff Training)

_____
_____
_____
_____
_____
_____
_____
_____
_____

AVADE® Level II Self-Defense Tactics (Staff at Risk)

_____
_____
_____
_____
_____
_____
_____

AVADE® Level III Defensive Control Tactics (High-Risk Staff)

_____
_____
_____
_____
_____
_____
_____

Creating an Effective Workplace Violence Prevention Plan

The Three Categories of an Effective Workplace Violence Prevention Plan

There are many components to the administrative policies, practices, and procedures for a successful workplace violence prevention system.

Administrative Protocols and Procedures

Workplace Violence Prevention Policy: A comprehensive zero-tolerance policy that strictly prohibits violence and threats against those in the workplace, as well as other behaviors deemed inappropriate, is the foundation of preventing workplace violence.

No Reprisal Reporting Policy: It's vital to create an atmosphere where employees feel safe reporting strange, threatening, or abusive behavior. If employees fear reprisal, people in authority may never know that an employee, client, or guest is behaving in a threatening manner. Some employers have instituted anonymous caller lines, where employees can leave information and keep their anonymity.

Documentation and Record-Keeping: Documentation is essential in reducing the liability an agency could be exposed to. If an employee needs to be terminated or a client or guest needs to be barred from the premises, documentation of inappropriate behavior will be necessary for legal purposes. Proper documentation also allows companies to mitigate risk in certain areas that have been identified through tracking and trending.

Incident Reporting Procedures/Structures: Many states require that all workplace incidents/injuries be reported to the Department of Labor and Industries or other regulatory agencies. Proper reporting structures must be in place for managers and supervisors. Employees need to be trained to identify and report incidents that could be indicative of an emerging problem.

Security Management Prevention Plan: A security management plan helps employers identify risk factors and risk areas. Once identified, a well-trained security manager and the team can respond to, and more importantly, prevent situations from escalating to violence. This proactive response planning identifies potential risk factors with strategies to prevent, reduce, and eliminate risks to staff, clients, and guests.

Management Commitment and Employee Involvement: **AVADE** training has many components ranging from basic employee awareness training to advanced training. We recognize that security, management, supervisors, human resources personnel, and department directors play a unique role in workplace violence prevention and will need more tools. Using **AVADE®** training and principles, everyone in an organization can participate in keeping the workplace safe. Overall, to successfully prevent and mitigate workplace violence, the commitment must come from the top down. It's essential to get leadership buy-in.

Emergency Code Procedures and Response: Module 10 discusses some common emergent situations that happen in all industries. Lives can be saved by things as simple as knowing where your exits are, knowing how to dial 911 out from a company line, and knowing where alarm buttons are. Proper training in emergency codes and response is critical.

Departmental Risk Level Assessment: Certain risk factors help us identify if a department is a low, medium, or high risk. Department managers must also have the training to identify potentially dangerous situations and know the procedures for responding to and reporting them. Many companies utilize the security management plan to help identify risk factors in all departments and work areas.

Workplace Violence Program evaluation: Workplace violence is a three-pronged process: *administrative, behavioral, environmental*. An employer's overall program should be reviewed periodically to ensure its effectiveness. As the environment changes in the workplace, so will the plan needed to reduce potential risks.

Human Resources: HR plays an integral role in the development and implementation of successful workplace violence prevention, mitigation, and intervention planning. Policy development, staff training, incident tracking and reporting, union negotiations, departmental coordination efforts, and disciplinary actions to enforce policies are key components in which human resources involvement is necessary.

Human Resources Hiring and Termination Protocols and Procedures: With consistent, careful pre-employment background checks, many problems can be averted. Termination procedures should be handled correctly and consistently by trained individuals who understand the potential risk factors and warning signs of workplace violence.

Legal Counsel: Using in-house or an outside firm for an understanding of the legal obligations related to workplace violence is essential to an organization.

Threat Assessment Team: A threat assessment team is a group of individuals, usually comprised of security management, human resources, department heads, administration, and others. This team evaluates the risk factors of an individual with warning signs who have been recently disciplined, terminated, or is being investigated for workplace violence. The team collaborates and determines the best course of action. During high-risk assessments, a clinical psychologist specializing in workplace violence may need to be retained from an established reputable consulting firm.

Staffing Levels: Particularly in retail and health care settings, it's vital that sufficient personnel are present for the safety of employees. The old saying holds true, "there is safety in numbers."

Behavioral Training

Training and Education: AVADE® **Workplace Violence Prevention** training is perhaps the most important component in a **Workplace Violence Prevention Program**. Understanding risk factors and what constitutes potentially dangerous behavior—and how to deal with it—is the first line of defense against workplace violence.

Post Incident Response Procedures: If a workplace violence incident DOES occur, policies and procedures need to be in place beforehand so that employees have a clear course of action and know what to do. See Module 5 for information on how to respond after an incident has occurred.

Post-Incident Reporting Procedures: For the legal protection of yourself, your co-workers, and your company, proper post-incident reporting is essential. Follow-up-to incidents can help reduce and even eliminate re-occurrence if action steps are taken.

Self-Defense and Appropriate Use of Force: We all have the right to defend ourselves. Proper training and education in self-defense techniques, and an understanding of the appropriate use of force, very often reduce injury, saves lives, and reduce liability exposure. Certain industries will need comprehensive training in controlling and restraining individuals. Health care, security, law enforcement, and behavioral health typically need additional training in this category, as their workers are at higher risk.

Environmental Considerations

Creating a physically safe environment for employees has been shown to minimize threats to employees, guests, and clients/customers. Rather than industrial concerns (such as ensuring heavy equipment is safe to use), here we're talking about environmental components that promote and support the **Workplace Violence Prevention Program.** See Module 9 for information on the environmental tools in your environments that can help keep you safe.

Worksite Audit/Analysis: An audit/analysis is similar to a security management plan but specific to all areas of the workplace and anywhere employees are. Many employers use audits and analyses of workplace violence incidents to help identify, prevent, and mitigate risk. An environmental analysis would include evaluating areas outside of a workplace, where someone could hide out in the shrubbery, etc.

Panic Alarms: It's essential to place panic alarms strategically, especially in high-risk areas, and to educate all staff on their use. Do you know where your panic alarms are? Do you even have panic alarms? If so, do you know how to use them, and what happens after they have been activated?

Access Controls: Door locks and security devices on doors are designed to keep people out and are only good when employees and staff use them properly. Doors propped open, piggybacking, and access numbers written above the lock fail to ensure a safe work area.

Physical Lighting: Criminals don't like lights! Things as simple as ensuring there are no broken/unusable lights in bathrooms, dark hallways, and parking lots can keep people safe from a violent incident and reduce crime.

CPTED = Crime Prevention Through Environmental Design: This concept is gaining ground around the world. CPTED promotes things such as lighting, ensuring pedestrian routes are open and visible, and even minimizing shrubbery in vulnerable areas so that assailants have no place to hide. Many corporations utilize CPTED in the design of new construction. It can also be utilized in environmental security audits and analyses as well as the security management plan.

Proactive Response Planning = Prevention and Intervention

Proactive vs. Reactive

Prevention and interventions are essential to eliminating and mitigating security risks in the workplace. Employers now recognize the importance of being proactive in their implementation of workplace violence policies and procedures, conducting worksite audits/analyses, tracking and trending incidents, training and educating staff, as well as other proactive measures to reduce the risk of violence to guests, staff, clients, patients, and visitors. A well-thought-out plan for the prevention of workplace violence takes a proactive approach versus an after-the-fact, reactive-driven response.

Personal Safety Habits

Whose Responsibility is Your Personal Safety?
Your **personal safety** is **your responsibility**; it always has been.

Personal safety involves maintaining a balance and awareness in all areas of your life while creating habits: mentally, physically, spiritually, and for all of your environments.

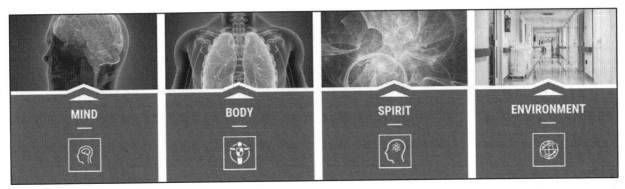

MIND   BODY   SPIRIT   ENVIRONMENT

Personal Safety Habits: *What is a Habit?*

"We are what we repeatedly do; therefore, personal safety is not an act, it is a habit." – David Fowler

Habits are our acquired patterns of behavior that occur automatically without thought, things we repeatedly do over and over. They can be either good or bad.

We Are Creatures of Habit!
You get up in the morning in a certain way and get ready for your day. You brush your teeth, comb your hair, put on your clothes, etc., the same way every day. You don't even think about it; you just do it. The way you answer the phone, greet people, shake hands, gesture, smile, or don't smile are also all your habits. Habits are ingrained in you and stamped into your unconscious mind.

Habits are powerful factors in our lives. They are consistent, unconscious patterns that constantly and daily express our character and produce our effectiveness…or ineffectiveness. Habits determine your future—and your safety!

> **"Sow an act and you reap a habit. Sow a habit and you reap a character. Sow a character and you reap a destiny."**
>
> **-Charles Reade, English Novelist, (1814-1884)**

How do you rate your personal safety habits? _____

Developing Personal Safety Habits

- **Identify Limiting Habits**
- **Let's Play "21"**
- **Creating New Habits**
- **Taking Action (visualize)**
- **No Retreat, No Surrender Policy**
- **Evaluate Yourself**
- **Benefits and Commitment**

Habits = Automatic Responses

A Habit is something that we repeatedly do over and over, an acquired pattern or behavior that occurs automatically without thought.

Identify Your Limiting Personal Safety Habits: Do you have habits that leave you unsafe? Such as leaving your car unlocked, working late, and cutting through unlit areas? Take a hard look at your daily habits and see what little things you can do to ensure your own safety. Once identified, you can begin to change and improve them.

The 21 Rule: This is the process of making small adjustments in your behavior—21 days of repeatedly doing what you intend to do to create a new habit. The 21 Rule is not applicable to a habit that we have had for an extended time. Long-term habits have roots like trees and run very deep. Changing or eliminating long-term habits could take as long as a year or more to develop or break.

Creating New Habits: Write out your new personal safety habits. Once you identify your limiting and successful habits, you can clearly decide to change them or make new, more productive, and empowering personal safety habits. Having a clear, defined personal safety goal is the first powerful step to creating a new habit.

Take Action with Visualization: Written words are powerful—but only when you look at them and make an effort and a commitment to follow through. Focus on your new personal safety habits often; focus on the benefits of your new habits. Use the process of visualization to add more repetitions to your successful new habit—more on this in the section on Awareness, using mental movies.

The No Retreat, No Surrender Policy: The no-retreat, no-surrender policy means that you will do whatever it takes to change or accomplish your personal safety goal. This policy is about doing it even when you don't feel like it—when you're tired, sick, hungry, or stressed. You do it no matter what; you make the commitment!

Evaluate Yourself and Ask for Help: Ask yourself, could I do more to improve my general personal safety and overall sense of safety? Ask for help and get more training. A good trainer will gladly let you know the areas that you could improve upon. Look to improve in all the areas in which you received negative feedback, too. Negative feedback is not necessarily "bad." Consider negative feedback as a way to add safety and self-improvement to your personal life. It's about taking responsibility for yourself and your circumstances.

Commitment Exercise

COMMITMENT	EXERCISE
If you change or add one new, empowering habit every other month. In five years, you will have thirty new habits. Remember, habits are something we unconsciously do; once they're ingrained, you don't even have to think about them.	Commit to developing at least one habit for each workplace violence prevention module. ▪ Write it down in your **AVADE® Workplace Violence Prevention Training Manual.** Focus on it often

Habits are ingrained in you and stamped into your unconscious mind.

Benefits of AVADE® Workplace Violence Prevention Training

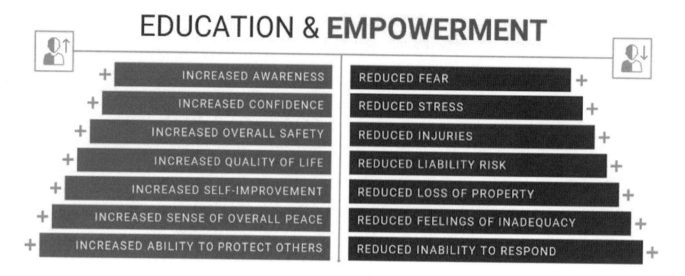

After going through an **AVADE® Workplace Violence Prevention Training Program**, refer back to your textbook "AVADE® Workplace Violence Prevention" as their personal refresher course.

The AVADE® manuals and student guides on workplace violence prevention will help remind you how to recognize emerging situations, how to deal with someone before they become violent, how to survive and escape a violent attack, and much-much more. ***Read and study carefully***. Integrate the lessons you learn here. Unfortunately, one day you may be responsible for saving your own life—and the lives of your co-workers.

Module One: Awareness

The First Principle of the AVADE® Training Program

Everything in life begins with **Awareness**. Have you ever said this to yourself: "I would have done that if I had been aware of it." The goal of this module is to help you understand what awareness is and how you can increase yours. There are many levels of awareness, and we will briefly look at them and why they are important to your safety in the workplace.

Awareness: A **mental state** or **ability** to **perceive, feel**, or be **conscious** of people, emotions, conditions, events, objects, and patterns.

The **key to awareness** in regard to your safety is **knowledge** and **understanding** of **your risks to violence**. Once achieved, this **gift of awareness** gives you the **wisdom** to **prevent** and **mitigate violence**.

When you develop and increase your awareness, you can change your life!

> "Every human has four endowments - self-awareness, conscience, independent will, and creative imagination. These give us the ultimate human freedom... the power to choose, to respond, to change."
> - Stephen R. Covey, *The 7 Habits of Highly Effective People*

Increase Your Awareness of Risks to Workplace Violence

- **Not having training in WPV prevention and de-escalation:** The biggest risk is not recognizing that an individual is escalating and not knowing how to avoid the situation or how to use your interpersonal communication skills to de-escalate that person.

- **Working alone (home care visits) or working in isolated areas:** When working alone or in high-risk areas, remember to increase your 360-degree view of awareness to keep yourself safe. Practice what police officers do when dealing with a person in conflict—get back-up!

- **Not using or having electronic safety measures:** Electronic safety measures (alarms, access controls, etc.) are only as good as the people using them. Unrestricted movement of the public can put workers at risk. Know and understand how the safety controls in your environment work. If not sure, as questions— get training.

- **Contact with individuals who are mentally ill, intoxicated, prisoners, and persons with a history of violence:** Some industries have a higher prevalence of contact with these individuals. However, any of us can be exposed to mentally ill consumers, ex-inmates, and violent perpetrators. Be aware and have a plan.

- **Low staffing levels and increased consumer waiting:** It's a fact of life in our current economy; we are all expected to do more with less. This means our consumers may have to wait for our services or products. Mealtimes, visiting hours, and overcrowded-uncomfortable waiting rooms may precipitate the risk. Use interpersonal communication skills and de-escalation skills when dealing with consumers who are upset.

- **An increase and prevalence of weapons in society:** Weapons are everywhere; they can be common everyday tools we use at work. Increase your awareness of what is around you and how it may be used as a weapon to inflict harm. Guns and knives are not the only threat we face today.

- **Presence of gang members and high crime areas:** Demographics of where we live, commute, and work are factors that predispose us to crime and violence. Be aware of these potential areas of risk and avoid them if possible.

- **Access to pharmaceuticals/drug seekers:** One thing is for certain; people will continue to seek and use drugs. Working with pharmaceuticals can put you at risk. Increased awareness is needed for industries that prescribe or administer drugs.

- **Drug and alcohol use among consumers:** Working with people who are under the influence of alcohol or prescribed and non-prescribed drugs may expose a person to an increased risk.

- **Distraught family members and visitors:** Stressed individuals may escalate into higher levels of the assault cycle. Recognizing that a person is distraught can increase your ability to de-escalate them.

- **Handling of money/transactions:** Anytime you work with valuables or money, there is an increase in risk. Assaults and robberies take place daily due to the fact that certain individuals will commit crimes to get those assets.

- **Public access (24/7 operations) to include late and early work hours:** Any workplace that is open to the public around the clock exposes employees to certain risks. An increase in criminal behavior occurs more often during certain times of the day than at other times. When workers arrive or leave work late at night or early hours, it may expose them to an increased risk of workplace violence. Workers are encouraged to get security escorts if available and travel to and from parking areas with co-workers.

- **Lack of, or inadequate security and mental health personnel on-site:** Working with individuals who have a history of violence predisposes staff to risk. This risk is increased if Security and Mental Health personnel are not available to deal with individuals with violent behaviors. Appropriate training and mental preparation prepare staff for increased risk factors.

- **Transporting patients and clients:** Individuals who transport patients and clients should be vigilant as they are often alone and in multiple environments. Stay Aware!

- **Poor environmental design and a lack of emergency communications:** Poorly lit corridors, parking lots, or other areas where objects block employees' vision. Without procedures and tools to communicate for help, workers are affected as an emergent response is delayed or absent. Panic alarms, cell phones, blue phones, radios, paging, and other methods of communication should be utilized if available. Stay vigilant and use your environmental awareness. Training for emergency codes and procedures; see module 10.

- **The perception that violence is tolerated:** A perception that victims will not or cannot report the incident to police, security, or management and press charges is a precipitating factor that often leads to more acts of violence on staff.

  o **A NO tolerance policy for violence should be established and enforced. Violence will NOT be tolerated!**
  o **The posting of signage/notifications that threatening and assaultive behavior will not be tolerated have become more and more prevalent in healthcare, corporate, and social service settings.**

Note: Each risk factor only represents the potential for an increased likelihood of violence. No risk factor, or combination of risk factors, guarantees that violence will occur or that its incidence will increase. However, the presence of these risk factors, particularly several in combination, increases the likelihood that violence will occur.

INCREASE YOUR LEVELS OF **AWARENESS**

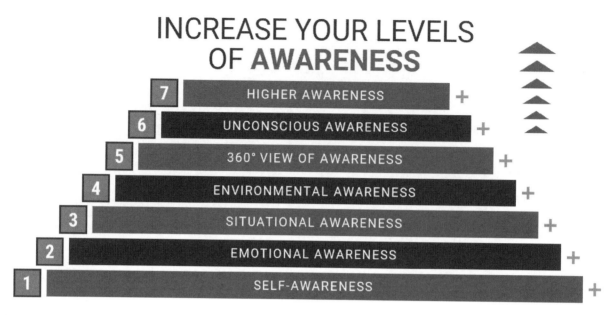

7	HIGHER AWARENESS	+
6	UNCONSCIOUS AWARENESS	+
5	360° VIEW OF AWARENESS	+
4	ENVIRONMENTAL AWARENESS	+
3	SITUATIONAL AWARENESS	+
2	EMOTIONAL AWARENESS	+
1	SELF-AWARENESS	+

Self-Awareness

This conscious awareness allows you to think, reason, choose, exercise free will, evaluate options, and make decisions. Through your self-awareness, you have communication with your body through the sensations of sight, sound, smell, taste, and touch. You are using your self-awareness right now as you look at these words, decipher the meaning, think about the message, and make decisions about their validity.

Emotional Awareness

Your ability to recognize and feel the emotions and feelings of others, as well as your own, is your emotional awareness.

When you are aware and in control of your emotions, you can communicate with compassion and empathy. When you are emotionally aware, you also recognize the patterns and changes in others around you. This ability to know that a co-worker or regular client's behaviors have changed can give you the opportunity to intervene, report your concerns, or distance yourself from the individual.

Emotions are **"the glue" connecting people** to one another. They are the foundation of our ability to **understand ourselves** and **relate to others**. When you are aware and in control of your emotions, you can think clearly and creatively; manage stress and challenges; communicate well with others; and display trust, empathy, compassion, and confidence.

When we lose control of our emotions, we spin into confusion, isolation, and doubt. By learning to recognize, manage, and deal with your emotions, you'll enjoy greater happiness, health, and better relationships.

Your emotions help you:

- Understand yourself, including your deeply-felt needs
- Understand and empathize with others
- Communicate clearly and effectively
- Make decisions based on the things that are most important to you
- Get motivated and take action to meet goals
- Build strong, healthy relationships

Understanding the emotions in others as well as yourself helps you evaluate the behaviors of others and how you feel about those behaviors. How does all this relate to your safety in the workplace? Simple: trust your feelings/emotions. If a situation or someone, in particular, is raising your level of fear or anxiety, trust that feeling and take the appropriate actions.

Situational Awareness

Situational Awareness means being **aware** of what is **happening around you**. It means understanding how information, incidents, and your own actions will affect your goals and objectives, both now and in the near future. Lacking situational awareness or having inadequate situational awareness has been identified as one of the primary factors in accidents attributed to human error. **It is best explained in a simple equation:**

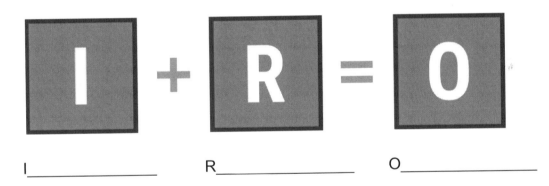

I_____   R_____   O_____

If an individual is angry and escalating (*incident*), knowing how to respond (*response*) to the situation can lead to a non-violent *outcome*. You can increase your personal safety by taking responsibility for all the situations you are in and by making conscious, informed choices and decisions about your environments, the people around you, and the places you frequent.

Environmental Awareness

Environmental awareness is the ability to understand and recognize the many factors relating to your environment and how they can benefit you or limit you.

It also means having: An understanding that your **external physical conditions** can affect and influence your growth, development, and physical survival.

360-Degree View of Awareness

Creating an awareness of what is around you at all times is described as a 360-degree environmental awareness.

This means being aware of your surroundings as much as possible at all times. Using a 360' view increases your conscious awareness of the environment and what is occurring. These are simple observations. What are the normal and abnormal activities around you? What are the normal sights and sounds of the environment you are in? You should also be aware of what security measures are in place and whether they are functioning as designed. Also, you should be alert to distractions that divert you from maintaining a 360' view. The more you focus on the 360' view, the more the non-conscious mind develops an automatic analysis of the environment, alerting you to potential danger.

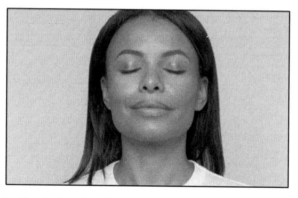

Unconscious Awareness

Unconscious awareness is the part of the mind that directs the involuntary and automatic processes of the body. Through its operation, it automatically rebuilds, repairs, and operates your body.

Your unconscious awareness is the storehouse of your memory, habits, beliefs, instincts, emotions, and knowledge.

In the introduction, we discussed the importance of personal safety habits. Knowing that habits reside in this part of our awareness gives us the opportunity to program our automatic responses by using mental movie techniques to create personal safety habits.

Pre-Planning

As humans, we have the ability to pre-plan events in our minds-eye. We are the only species that has this ability. When working in environments where you are predisposed to risk factors, it is crucial to have pre-planned responses to situations that may occur. Most people, when stressed or in fear, will either under-react or over-react. Neither is acceptable. When you are mentally prepared and have pre-planned the situation, you can respond automatically and appropriately.

Mental Movies and Impressing the Unconscious Mind

As humans, we have the ability to pre-play events in our minds. We also have the ability to replay past events in our minds. Most people have experienced both facets of playing mental movies and impressing the non-conscious mind. Unfortunately, most people spend far more energy pre-playing negative events (worry) and re-playing negative events (past events that were negative) than visualizing positive outcomes.

We all heard the old sage wisdom -
"He who fails to plan- plans to fail." Have a plan!

Make a conscious choice to pre-play events to your liking and re-play positive events. Here is how we impress the unconscious mind so that we can respond automatically without having to stop and think about what we need to do. A preplanned response can literally save your life.

Stage 1: Create the scene of the event, incident, or situation in your mind's eye.

Stage 2: Make the scene as clear and colorful as possible. Focus your mind's eye as you create this clear, concise mental scene.

Stage 3: "Lights, Focus, Camera, and Action!" Now that the scene is clear and focused, give it action. As the director of your mental movie, you direct everything in it.

Stage 4: The plot/outcome is up to you! You decide what happens when it happens and who it happens to. You are the hero of your mental movie. You always win in your mind's eye when you create, direct, and choreograph the mental movie.

Stage 5: Feel what it is like to be the star of your mental movie. Positive energy helps build, reinforce, and utilize the mental power we all have. This ultimately makes us stronger, more decisive, and automatic in our responses.

Stage 6: Remember to **Pre-play** your mental movie prior to any future situations you may be concerned about. We are the only creatures with this ability. **Re-play** positive outcomes, and try not to re-play negative outcomes of real situations. If you do re-play negative situations in your mind's eye, make sure to always change the outcome of your choosing.

Exercise: Guided Imagery

- Have your class relax and close their eyes while you create a scene for them where they take part in the mental movie.

- Use the steps above; make the scene very clear for them with your explanation.

- Have them escape from a dangerous situation or have them use defensive interventions.

- Use scenarios that are familiar or relevant to your audience.

- Remember that not everyone sees (visualizes) themselves in their mind's eye. Some people can only imagine (feel) what it would be like. There is no right or wrong way.

- Congratulate them on their success and encourage them to practice on their own.

The Amazing Mind

The **human mind** is the most **complex and powerful** machine in the universe. Properly **preparing your mind** through **mental movie exercises** is one of the most important aspects of violence intervention. Your physical body's performance is increased through **mental training**.

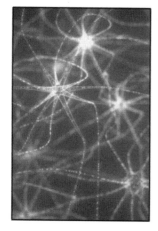

Higher Awareness:

Many, if not most, people believe in some form of infinite and eternal energy from which all things proceed. It is the reality that underlies all existence and is everywhere present. This **state of awareness** is the **highest**, as it **encompasses all levels of your awareness** as well as your **spiritual/energetic** awareness. Some people call this awareness a sixth sense, and many people have credited it with keeping them out of dangerous situations or even saving their lives.

Constant Communication

Our self-awareness, emotional awareness, situational awareness, environmental awareness, unconscious awareness, and higher awareness are in a constant state of communication with each other. Even though we are not cognizant of this, it is continuously present. Just knowing this is the beginning of increased awareness.

Developing & Increasing Awareness

Developing and increasing your awareness does not mean becoming paranoid or hyper-vigilant. It simply means using all your senses.

Improve and Increase Your Awareness

There are several ways to improve and increase your awareness.

- **Planning and preparing** for situations that haven't happened yet. This is done by pre-playing (mental movies) what you would do if faced with a crisis situation.

- **Being Responsible** or **"Response-able"** is the ability to choose your awareness, responses, and attitude towards incidents, yourself, and others.

- **Pay Attention** to what is going on inside of you and outside of you.

- **Be Present.** You don't have to keep your mind constantly busy thinking about all the possible things that can go amiss. Being present or in the moment allows your awareness to be at its most optimal state.

- **Be Proactive.** Recognize the importance of responsibility and awareness. Proactive people don't blame circumstances or conditions for their behavior or outcomes. Their behavior and outcomes are a product of their own conscious choices, based on their knowledge and values rather than their circumstances.

- **Attitude Is Everything.** Your success in everything you do depends on your attitude. Creating a positive attitude about life and all of the events you will experience will help develop and enhance your awareness.

Make small commitments and keep them.
Be a light, not a judge. Be a model, not a critic.
Be part of the solution, not part of the problem.

Module Two: Vigilance

The Second Principle of the AVADE® Training Program

Vigilance is the <u>practice</u> of paying attention to our internal and external messages with regard to ourselves, other people, things, and events.

Vigilance is taking your awareness and putting it into action.

What is Vigilance?

Vigilance: The **practice of paying attention** to our **internal** and **external** messages with regard to ourselves, other people, things, and events.

Vigilance is putting awareness into action. It is your ability to:

- **Be Alert**

- **Be Cautious**

- **Pay Attention**

- **Trust Your Gut Feelings**

- **Use All of Your Senses**

Hyper-Vigilance

NOTE: Hyper-vigilance is a negative condition of maintaining an abnormal awareness of environmental stimuli that causes anxiety, leads to exhaustion, and causes us to startle easily. Hypervigilance is counter-productive and unhealthy. Learning the AVADE® principles will give you the tools you need to live a happy, safe life without allowing fear to consume you.

All great men are gifted with intuition.
They know without reasoning or analysis, what they need to know."

- Alexis Carrel, French Biologist, and Noble Prize Winner, 1912

The Five Senses: Taste, touch, hear, smell, and sight are the mental connections through our bodies to the outer world. Our senses can also alert us and keep us safe from danger. Many people believe that there is a sixth sense.

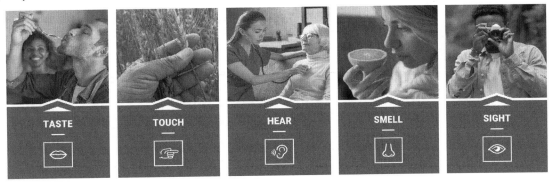

TASTE	TOUCH	HEAR	SMELL	SIGHT

Is There a Sixth Sense?

Trust your intuition, your sixth sense. Intuition is knowing without knowing why you know. Intuition communicates with us through symbols, feelings, and emotions. It's like a radar for sensing, seeing, or feeling danger before it becomes obvious.

Trust your intuition!
Intuition is a **personal security system** that is **always on** and **ever vigilant**, surveying not only danger but everything else as well.

Intuition is a process of gaining information that does not rely on your senses, memory, experiences, or thought processes.

"They that are on their guard and appear ready to receive their adversaries are in much less danger of being attacked than the supine, secure and negligent."

– Benjamin Franklin, author, scientist, and a founding father of the USA

Using Your Intuition

The ability to **read a person's attitudes** and **thoughts** by their **behaviors** was the **original communication system** used by humans prior to spoken language.

In his book, *Body Talk: The Meaning of Human Gestures*, author Desmond Morris lists more than fifty body signals (messages) that are universal to all human beings in every culture. The majority of these messages are communicated unconsciously. Just as communication is unconscious, so is our ability to read this non-verbal communication. If you were asked to identify just ten of the non-verbal messages, you may find it difficult, but we all know them and respond to them intuitively. The key to using your intuition more effectively is to bring the unconscious data it supplies to a place where your conscious mind can interpret it. Intuition is always communicating with you. Occasionally it may send a signal that turns out to be less than dangerous, but everything it communicates to you is meaningful.

Intuition might send any of several messengers to get your attention, and because they differ according to urgency, it is good to know the various messages.

Messages of Intuition

"If there is anything intuition demonstrates, it's the interconnectedness of everything."
- Carl Jung, Synchronicity

- **Synchronicity:** This is the message all of us get. It is the connectedness we all have and write off as airy-fairy. The best example of this is a phone call. All of us have been thinking about that particular someone when the phone rings, and it's them. This happens to all of us in many ways every day.

- **Nagging Feelings:** When we experience nagging feelings about someone or something, it is our unconscious awareness telling us to wait and question what is going on.

- **Hunches:** A hunch is a feeling that a particular event or situation will go a certain way.

- **Gut Feeling:** A term many of us like to use in regard to predicting something that may or may not happen. For some of us, a gut feeling is visceral; we can literally feel it.

Messages of Intuition

- **Hesitation/Doubt:** When we hesitate, when we doubt, we are stalling for more time and questioning the situation.

- **Suspicion:** For some, being suspicious is their internal radar that says, "Something isn't right here."

- **Physical Changes:** Like other species, we, too, change physically when exposed to internal and external intuitive messages. When the hair stands up on the back of your neck or when you get goosebumps, your body is telling you something.

- **Sense of Danger:** The intuitive messenger with the greatest urgency is a sense of DANGER. When you know with all of your being that you are in trouble or a situation is imminent, this is the intuitive message of danger.

Developing Intuition

Learning to read body language teaches us to be more sensitive to people's feelings and emotions, provide better customer service, or care to those who rely on us, and increase our personal safety.

Developing your intuitive ability begins with paying attention to what's going on inside of you so that you can become aware of these inner signals and catch them when they are happening or shortly afterward.

NOTE: The enemy of intuition is worry. When you play or replay negative situations, spending energy on things that have already happened or might happen soon, you don't have the mental space to acknowledge and act on signals your intuition is trying to send to you!

Stop-Look-Listen
Developing and using your intuition means you need to stop, look, and listen occasionally to what your feelings, senses, perceptions, and the contexts of situations are telling you at that present moment. Listening to, trusting, and acting on your intuitive inner guidance is an art. And like any art or discipline, it requires an ongoing commitment. Challenge yourself to develop a deeper understanding of self-awareness.

Intuition Exercise:

"Is someone staring at me?" – Awakening your Intuitive Ability

"They that are on their guard and appear ready to receive their adversaries are in much less danger of being attacked than the supine, secure and negligent."

– Benjamin Franklin, author, scientist, and a founding father of the USA

Module Three: Avoidance

The Third Principle of the AVADE® Training Program

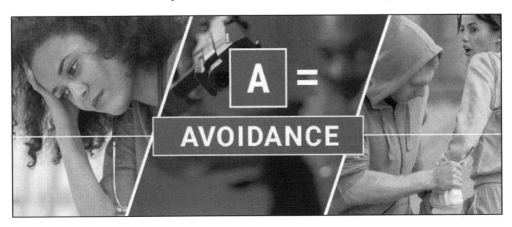

Who Commits Violence? People do! The types of individuals who commit violence are categorized into five areas: stranger violence, patient/client violence, lateral violence, domestic violence, and extreme violence.

Characteristics of Individuals Who Commit Violence

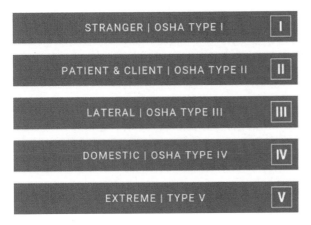

STRANGER | OSHA TYPE I — I

PATIENT & CLIENT | OSHA TYPE II — II

LATERAL | OSHA TYPE III — III

DOMESTIC | OSHA TYPE IV — IV

EXTREME | TYPE V — V

After examining these characteristics, we will look at strategies to prevent, mitigate, or eliminate your risk of violence from these individuals.

OSHA Type I - Stranger Violence

Type I Stranger Violence is where the perpetrator has no legitimate relationship with the business or its employees. **The offender is usually involved in committing a crime in conjunction with the violence.** Examples include perpetrators who are looking to:

- **Rape**
- **Robbery**
- **Assaults (verbal and physical)**
- **Bomb Threats**
- **Gang Violence**

- **Homicide occurs when one human being causes the death of another human being.** Homicides can be divided into types: murder, manslaughter, justifiable, etc.

Stranger violence also includes verbal threats, threatening behavior, or physical assaults by an assailant who has no legitimate business or relationship to the workplace. This person may enter the workplace to commit a criminal act, e.g., robbery. In most states, violence by stranger's accounts for most of the fatalities related to workplace violence.

Stranger violence occurs between offenders and victims who have no prior relationship. Unlike crimes that take place between family members, friends, business partners, or acquaintances, stranger violence occurs when the offender is not known to the victim in any way. Violent crime refers to crimes including, but not limited to, homicide, sexual assault, assault, robbery, and other violent offenses. While most violent crimes are perpetrated by offenders known to the victims, violence between strangers is still thought of as one of the most frightening forms of violence.

Robbery Prevention and Response (see Robbery Code –Module 10)

Stranger Violence = Predator

What is a Predator?

A correlation can be made between predators in the wild and human predators in our society. A number of similarities are present with both animals and humans.

> ### Human Predators Want Three (3) Things
> 1) *Valuables (money, assets, possession, drugs etc..)*
> 2) *Bodies (physical/sexual assault –rape)*
> 3) *Lives (homicide-murder)*

Fortunately, we and others (species) have learned to adapt (adaptation) and overcome predators.

Predator-Prey & Adaptation

Adaptation is a **basic phenomenon** of **biology** and also refers to characteristics that are especially important to an **organism's survival**.

Adaptive traits can be structural, behavioral, psychological, and physiological.

- **Structural:** We, as humans, secure our homes, cars, and workplaces with locks, solid doors/windows, and use security devices, etc., to keep us safe.

- **Behavioral:** We have the ability to recognize threatening behaviors in others, as well as behave in ways so as not to cause unwanted attention or portray ourselves as easy targets.

- **Psychological:** It all starts with having a mindset of awareness and vigilance.

- **Physiological:** Its self-awareness of our physical ability to use our senses and to take physical action, such as running or defending ourselves if needed

Predator Characteristics

(A characteristic is an attribute or trait of an entity with many particular meanings.)

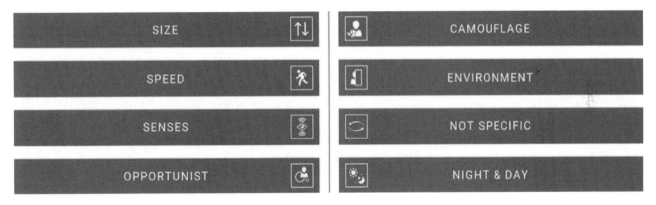

SIZE	⇅	CAMOUFLAGE
SPEED	🏃	ENVIRONMENT
SENSES	👁	NOT SPECIFIC
OPPORTUNIST		NIGHT & DAY

Predator and Prey:

A predator may be larger than its prey, stronger, and sometimes faster. **Predators develop their senses and always seek opportune times to strike.** They will camouflage themselves using their environment and behaviors. And a predator is not always specific in regard to its prey; often, it will seek more than one prey or type of prey. Most crime and violence occur during evening and nighttime hours. But be cautious, as some predators will choose daytime to prey upon their victims as well.

The predator doesn't want someone who will resist, so he or she will select prey that is older, weaker, or very young. The predator's prey can be either male or female. The predator knows that a person's presence sends a message about their confidence and ability; people who are unaware become easy prey for predators. People who stand out or call unnecessary attention to themselves are advertising themselves as prey. Those who are distracted can also be victimized. And isolation gives the predator protection from unwanted attention.

Intentions are a reflection of a person's thoughts coming from their face, body, posture, the position of hands, and clothing. Intentions can also show an individual's level of confidence, emotional state, motives, and attitudes. **Pay attention to intentions!**

Don't Be Easy Prey

Don't be a victim. Don't be prey. Any of the mental states or what is known as **Prey (Victim) Paradigms** listed below may leave you vulnerable to observant predators. They'll know you're an easy target. Do not fall into this mental state—that's one of your best defenses for avoiding violence.

- **Un-Aware Unconsciously:** An unconscious state of unawareness of a person's surroundings and the people they encounter. This unconscious state *is not knowing that you don't know.* But remember, ignorance is not a good defense.

- **Un-Prepared:** A higher state of conscious awareness than being unaware but lacking in preparedness for potential situations. Have you ever said to yourself, "I'm just not that prepared for the day"?

- **Un-Secured:** Not using the precautionary security tools and equipment in a person's environment. Environmental components are in place to keep you safe. Not knowing where they are or how to use them is not a good defense.

- **Un-Aware Consciously:** The most serious unawareness is a dangerous state of denial — the "nothing can happen to me" mentality. It's when you just don't care and are consciously choosing to be unaware.

- **Un-Fortunate:** Being in the wrong place at the wrong time. This paradigm mindset is the least likely event to happen; however, by increasing your awareness and your vigilance, you can lessen your chances of being in the wrong place at the wrong time.

Prey (Victim) Characteristics (EASY TARGET)

- Predators will always choose the easier target as they are **unaware** and **distracted.**
- Easy targets are easily identifiable due to their **non-confident presence: eyes being down, slumped posture, lackadaisical stride, and non-specific actions.**
- East Targets appear have a **timid and submissive presence**.
- Predators will target easy prey and avoid prey that is harder or more of a risk for them.

Hard Target vs. Easy Target

Understanding the characteristics of individuals who commit violence, as well as what predators look for in their prey, increases your awareness and vigilance. And remember: if it doesn't feel right, it almost certainly isn't.

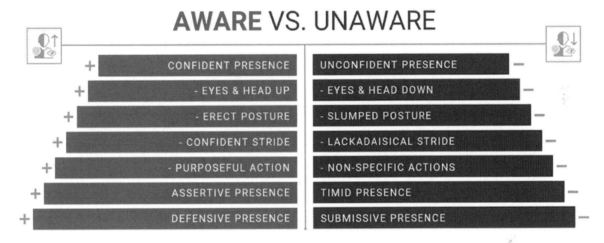

Confident-Assertive-Defensive Characteristics (HARD TARGET)

- Having awareness and a presence that says "confidence" is the first step in avoiding conflict with an assailant (predator).
- When it's obvious you are paying attention to what's around you; you are not an easy target.
- Hard targets are easily identifiable due to their head and eyes being up, walking with an erect posture, a confident stride, and purposeful action.
- Hard targets know when they need to shift their body language and attitudes from confident into assertive or defensive.
- Predators will target easy prey and avoid prey that is harder or more of a risk for them.

All of these characteristics display a confident presence rather than a weak or easy target presence.

- Do we unconsciously send messages to others that we are afraid and weak?
- Can we change these unconscious signals we send?

Assertive Presence*:* Assertiveness is the ability to exercise one's rights without denying the rights of others. We express our assertiveness with our body language, eye contact, and voice. The opposite of being assertive is to be inclined to timidity or lack of self-confidence. There are times when an assertive presence is needed in our interpersonal communications.

Defensive Presence*:* A defensive presence is only used when dealing with an aggressive individual(s). To avoid being seen as aggressive, stand with your body angled at forty-five degrees to another person. Most animals, when wanting to fight, will signal this approach by facing head-on.

The Law of Cause and Effect basically states that for every movement of energy—such as in a natural happening or a human thought that takes the form of an image, feeling, desire, belief, expectation, or action—there is a corresponding effect. For this reason, the Law of Cause and Effect influences every aspect of your living experience. To determine why your living experience is of a certain quality or why something has come into your life, you simply need to discover what causes preceded the effects. If and when you like the effects you are living with, then you keep the causes. If not, then you change the causes to create a different effect. ***How does this help you avoid violence?*** Using your confident, assertive, or defensive presence, even when you do not feel like it, can influence your thinking as well as the situation. The same is true with our thoughts; having confident, assertive, or defensive thoughts can influence our bodies and the situation.

OSHA Type II – Patient/Client Violence

Type II patient, client, or customer violence can involve verbal threats, threatening behavior, or physical assaults by an assailant who either receives services from or is under the custodial supervision of the affected workplace or the victim. **Violence** by **clients**, **patients**, **guests**, and **customers'** accounts for the majority of **non-fatal injuries** related to **workplace violence** in many states.

Examples of Type II Patient/Client Violence would include dealing with individuals who are:

Intoxicated

Mentally Ill

Angry/Aggressive

Stress/Confused

Physical Abnormalities

Sexually/Physically Aggressive

Type II violence is the most common in healthcare settings. Research shows that this type of violence occurs most frequently in emergency and psychiatric treatment settings, waiting rooms, and geriatric settings but is by no means limited to these areas.

Prevention/Mitigation of Type II violence will be addressed through the following interventions:

- Interpersonal Communications

- Trauma-Informed Care

- Understanding Communication Skills

- The 5 Habits of De-Escalation

- The Assault Cycle

- De-Escalating Upset (Stressed) Individuals

- De-Escalating Angry (Aggressive) Individuals

- De-Escalating Intoxicated (Drugs & Alcohol) Individuals

- Avoid Physically Combative/Violent Individuals

OSHA Type III – Lateral Violence

Type III Lateral Violence is often perpetrated by someone who was recently disciplined or discharged. It involves verbal threats, threatening behavior, or physical assaults by an assailant who has some employment-related involvement with the workplace.

Assailants could be current or former employees, supervisors, managers, or contractors. **Any workplace can be at risk of violence by a co-worker.**

Examples of Type III Lateral Violence would include dealing with individuals that display:

Bullying Behavior

Intimidating Behavior

Angry and Aggressive

Sexually/Physical Aggressive

Recently Disciplined

Discharged Employee

An assailant who commits a threat or assault may be seeking revenge for perceived unfair treatment. Lateral workplace violence fatalities can receive a lot of media attention but only account for a small portion of all workplace violence-related fatalities.

Any aggressive or threatening behavior committed by an employee should be immediately reported to human resources, security, supervision, management, etc. Early warning signs may be a pre-incident indicator for cause and concern. **See it, Hear it, Report it**

Pre-Incident Reporting: Signs of lateral violence should be reported via your incident reporting procedures.

Warning Signs of Type III Lateral Violence

EARLY WARNING
SIGNS OF VIOLENCE

A single **early warning sign** may not be a **red flag** (or it may), but a combination of any of the following signs should be cause for concern and action. **Recognize early warning signs of violence** and **report** what you **see** and **hear!**

- Direct or verbal threats of harm
- The recent acquisition of weapons
- Sudden change in social media behavior
- Empathy or admiration with individuals committing violence
- Intimidation of others by words and/or actions
- Increased use of alcohol and/or illegal drugs
- Unexplained increase in absenteeism; vague physical complaints
- Noticeable decrease in attention to appearance and hygiene
- Depression/withdrawal and/or expression of extreme desperation over recent problems
- Resistance and overreaction to changes in policy and procedures
- Repeated violations of company policies or refusing to follow policies
- Increasing in number or severity of mood swings
- Noticeably unstable emotional responses
- Explosive outbursts of anger or rage without provocation
- Suicidal; comments about "putting things in order."
- Paranoia/paranoid behavior ("everybody is against me"), hypersensitivity/extreme suspiciousness.
- Increasingly talks of problems at home
- Escalation of domestic problems into the workplace; talk of severe financial problems
- Talk of previous incidents of violence
- Increase in unsolicited comments on firearms, dangerous weapons & violent crimes
- Extreme moral righteousness
- Inability to take criticism regarding job performance
- Holding a grudge, especially against a supervisor
- Repeatedly verbalizing that something will happen to someone against whom the individual has the grudge
- Intentional disregard for the safety of others
- Destruction of property

OSHA Type IV - Domestic Violence

Type IV Domestic Violence (DV) is the willful intimidation, physical assault, battery, sexual assault, and/or other abusive behavior as part of a systematic pattern of power and control perpetrated by one intimate partner against another. It includes physical violence, sexual violence, threats, economic and emotional/psychological abuse. The frequency and severity of domestic violence vary dramatically.

DV in the workplace can involve verbal threats, threatening behavior, or physical assaults by an assailant who has a personal relationship with someone in the workplace; the assailant may or may not work there. The assailant's actions may be motivated by real or perceived difficulties in the relationship or by psychosocial factors specific to them.

Examples of Type IV Domestic Violence include:

Partner (Significant Others)   **Family Members**   **Child Custody Issues**

Stalking   **Enemies**   **Friends**

According to the National Coalition Against Domestic Violence (www.ncadv.org)

- In the US, more than 10 million adults experience domestic violence annually. (every 3 seconds) DV is most common against women between the ages of 18-24.
- 1 in 4 women and 1 in 10 men experience sexual violence, physical violence, and/or stalking by an intimate partner during their lifetime.
- Approximately 1 in 5 female victims and 1 in 20 male victims need medical care because of domestic violence.
- 23.2% of women and 13.9% of men have experienced severe physical violence by an intimate partner during their lifetime.
- On a typical day, domestic violence hotlines nationwide receive over 19,000 calls.

Possible Signs of DV Victimization

Studies by the ABA **http://www.americanbar.org** and the FBI **(https://www.fbi.gov/stats-services/publications/workplace-violence**) cite these things as indicators of possible domestic violence or stalking.

The Following Observable Behavior May Suggest Possible DV Victimization

Domestic violence is prevalent in every community and affects all people regardless of age, socioeconomic status, sexual orientation, gender, race, religion, or nationality. Physical violence is often accompanied by emotionally abusive and controlling behavior as part of a much larger, systematic pattern of dominance and control. Domestic violence can result in physical injury, psychological trauma, and even death. The devastating consequences of domestic violence can cross generations and last a lifetime.

National Domestic Violence Hotline: 1-800-799-SAFE (7233)

More and more, domestic violence is spilling over into workplace violence. This is a terrifying trend because you and your employees or co-workers could be in danger from someone you've never met and may not even recognize if he/she came into your workplace.

Protecting the Victim and Workplace from Domestic Violence

1. **Institute a culture of safety in your workplace**—that means making people feel SAFE about reporting abuse/victimization. It is a federal law that employers must make concessions for a victim of domestic violence. Employers must balance any such steps with the employee's right to privacy and confidentiality.

2. **If an employee comes to you to report abuse, TAKE IT SERIOUSLY.**
Abusive husbands, boyfriends, wives, girlfriends, and stalkers are pursuing their victims into their places of work. This can put you at risk! As well as everyone who works with you, including your patients, customers, and clients.

3. **Refer employee (victim) to EAP (employee assistance program).**

4. **Refer employee (victim) to a DV (domestic violence) assistance program.**
https://ncadv.org/resources (National Coalition Against Domestic Violence)

5. **Remember, the victim IS a victim.** Be sensitive and considerate when discussing what is going on in her/his home life. Explain that this DOES affect the workplace and that, for their safety AND all co-workers, there are steps that need to be taken to mitigate the risk to all. Again, please remember you are dealing with a victim. Do not victimize her/him again.

6. **Arrange for a security officer to escort the victim to and from parking areas.** If possible, have the victim park in a designated parking area (physicians parking, valet, etc.).

7. **Get the name, description, and, if at all possible, a photo of the abuser.** Abusers may have a criminal record, with information in the public domain. Make sure ALL relevant personnel (security) have this photo/information and that they know what steps to take. If abuser comes on-site and the victim has filed a restraining order, personnel need to DISCREETLY call 911.

8. **Consider changing the employee's work schedule, location, and hours.** Abusers know his/her schedule and location. If possible, move front-line employees to more secure areas.

9. **Offering training resources to the employee (victim).** Training can create confidence, empowerment, and life safety skills for victims of DV.

10. **Consider installing remote panic alarms at the employee's workstation.** These silent alarms can alert security to an emergent situation. Proper training on the use of the alarm system is crucial.

11. **Consider furloughing the employee as it may be the best solution for the workplace.** If the threat is serious enough to furlough the employee, law enforcement should be involved as well as your threat assessment team, legal, human resources, etc.

12. **If furloughing is not possible, consider providing armed officers to protect the employee and others.**

13. **Consider using technology to monitor the victim and abuser's social media.** Using technology while creating a geo-fence around your organization could be beneficial.

Imminent Threat of Domestic Violence

1. **Alert the police.** If your employee has resisted filing a police report about the abuse, this may be the time to insist and remind her/him that OTHER people are now at risk. At the very least, you can alert the police, even if there is nothing they can act on.

2. **Train your employees in EXACTLY what to do if they see the abuser/stalker on work grounds, in the parking lot, or anywhere near your place of business.** This response will vary based on the exact circumstances, i.e., if a restraining order has been filed, call 911 and report her/his presence. If you have trained security personnel, they should be alerted first. That's something you need to determine.

3. **Under NO circumstances should UNTRAINED personnel approach the abuser/stalker.** Only personnel properly trained in de-escalation, such as **AVADE®** techniques, **https://avadetraining.com,** should engage her/him. The proper techniques will defuse a situation; an improper approach could escalate it.

4. **If at all possible, consider locking the doors of your establishment and "buzzing" people in.** This is becoming more and more common, so there is no need to go into great detail about it with your customers/clients. At the very least, lock all doors NOT used by walk-in clients. There's no reason to leave back doors propped open or unlocked.

5. **Panic buttons are not necessarily cost-prohibitive to install anymore, and they can be portable and look like a key fob.**

6. **Consider posting/hiring extra security.** Good security services can assess the threat and provide the appropriate level of security (whether that's plain-clothed or uniformed personnel), coordinate with police, and establish guidelines for all your employees to follow.

7. **Offer your employee paid leave, if possible, and encourage her/him to stay somewhere the abuser/stalker does not know about,** even if it is just for a short while, which may be enough time for the situation to de-escalate.

8. **Find out what your legal obligations are.** If you are a business owner and you know an employee has been threatened, you MAY be legally obligated to inform clients, post a photo, etc. If you share a building with another organization, you may be legally obligated to alert them, too. It may be worth it to consult an attorney. (Upfront consultation fees cost less than wrongful-death lawsuits.)

Type V - Extreme Violence

Extreme violence goes beyond our human understanding of how and why members of the same species can inflict such pain and harm on one another.

Examples of Type V Extreme Violence include:

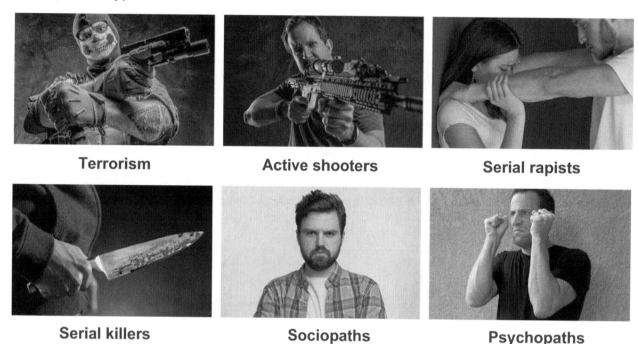

Terrorism	**Active shooters**	**Serial rapists**
Serial killers	**Sociopaths**	**Psychopaths**

Terrorism: the use of violence and intimidation in the pursuit of political aims.

- **Active Shooters:** an individual(s) actively engaged in killing or attempting to kill people in a confined and populated area. Active Shooter awareness, preparedness, and responses will be covered in depth in module 10.
- **Serial Rapist:** a person who forces a series of victims into unwanted sexual activity.
- **Serial Killers:** a person who murders three or more people, usually in service of abnormal psychological gratification.
- **Sociopaths:** a person with a personality disorder manifesting itself in extreme antisocial attitudes and behavior with a lack of conscience.
- **Psychopaths:** a person suffering from a chronic mental disorder with abnormal or violent social behavior.

Public safety and security are everyone's responsibility. If you see suspicious activity, report it to local law enforcement or a person of authority using the "5W's".

Describe specifically what you observed, including:

- **Who Did You See?**
- **What Did You See?**
- **When You Saw It?**
- **Where It Occurred?**
- **Why It's Suspicious?**
- IF THERE IS AN EMERGENCY, CALL 9-1-1.

if you
SEE | SAY
something something™

Developing Your Avoidance Ability

Of course, you have a lot more tools for avoidance than just a confident presence. Learning to use all the tools at your disposal will help you develop your avoidance ability.

STRUCTURAL AVOIDANCE

BEHAVIORAL AVOIDANCE

PSYCHOLOGICAL AVOIDANCE

- **Structural Avoidance**
  The use of any barrier, shield, device, or protective layer around you. Most commonly, these are your home, vehicle, and workplace and the security that they afford you.
- **Behavioral Avoidance**
  The ability to recognize behaviors through reading body language is the oldest communication system. Trust in your ability to read others and know that you, too, are sending a message.
- **Psychological Avoidance**
  Mental awareness is having the ability to recognize dangers and make decisions, choices, and responses that always keep you safe.

PHYSIOLOGICAL AVOIDANCE

ENVIRONMENTAL AVOIDANCE

INTUITIVE AVOIDANCE

- **Physiological Avoidance**
  Having the ability to physically and defensively intervene in a situation. Your confident presence is also a huge physiological deterrent.
- **Environmental Avoidance**
  Using safety awareness for the different types of environments you find yourself in—similar to structural avoidance but broader in scope, as our environments are broad.
- **Intuitive Avoidance**
  When you are truly present in the moment, you can receive messages internally and externally. Trusting and acting on these messages will keep you aware and safe.

Module Four: Interpersonal Communications

COMMUNICATION IS KEY

Interpersonal communication is a transactional process through which people share their ideas and feelings by simultaneously sending and receiving messages.

- It's a complex and dynamic process in which individuals interact with one another, usually face-to-face.
- Messages may be exchanged verbally or non-verbally and may be sent intentionally or unintentionally.

"The meeting of two personalities is like the contact of two chemical substances: if there is any reaction, both are transformed."
- Carl Jung, Swiss Psychologist, 1875 – 1961

How do you rate your ability to communicate with others on a scale of 1-10? _____

Interpersonal Communication Fundamentals

Our ability to communicate with others can significantly reduce the potential for conflicts.

Interpersonal communications fundamentals involve the following:

ACTIVE LISTENING

ASSERTING

INFLUENCING

PERSUADING

EMPATHIZING

COMPASSION

SENSITIVITY

DIPLOMACY

TRAUMA-INFORMED CARE

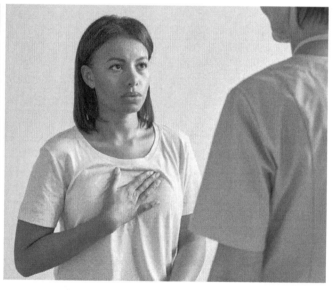

Active Listening: Active listening is a structured way of listening and responding to others. It focuses attention on the other person. Active listening is, arguably, the most important communication skill of all because, without it, no other technique, theory, or principle will work.

- Webster defines **Active** as: "involving action or participation"
- Webster defines **Listen** (verb) as: "to hear something with thoughtful attention, give consideration"

When we use active listening, we are actively involved in hearing and paying attention to what the other person is saying.

When using active listening, you should:

- Pay attention to the inflection of the person's words.
- Pay attention to the context of what they are saying.
- Use supportive body language – eye communication (shows you are interested).
- Avoid rolling your eyes.
- Avoid repeatedly rubbing your neck.
- Avoid looking away often.
- Avoid unconsciously shaking your head back and forth (this says "no").
- Avoid shuffling your feet.
- Avoid crossing arms, tapping fingers, biting lip, etc.
- Avoid checking your cell phone, writing notes, texting, etc.

Asserting: To state or express positively one's rights, beliefs, or positions. The caveat to this communication skill is that our rights and beliefs should not affect another person's rights and beliefs. When we are assertive, we state our position in a strong and definite professional way. There are times (not all the time!) in our communication where we must be assertive.

Influencing: Our power to affect people, actions, and events. The ability to influence others is more than just using words; it involves our body language and our para-language (tone and inflection).

Persuading: To succeed in causing a person to do, or consent to do, something. We are all in the SALES business. We are either selling an idea, a product, or a service. In some cases, we are selling all three. Your ability to communicate through persuasion helps you accomplish your goal of serving others, getting your idea across, or selling your product. To be persuasive, one MUST believe in what one is doing, selling, or providing. It's not what you do; it's how you do it that influences and persuades others.

Empathizing: To sense and understand someone else's feelings as if they were your own. In other words, you are putting yourself in another person's shoes. This can be difficult at times, as some situations make it extremely difficult to imagine being in that person's shoes. However, the key to these situations is to "try" to put yourself in their shoes. When we "try," it comes across in our verbal and non-verbal communication, and people recognize our empathy. **Caution: Do not confuse "sympathy" with "empathy."**

Empathy is the capacity to understand or feel what another being is experiencing from within the other person's frame of reference. Using empathy fulfills a person's need for psychological survival. We all need to feel understood.

Compassion: Is a relational process that involves noticing another person's pain, experiencing an emotional reaction to his or her pain, and acting in some way to help ease or alleviate the pain. **Compassion fatigue is a major concern.** Compassion fatigue is a condition characterized by emotional and physical exhaustion leading to a diminished ability to empathize or feel compassion for others, often described as the negative cost of caring.

Sensitivity: Being cognizant of emotional feelings (of self and others). A person who is not sensitive in their communication comes across as callous and not caring. Being sensitive when communicating with others demonstrates that you truly care for them. Sensitivity is expressed in our words, tone, inflection, and body language.

Diplomacy: Having tact and skill in dealing with people in an effective way. Not having diplomacy in our communications is communicating ineffectually. A person who has tact and diplomatic skill will **not** always say what's on their mind. The opposite of this is a person who has no filter and says whatever's on their mind. Being mindful of what we say is the key to diplomacy. In relationships, business deals, and in situations where we deal with difficult people, diplomacy is absolutely necessary.

Trauma-informed Care is an approach to providing care that **recognizes** and **responds** to experiences of **trauma**. It acknowledges that **trauma** is **widely experienced** and **often stigmatized.** It helps staff and clients to understand the diverse ways that trauma can impact an individual. Trauma-informed care can help survivors begin to rebuild a sense of personal safety and empowerment.

What do we mean by trauma?

"Trauma" is typically understood to be **caused by an event** (or a series of events) that is experienced by someone as being harmful—physically or emotionally—and that has long-term negative effects on the person. Common forms of trauma include abuse, neglect, and household dysfunction. Sometimes traumatic events are so harmful that they are even life-threatening.

Trauma is widespread. For example, 84% or more of adult mental health clients have histories of trauma[12], yet the topic of trauma has often been ignored—a source of shame and denial. But it is now increasingly accepted that trauma should be addressed in health care and social service settings, particularly (but not only) when serving patients who have behavioral health disorders.

What are some of the short- and long-term effects of trauma?

---

[12] Mueser, K.T., Salyers, M.P., Rosenberg, S.D., Goodman, L.A., Essock, S.M., et al. (2004). Interpersonal Trauma and Posttraumatic Stress Disorder in Patients with Severe Mental Illness: Demographic, Clinical, and Health Correlates. Schizophrenia Bulletin, 30 (1), 45-57.

Trauma has wide-ranging physical, emotional, psychological, and behavioral effects. It affects the brain—especially the developing brain. It adversely affects both short-term and long-term well-being and overall functioning and has been associated with mental health disorders, addiction, and other impairments that affect an individual's physical and mental health. Trauma can make it hard for someone to cope with future distress and to form healthy relationships. Trauma can also produce "triggers," situations that remind trauma survivors of the events that originally harmed them. These triggers can cause someone to essentially "relive" the traumatic event and become highly distressed, which can pose a safety hazard to that person and to others. The person may start to have a strong negative emotional, physical, or behavioral reaction.

What can you do to provide trauma-informed care?

According to the Substance Abuse and Mental Health Services Administration (SAMHSA), the key elements of being trauma-informed include:

1. *Realizing* the widespread impact of trauma and understanding potential paths for recovery;
2. *Recognizing* the signs and symptoms of trauma in clients, families, staff, and others;
3. *Responding* by integrating knowledge about trauma into policies, procedures, & practices;
4. Seeking to actively resist *retraumatization*.[13]

Always try to **ask yourself: How is a person's current behavior potentially influenced by their past experiences of trauma? What support might they need?**

Be mindful of the following six principles:

1. **Safety:** Organizations can strive to create environments where staff & clients feel safe, both physically & psychologically
2. **Trustworthy & Transparent:** Decisions should be made in a transparent way, with the goal of building trust with & between clients & staff
3. **Peer Support:** Trauma survivors can support one another to build a climate of safety, recovery, & hope
4. **Collaboration & Mutuality:** By attending to power imbalances in an organization or between staff & clients, we recognize the importance of shared decision making & that everyone has a role to play on the path to healing
5. **Empowerment, Voice, & Choice:** Recognize the unique strengths of trauma survivors & believe in the possibility of recovery. Support client's participation in goal-setting & self-advocacy
6. **Cultural, Historical, and Gender Issues:** Recognize and address cultural biases and stereotypes, as well as historical trauma. Be attentive to the needs of different people based on their gender identity, sexual orientation, age, race, ethnicity, or other aspects of their backgrounds.

---

[13] https://www.samhsa.gov/nctic/trauma-interventions

Some examples of specific ways to build trauma-sensitive practices include:

- Provide a calm environment. Take your time.
- Don't rush into the services you provide.
- Be relaxed.
- Screen for trauma.
- Provide people with brief responses that show empathy and that validate their experiences.
- Encourage people to voice their questions or concerns.
- Let people know that their concerns are normal and make sense.
- Explain what you're going to do before you do it.
- Give people as much control and choice as possible.
- Let people know their choices and their ability to leave or to not participate in certain activities or services.
- Teach people about self-care.
- Identify your own "triggers" and biases and how they affect your behavior.

Key Resources:

- National Center for Trauma-Informed Care
  https://www.samhsa.gov/nctic

- SAMHSA's Concept of Trauma and Guidance for a Trauma-Informed Approach
  https://store.samhsa.gov/product/SAMHSA-s-Concept-of-Trauma-and-Guidance-for-a-Trauma-Informed-Approach/SMA14-4884

Understanding Interpersonal Communication Skills

Communication skills involve much more than just speaking well. Albert Mehrabian was a pioneer researcher of body language. In his book, *Nonverbal Communication,* he explained that most of our communication in a face to face encounter is nonverbal.

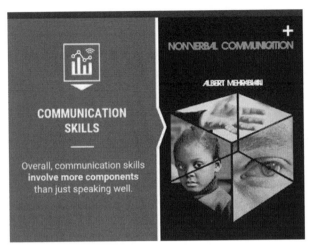

ATTITUDE & EMOTION

Albert Mehrabian was a pioneer of **body language** research. In his book, **Nonverbal Communication,** he explained that:

55%	**38**%	**7**%
NONVERBAL	VOCAL TONE | INFLECTION	VERBAL WORDS ONLY

Our attitudes and emotions are continuously revealed on our faces—and most of us are completely unaware of it. Most people form 60% to 80% of their initial opinion about a new person in just a few minutes or less. To communicate effectively, you need to understand the 93% of communication that isn't verbal. Know what message you're sending—and accurately read the message being sent to you.

It's well known that good **communication** is the foundation of any successful relationship, be it personal or professional. It's important to recognize, though, that it's our **nonverbal communication**—our facial expressions, gestures, eye contact, posture, and tone of voice—that speak the loudest.

"Actions speak louder than words."
"It's not what you say, it's how you say it."

- Over 90% of our communication is non-verbal.
- Most people are unconscious of their non-verbal communication.
- When reading another person's non-verbal communication, look for clusters.
- When individuals are stressed, angered, intoxicated, or combative, they will focus more on your non-verbal communication and less on your spoken words.
- Failure to pick up on incongruent verbal and non-verbal messages can be tragic.

Facial Expressions & Eye Communication

A Smile is worn on every friendly face.

Smiling and laughing are universally considered to be signals that show a person is happy. Smiling serves much the same purpose as it does with other primates: it tells another person you are non-threatening and asks them to accept you on a personal level.

Eye Contact: The Three I's of Eye Communication

- **Intimate** (signals interest in a person)
- **Intimidating** (a person will stare to intimidate or dominate another)
- **Interested** (eye contact recommended for appropriate interpersonal communications).

Give the amount of eye contact that makes others feel comfortable and that you are interested in them. When talking, we maintain 40% to 60% eye contact, with an average of 80% when listening. To build a good rapport with people, your eye contact should meet theirs about two-thirds of the time. (The exception to this is Japanese and some Asian and South American cultures where extended eye contact can be seen as aggressive or disrespectful.)

We have all heard that the eyes are the window to the soul. But what does this really tell us?

Reading Eye Communications

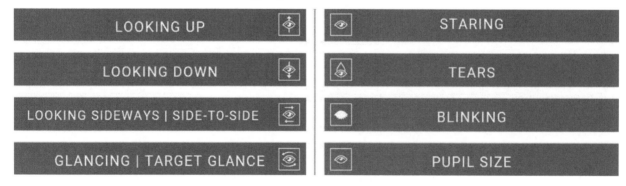

- **Looking up:** indicates a person is thinking.
- **Looking down:** a signal of submission.
- **Looking sideways:** can indicate distraction, showing interest in something, or irritation.

- o **Side-to-Side:** shiftiness, lying, or looking for an escape route.
- ▪ **Glancing:** may indicate a person wants something.
- o **Target glance:** indicates a person is looking at the striking area.
- ▪ **Staring:** may indicate shock, disbelief, aggressiveness, or derangement.
- ▪ **Tears:** indicates sadness, extreme fear, or tears of joy.
- ▪ **Blinking:** blinking a lot can indicate significant stress—non-blinking can indicate attack
- ▪ **Pupil Size:** the pupils are affected by light and can also be affected by intoxication.
- o **Dilated:** cocaine, crack, meth, hallucinogens, and other stimulants
- o **Constricted:** heroin, depressants, and opioids

Body Language

- ▪ **Body language is an outward reflection of a person's emotional condition.**

When a person has a nervous, negative, or defensive attitude, it is very likely they will fold their arms firmly on their chest, displaying that they feel threatened.

- ▪ **Crossed arms on the chest are universally perceived as defensive or negative.**

Gestures: Be expressive, but don't overdo it. Keep your fingers closed when you gesture, hands below chin level, and avoid arm or feet crossing. Nodding the head is almost universally used to indicate "yes" or agreement. Using multiple nods can be a persuasion tool. Research shows that people will talk three to four times more than usual when the listener nods their head at regular intervals.

Hands: The hands have been the most important tools in human evolution. There are more connections between the brain and the hands than between any other body part.

Throughout history, the open palm has been associated with truth, honesty, allegiance, and submission. Hidden palms may give a person an intuitive feeling that the person they are communicating with is untruthful. **Universal hand signals are...**

Cultural Differences:

The biggest cultural differences exist mainly in relation to territorial space (distance), eye contact, touching, and insult gestures. The regions that have the greatest number of different gestures are Arab countries and parts of Asia and Japan. Be sensitive to cultural differences if they exist.

The "Right" Angle

When approaching individuals who are in the assault cycle (stressed, intoxicated, angry, combative), we should approach them at a 45-degree angle versus approaching them head-on. This type of approach reduces tension and is a lot safer.

The 5 Habits of De-Escalation Exercise

When approaching individuals who are in the assault cycle (stressed, intoxicated, angry, aggressive, and escalated), we should approach them at a 45-degree angle versus approaching them head-on. This type of approach reduces tension and is a lot safer.

- Habit I – 360° View of Awareness & Plan "E"scape

- Habit II – Approach 45° & Blade your Body 45°

- Habit III – Hands Open (palms up)

- Habit IV – Introduce Yourself & Get the Individuals Name

- Habit V – QTIP = Quit Taking It Personally

The Assault Cycle

The cycle of assault is a theory that describes how aggressive incidents happen over a period of time, developing through five specific stages or phases. This concept reminds us that violent events rarely happen without any warning signs, and it helps us to understand and manage people who have the potential to become violent. It highlights, in particular, the important role played by de-escalation techniques in preventing aggressive incidents from spiraling into violence.

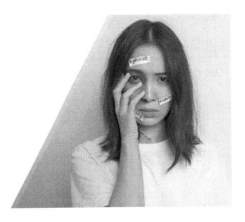

What are the stages in the cycle of assault?

The Triggering Phase (STRESSORS) This is the initial stage where an individual is triggered by an event or sequence of events that have a threatening effect upon them. Typically, the event either causes the person to feel stressed, fearful, or frustrated. This stage is very prevalent in the healthcare industry but can be seen in any workplace.
- In this early stage, proper communication and de-escalation interventions tend to work best.
- Without early interventions, an individual may escalate to the next phase.

Escalation Phase (ANGER) In this phase, the person becomes increasingly tense, angry, and verbally aggressive. He or she may do things like pace, bang objects, yell, taunt, etc. The escalation phase, also known as anger, is a feeling related to one's perception of having been offended or wronged and a tendency to undo that wrongdoing by retaliation.
- All of us have been escalated and angry. How we handle our anger and deal with another person's anger can determine the kind of outcome we want.
- Anger may lead to a person becoming combative if the person is unable to maintain control.

Crisis Phase (VIOLENCE) This is the peak of aggressive/violent behavior. The aggressor may hit, kick, throw things at people, or explode in other forms of physical assault. This combative physical aggression is described as behavior between members of the same species which is intended to cause pain or harm.
- In the crisis phase, the best strategy and intervention is to escape immediately.
- In this fight-flight phase, the aggressor will have a spike in adrenalin, cortisol, and norepinephrine, which is typically short-lived, bringing them to the recovery phase.

Recovery Phase (SUBMISSION) In this phase, the person's body and mind begin to relax and recover. They seem to have ended the combative behavior, though sometimes it's unclear whether or not this is only temporary. During this stage of submission, it is important to recognize that the individual is not completely void of their stress hormones and could re-escalate.

Post-Crisis Depression Phase In this phase, the aggressor feels the emotional and physical toll that his/her actions have taken. They may experience fatigue, depression, and/or guilt because of their actions. This phase is important to understand for staff who have patients on a long-term basis.

Recognizing how to intervene in the cycle of assault: There are several ways to calm down a situation before it moves from the Trigger Phase and Escalation Phase to the Crisis Phase (physical assault). It's critical to watch for signs of escalating anger and aggression. The assault cycle can include any of the perpetrators of violence: stranger, client/patient, lateral and domestic aggressors.

The *Assault Cycle* is the predictable behavior that leads to violence.

AGGRESSIVE BEHAVIOR

The **Assault Cycle** is the predictable behavior that leads to violence. It includes individuals who are **stressed, intoxicated, angry, physically combative,** and **submissive**.

▪ **Caution** when dealing with these behaviors as they can be **violence predicting factors**.

Key Resource: 1 Kaplan, S. G., & Wheeler, E. G. (1983). Survival skills for working with potentially violent clients. Social Casework.

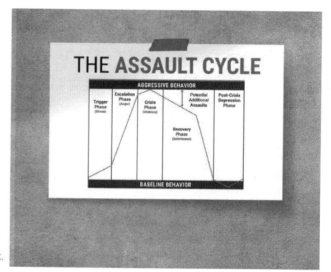

Understanding the assault cycle and the phases of it are crucial to know to de-escalate and defuse a potentially dangerous situation so you can break the cycle before violence occurs or escalates.

Your ability to recognize what phase a person is in is essential to your personal safety and intervention efforts. The assault components/cycle include individuals who are **stressed, intoxicated, angry, physically combative, and submissive**. Caution should be exercised when dealing with any of these behaviors as they can be violence-predicting factors.

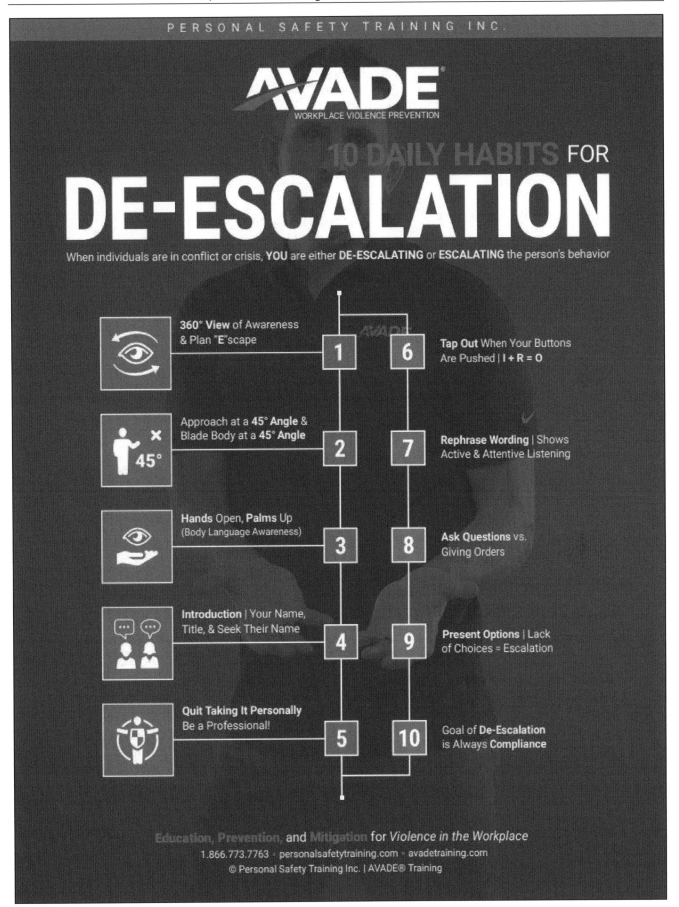

The Triggering Phase - Upset (Stressed) Individuals

Regardless of your profession, we all end up dealing with stressed people in various ways and situations. This can mean working with upset, escalated, and challenging individuals in many ways. Learning how to recognize the person's behavior, control your responses, and have pre-planned de-escalation techniques for the situation is a win for all.

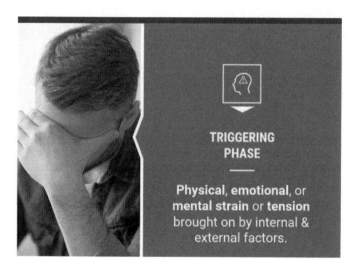

POTENTIAL ESCALATION

The following information can assist you in **recognizing** that an individual has been **triggered** and is now **upset** or **stressed** and has the **potential to escalate**.

When **interventions** are used to **de-escalate** and **defuse**, there is less of a chance that the individual will spiral into the escalation phase of the **Assault Cycle**.

TRIGGERING PHASE

Physical, emotional, or **mental strain** or **tension** brought on by internal & external factors.

Signs and Symptoms of Stress (Escalation, Aggression, & Violence Predicting Factors)

EMOTIONAL

Agitated, frustrated, moody, feeling overwhelmed, difficulty relaxing or quieting the mind, low self-esteem, feeling depressed, avoiding others, etc.

PHYSICAL

Change in facial expression, change in eye contact, low energy, medical symptoms (headache, upset stomach, etc.), nervousness, dry mouth, clenched jaw, grinding teeth, shallow breathing, etc.

COGNITIVE

Constant worrying, racing thoughts, inability to focus, poor judgment, pessimism, acting distracted or confused, etc.

BEHAVIORAL

Change in appetite, change in speech, procrastinating & avoiding responsibilities, increased use of alcohol & drugs, nail biting, fidgeting, pacing, etc.

What are some additional emotional, physical, cognitive, and behavioral signs and symptoms you might recognize?

Stress De-Escalation Techniques

Use these verbal and physical maneuvers and interventions to defuse and de-escalate and to avoid escalation and violent behavior:

- **Habit I – 360° View of Awareness & Plan E"scape**

- **Habit II – Approach 45° & Blade your Body 45°**
  (relaxed 45° with 4-6 feet away)
  - **Blade Your Body,** so the other person does not feel threatened.
  - **The Bladed Stance:** When dealing with people who are stressed, angered, intoxicated, or escalated, always BLADE your body. The bladed stance is done by simply turning your body slightly to the side. This stance protects your vulnerable line (nose to groin) as you are now in an angled position. This position is less threatening to others and provides less of a target to an aggressor if the situation escalates. The bladed position can also be done from a seated position.
  - **Assess the Area and Space** you're in and **stay at least 4-6' away.** Know your escape routes. Getting too close to people can escalate them.

- **Habit III – Hands Open (palms up)** (this approach is less threatening to people)
  - **Assess your Body Language:** What signals are you sending? Avoid being rigid. Staying relaxed will encourage the other person to relax.
  - Remember, over 90% of communication is non-verbal.

- **Habit IV – Introduce Yourself & Get the Individuals Name.** (use your name, seek their name, use their name when explaining why you are there)
  - **Use Your Voice:** Use a slow, quiet, and confident tone.
  - **Use Names (the individual's and yours):** Introduce yourself and ask the individual his or her name. Personalizing a situation can reduce tension and establish a bond.

- **Habit V – QTIP – Quit Taking It Personally**
  (no matter what is said or what happens, be a professional)
  - **Control your Behavior:** If you get upset or agitated, you will escalate the situation. Do not get sucked into the issue. Remember, **I + R = O, and be a professional.**

- **Do Not Touch the Individual:** Touching a person may escalate the situation.

- **Break Eye Contact** to remain non-threatening. And use your interested eye contact when you do look the person in the eye.

- **Use Attentive Listening:** Make sure the individual feels like he/she is being listened to (use paraphrasing).

- **Do NOT Make Promises** that you cannot keep. Medications and service times are particularly relevant triggers in regard to promises.

- **Clarify Communications, and Ask for Specific Responses**
"You want _____, is that correct?" "What can I do to help you?" "I sense you are upset?" "Do you have any questions for me?" "Are you understanding everything, ok?"

- **Express Your Intention to Help:** "I am here to help." "Is there anything I can get you?"

- **Redirect Environment:** We redirect environments by getting people to move to a new location or area. Moving a person to another location allows them to "save face" (respect) if there are friends and family nearby. It may also provide you with a safer location to deal with them.

- **Redirect Thoughts:** We redirect thoughts by asking questions, and questions are powerful. Properly asked questions can enable the person posing them to de-escalate the entire situation. **RAQ = Random Asked Question.**

Learning to Ask the Right Questions

By learning to ask the right questions at the right time, you will be able to:

- Make a positive first impression.
- Positively direct the interaction/situation.
- Control the conversational cadence.
- Stay on task and not get distracted or sucked into the situation.
- Interrupt the negative momentum.
- Influence another person's behavior as well as your own.
- Direct another person's focus as well as your own.
- Motivate others as well as yourself.
- Develop relationships.
- Establish rapport.
- Set clear goals and make decisions.

✓ **When it comes to establishing and understanding effective communications, questions are critical!**

✓ **Asking a question based on something the other person said demonstrates that you listened.**

The Escalation Phase - Angry (Aggressive) Individuals

Anger is a normal emotion that everyone experiences from time to time. However, if a person is unable to control their anger, it can cause problems in relationships both at home and at work. Individuals can become angry for many reasons, and everyone experiences anger differently. When interventions are used to de-escalate and defuse, there is less of a chance that the individual will spiral into the escalation phase of the assault cycle.

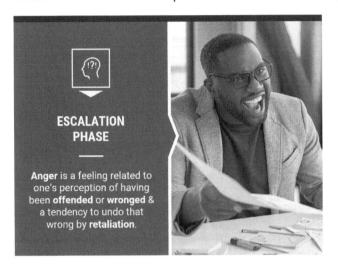

ESCALATION PHASE

Anger is a feeling related to one's perception of having been **offended** or **wronged** & a tendency to undo that wrong by **retaliation**.

ANGER SPIRAL

Individuals can become **angry** for many reasons, and everyone experiences anger differently. When **interventions** are used to **de-escalate** and **defuse**, there is **less of a chance** of the individual spiraling into the **Escalation Phase** of the **Assault Cycle**.

Signs and Symptoms of Anger (Escalation, Aggression, & Violence Predicting Factors)

- **Loud Voice**

- **Challenging Statements**

- **Foul Language**

- **Verbal Threats**

- **Dealing with a Veiled Threat:**

  "What do you mean by_____?"

- **Physically Acting Out (Pacing & Tense)**

- **Personal History of Violence** (Knowledge of a person's background and history can be extremely important as it can be a pre-incident indicator of escalation to violence.)

- **Exaggerated Movements** (stomping, hitting objects, posturing)

- **Demanding Expressions** (finger-pointing, lips pressed or pushed forward, nose wrinkled, and posturing)

- **Demanding** (unnecessary services, unnecessary attention, entitlement)

- **Acting Disgruntled** (may be passive aggression)

- **Attempting to Intimidate** (by invading a person's personal space)

Anger De-Escalation Techniques

Use these verbal and physical maneuvers and interventions to defuse and de-escalate and to avoid escalation and violent behavior:

- **Habit I – 360°View of Awareness & Plan "E"scape)**

- **Habit II – Approach 45° & Blade your Body 45°** (relaxed 45° with 4-6 feet away)
  - ○ **Blade Your Body,** so the other person does not feel threatened.
  - ○ **Assess the Area and Space** you're in, and **stay at least 4-6' away.**

- **Habit III – Hands Open (palms up)** (this approach is less threatening to people)
  - ○ **Assess your Body Language:** What signals are you sending? Avoid being rigid. Staying relaxed will encourage the other person to relax.
  - ○ Remember, over 90% of communication is non-verbal.

- **Habit IV – Introduce Yourself & Get the Individuals Name.** (use your name, seek their name, use their name when explaining why you are there)
  - ○ **Use Your Voice:** Use a slow, quiet, and confident tone.
  - ○ **Use Names (the individual's and yours):** Introduce yourself and ask the individual his or her name. Personalizing a situation can reduce tension and establish a bond.

- **Habit V – QTIP – Quit Taking It Personally**
  (no matter what is said or what happens be a professional)
  - ○ **Control your Behavior:** If you get upset or agitated, you will escalate the situation. Do not get sucked into the issue. Remember, **I + R = O, and be a professional.**
  - ○ When your buttons get pushed because you are being yelled at, cursed at, intimidated, etc., you end up taking things personally. **This never helps!** Remember to quit taking things personally; be professional and be nice.

- **Walk Away If Possible.** Yes, just walk away. **Tap Out**= Remove yourself or someone else.

- **Avoid Arguing.** No one ever really wins an argument. To avoid arguing and telling someone, they are wrong. Instead, use this powerful phrase: *"If I were in your shoes, I would probably feel the same way,"* angry/upset. With the information received, you may be able to offer a resolution (fix) to the problem.

- **Don't Interrupt—allow them to vent.** Interrupting a person is the quickest and surest way to tell them that you are not listening and that your thoughts and ideas are more important than theirs.

Remember, you can use all these interventions for stressed individuals as well.

- **Display Sincerity.** Sincerity means freedom from deceit, hypocrisy, or duplicity. The ancient word "sincere" means without wax. When we are sincere, we are real. **People know when individuals are fake. Be sincere!**

- **Seek to Agree—and get them to say "yes."** When we agree with another person or get them to agree with us, it builds a bond. **Example:** "You're right; this place is a bummer." "Yeah, it is overcrowded in here, huh."

- **Use a Collaborative Approach—using "we" and "us"—gives a person a feeling of belonging. Example:** "Why don't we sit down and talk about this." "Between us, we will come up with something." "Why don't we go outside and talk about this."

- **Identify the Problem. Ask them, "I sense you are angry/upset?"** Using this technique gets right to the heart of the problem versus dancing around the issue. There may be a simple solution or a way to fix it for the person who is angry. People who are asked this question ("I sense you are angry/upset") will generally tell you why they are angry/upset. With the information received, you may be able to offer a resolution (fix) to the problem.

- **Ask Questions Rather Than Give Orders!** What are the most common problems that you face in your workplace? Identify them. And instead of ordering a person to stop what they're doing, ask a question. **Examples:**
  Order: "You can't smoke here." vs. **Question:** "Did you know this is a non-smoking area?"
  Order: "You can't park your car here." vs. **Question:** "Did you know this is valet parking only?"
  Order: "You need to have a mask on your face." vs. **Question:** "Did you know that masks are required to be on in here?"
  - Asking a question versus giving an order gives a person an out. It allows them to save face, develops a rapport with them, and provides the compliance that you are looking for.

- **Give Options** People don't like absolutes; they prefer options. Always offer the best option first and less desirable options after. It puts the "ball in their court," so to speak.

- **Resist Being Defensive** (do not make threats and ignore challenges)
  When we are defensive or make threats and challenges, we become the aggressive individual. Remember QTIP, and don't go down in the mud with the individual. If you feel like you are getting sucked into the situation, remove yourself.

- **Set and Enforce Boundaries, but only ones you can enforce.** Initially, we allow people to vent. But when people vent, and vent, and continue to vent, you may need to intervene and set boundaries. If you say you are going to do something, you need to be able to back it up. In parenting, we call this tough love.

- **REMEMBER THE GOAL OF DE-ESCALATION = COMPLIANCE**

De-Escalating Intoxicated (Drugs & Alcohol) Individuals

Intoxication (also known as drunkenness, inebriation, being high, under-the-influence, etc.) is a physiological state occurring when an individual has a high level of alcohol or drugs in their bloodstream. Intoxication can lower inhibitions and impair self-control, which can lead to violence. Anyone under the influence of alcohol or drugs—prescription or otherwise— falls into this category. Intoxication can have dramatic effects on any of the components in the assault cycle: stress, anger, and physical combativeness.

UNDER THE **INFLUENCE**

Intoxication is a **physiological state** occurring when an individual has a **high level** of **alcohol** or **drugs** in their bloodstream.

This can **lower inhibitions** and **impair self-control**, which can lead to **violence**. Anyone under the influence of **alcohol** or **drugs** (prescription or otherwise) falls into this category.

Signs/Symptoms of Intoxication (Escalation, Aggression, & Violence Predicting Factors)

- **Slurred speech**
- **Impaired balance and/or poor coordination**
- **Flushed face**
- **Frequent rubbing of the nose or twisting jaw back and forth**
- **Abnormal eyes—red, glossy/glassy, pupils dilated or constricted**
- **Up & Down Attitudes—euphoria, despair, etc.**
- **Reduced inhibition, erratic behavior**
- **Acting paranoid or disconnected**
- **Odors, on breath and/or clothing**
- **Emotional response**
- **Argumentative**
- **Loud and Obnoxious**

Intoxication De-Escalation Techniques

Use these verbal and physical maneuvers and interventions to defuse and de-escalate and to avoid escalation and violent behavior:

- **Avoid** intoxicated individuals **when at all possible.** The best de-escalation for intoxicated individuals is avoidance.

- **De-Escalation Habits I-V**

- **Use Caution and Stay Aware.** When you can't avoid intoxicated individuals, be sure to stay aware. And use caution. When people are intoxicated, they are impaired. When impaired, people will do things they wouldn't normally do when sober.

- **Don't Argue.** Arguing with intoxicated individuals **can escalate** the situation. Arguing never helps the situation, especially with a person who is under the influence and, therefore, not necessarily rational.

- **Be Proactive in Your Responses.** Reactive responses are always delayed. Proactive people recognize that proactive responses are preferred.

- **Seek to Agree.** The intoxicated individual usually wants an ally. When we seek to agree with them, it builds that ally, which ultimately builds a rapport with them. Having a rapport equals less chance of escalation.

- **Express your Feelings**—expressing that you are frightened or scared of the person's behavior may de-escalate them.
  Example: "That really scared me when you said that."
  Example: "I am concerned, as I care about you and your safety."

- **Assess Area and Space for weapons and escape routes and maintain a proper distance.** With an intoxicated individual, anything may be a weapon. Be aware of what is around you and what is within reach of the intoxicated person. Know your escape routes. Remember, you need to be at least **4 feet** away from an individual to avoid an unarmed attack and much further away with weapon attacks.

- **Above all else, maintain your awareness!**

  Remember to use all stress and anger intervention techniques as well.

Crisis Phase - Physically Combative/Violent Individuals

Combative Physical Aggression is behavior between members of the same species that is intended to cause pain or harm.

PHYSICALLY VIOLENT ASSAULT FACTORS

The top **three factors** related to a physically **violent assault** on a staff person is:

- **Missing** the **signs** & **symptoms** of an imminent **attack**.
- Being **too close** to the **attacker**.
- Giving up your ability to **escape** the **environment**.

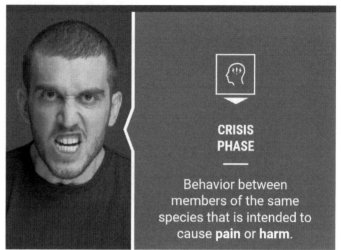

CRISIS PHASE
—
Behavior between members of the same species that is intended to cause **pain** or **harm**.

Signs/Symptoms of Combative Physical Aggression
(Escalation, Aggression, & Violence Predicting Factors)

- **Changes in Posture**—dropping into a fighting stance (pugilistic stance)

- **Preparatory Signals**—rolls sleeves up, takes the coat off, etc. – or stands up suddenly

- **Scanning Area by Moving Head Side to Side**

- **Non- or Slow-Blinking Pattern** ("thousand-yard stare")

- **Flanking Positioning** (finding a suitable position to attack)

- **Telegraphing Intentions**—arm swings or gets cocked before a punch is thrown

- **Looks at Striking Area**—an assailant will almost always look at the area they intend to strike before the attack (target glance)

- **Exaggerated Movements** (lunging in)

- **Changes in Verbalization**—either talking a lot more or suddenly talking less

- **Bracing Effect**—as though bracing to hit or be hit

- **Tightening of Body and/or Fists** (clenching)

- **Trying to Distract YOU**

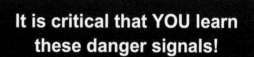

It is critical that YOU learn these danger signals!

Strategies to Avoid Physical Harm

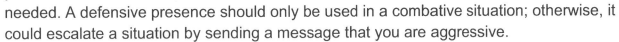

- **Escape Immediately.** That is the most important thing you can do. Once someone has reached the state of combative aggression, your number one priority is to get away. The best self-defense is not to be there! **Escape-Escape-Escape!**

- **Defensive Presence.** Show that you're ready to defend yourself by blading your body and hands. A defensive presence demonstrates that you are trained and ready to defend yourself if needed. A defensive presence should only be used in a combative situation; otherwise, it could escalate a situation by sending a message that you are aggressive.

- **Loud Scream or Yell** so you can attract attention. Yelling, "Stop!" can also arrest someone's attack. Yelling or screaming loudly will alert others, create witnesses, establish your authority, keep you breathing, can be used to distract the aggressor, provide direction to the aggressor, and reduce liability risk to you and your agency.

- **Use Distractions** to interrupt their focus and intent. Distractions buy us time to escape, defend or control. Distractions interrupt one or more of the five senses, giving you time to act. Distractions are sounds, movements, lights, and psychological interruptions. **Always Use Distractions!**

- **Stay Aware—Avoid Tunnel Vision.** When your heart rate exceeds 145 beats per minute, your vision narrows, causing what is called "tunnel vision." Knowing this, you can avoid it by physically turning your head from side to side.

- **Watch to see—what they are planning to do next.** Awareness is always a key component in dealing with combative individuals. Anticipating what the combatant will do next gives us time. And time is precious.

- **Get Help: Alert Others** by motioning or verbalizing. There is safety in numbers! Many agencies have "emergency codes" for combative persons. Know your codes and how to initiate them.

- **Last Resort: Defend or Control if escape is impossible!** If you cannot get away, you are left with only two options (being a victim is not an option), defend yourself and/or control the out-of-control individual. **Being a victim is not an option!**

The Recovery Phase - Submission

Submission: *To yield or surrender (oneself) to the will or authority of another.*

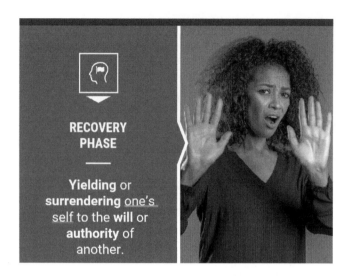

RECOVERY PHASE
—
Yielding or **surrendering** one's self to the **will** or **authority** of another.

FEAR & READINESS

Submission is displayed through a significant **cluster** of **body movements** that are used to signal **fear** and **readiness** to **submit**. This is common in both humans and animals.

Many animals **avoid fighting** themselves (which could maim or kill them) by displays of **aggression** or **submission**.

Just as important as knowing the signals of escalation (components of the assault cycle) is knowing the signs of submission. Submission is displayed through a significant cluster of body movements that are used to signal fear and readiness to submit. This is common in both humans and animals. Many animals avoid fighting amongst themselves (which could maim or kill them) by displays of aggression or submission.

Signs & Symptoms of Submission

- **Body Positions:** In fearful stances, the body is generally closed in on itself and may also exhibit other signs of fearfulness.

- **Self-Protection:** Hunching inwards reduces the size of the body, limiting the potential of being hit and protecting vital areas—for example, hands covering the crotch or chin pushed down to protect the neck.

  - In a natural setting, being small may also reduce the chance of being seen. Arms are held in. A crouching position may be taken, with knees slightly bent. This posture approaches the curled-up, regressive fetal position.

- **Lowering:** Putting the body in a lower position shows the other person that you are not a physical threat. This can include hunching down, bowing, kneeling, or even prostration. It is no surprise that these are typically used in formal greetings of a superior person. Even in sitting, a submissive person will choose a lower chair or slump in order to be lower than others are.

- **Motionlessness:** In a natural setting, staying still reduces the chance of being seen (which is why many animals freeze when they are fearful). And if exposed, it also reduces the chance of accidentally sending signals, which may be interpreted as being aggressive. It signals submission that you are ready to be struck and will not fight back.

- **Head Down:** Turning the chin and head down protects the vulnerable neck from attack. You also avoid looking at the other person in the face (since staring is a sign of aggression).

- **Eyes Down:** Widening the eyes makes you look more like a baby and hence signals your vulnerability. Looking attentively at the other person shows that you are hanging on to their every word.

- **Mouth (Smile):** Submissive people smile more at dominant people. However, they often smile with the mouth but not with the eyes.

- **Submissive Gestures:** The many gestures that show submission communicate that there is no intent to harm the other person. Hands out and palms up show that no weapons are held and are a common pleading gesture. Other gestures and actions that indicate tension may reveal a state of fear. This includes hair tugging, face touching, and jerky movement. There may also be signs such as losing color in the face and sweating.

  - **Small Gestures:** When the submissive person must move, they often make small gestures. These may be slow to avoid alarming the other person, although tension may make them jerky.

- **Submissive Verbalization:** Common verbalizations will be: "I'm sorry," "I shouldn't have…," "I didn't mean to," "I apologize," "What can I do?" "You're right; I'm wrong," etc.

- **Wanting to Shake Your Hand – Should YOU?** An individual may want to shake your hand as an expression of their submission. Caution! When shaking a person's hand, we are within the reactionary gap (4-foot zone) and may be vulnerable to an attack. This tactic could be a ploy to lead you into the attack zone.

> **Dealing with people who are stressed, angry, aggressive, intoxicated, mentally ill, or physically combative can be a frightening experience.**
> **For some, it is part of daily experience at their workplace.**
> **No matter what you do, your interpersonal communications can help you recognize and diffuse a potentially violent situation.**

Developing & Using Interpersonal Communication Skills for Customer Service

Some general things to keep in mind when communicating:

- **Be Clear and Concise When Speaking**

- **Avoid Using Slang and Jargon:** It helps avoid confusion, misdirection, complaints, and poor interpersonal relations.

- **Play the Part of the Scene You Are In...** "All the world is indeed a stage, and we are merely players." As the stage changes, play the appropriate part to keep yourself and others safe.

- **The Golden Rule (treating others as you would like to be treated)** Treating and speaking to people with respect is the universally accepted standard of behavior towards others. "Do unto others as you would have them do unto you."

- **Platinum Rule (treat others the way *they* want to be treated)**

- **Use Common Courtesies** consistently and repeatedly with all people, all the time.
    - Please.
    - Thank you.
    - Yes, please.
    - My pleasure.
    - You're welcome.
    - I am sorry to disturb you, but I need to speak with you for a moment.

- **People Watch and Pay Attention.** Watch and learn as you view the stage that others are on. Pay attention to what works and doesn't work for you and for other people.

- **Learn from your experiences and the experiences of others.**

    Experience is a great teacher!
    Knowledge, training, and experiences are the keys to understanding and avoiding situations that are threatening and unsafe. When faced with a situation that is both unavoidable and threatening, we may need to physically intervene to defend ourselves or another   person.

Module Five: Defense of Self and Others

The Fourth Principle of the AVADE® Training Program

The following information will provide a general understanding of what self-defense and use of force are, how you can legally protect yourself against assault, as well as the risk of liability associated with any type of self-defense or force.

What is Self-Defense?

Self-defense is the right to use **reasonable force** to **protect oneself or members of one's staff/family from bodily harm** from the attack of an aggressor if you have reason to believe that you or they are in **danger**.

Self-defense must always be your last resort. When it is used, the force used must be considered "reasonable,"; e.g., striking someone who yells an obscenity at you is not considered "reasonable force."

The best self-defense is to avoid the situation and getaway. If avoidance and escape are not possible, a reasonable defense would be lawful as a last resort. You have the right to defend yourself; however, **any use of self-defense must follow any agency policy and procedure**, as well as state and federal law.

The following information will provide a general understanding of what self-defense and use of force are, how you can legally protect yourself against assault, as well as the risk of liability associated with any type of self-defense or force.

This module will give you a basic understanding of self-defense, assault, reasonable force and basic legal definitions of force. Personal Safety Training Inc. makes no legal declaration, representation or claim as to what force should be used or not used during a self-defense or assault incident or situation. Each individual must take into consideration their ability, agency policies and procedures, and laws in the state and country in which they reside.

Types of Assault

Physical Assault: The attempt to cause injury, coupled with the present ability to cause injury.

Non-Physical Assault: Physical contact is not required to constitute an assault. In all states, threats are a separate crime. A verbal threat of physical harm is a threat with the intent to intimidate or scare, resulting in the alteration of any part of a person's normal life due to the threat.

To constitute an illegal threat, the following must be present:

- The threat must be serious, with the threat of definite injury
- The threat must be immediate and can be carried out in the immediate or near future.
- The threat must be credible; that is, the victim believes the threat and acts upon that belief.

Domestic Assault: This can involve battery that occurs between two parties who are related to some degree (family or intimate relationships).

Battery Assault: Battery is a criminal offense whereby one party makes physical contact with another party with the intention to harm them. In order to constitute a battery, an offense must be intentional and must be committed to inflict injury on another.

Sexual Battery: Any non-consensual physical contact that is sexual in nature.

Lawful Use of Defense

In order to be lawful in your defense of yourself and others, you must have a basic understanding of some legal definitions and how they apply to self-defense and our legal system.

- **Use-of-Force**
- **Reasonable Force**
- **Reasonable Belief**
- **Deadly Force**
- **Excessive Force**
- **Dangerous & Deadly Weapons**

Security / Law Enforcement Responses to Workplace Violence Incidents

SEEK ASSISTANCE FROM
SECURITY

- Ensure that you know how to contact **Security** in an **emergency**. Memorize their **number** & **extension**.
- **Security** can assist **Law Enforcement** with **contact**, **directions**, & proper **documentation**.
- **Security** should be **notified of all incidents** of **Workplace Violence**.

SECURITY PROFESSIONALS

In all cases of **Workplace Violence** or calling the **Police** notify **Security** & your **Supervisor** without delay.

Notes

_____

_____

_____

_____

_____

SEEK ASSISTANCE FROM
LAW ENFORCEMENT

- **Law Enforcement** is responsible for responding to potential or in-progress **criminal activity**, **reporting**, & **arrests** if warranted.
- If an employee believes the situation involves **dangerous criminal activity**, such as **assault** or **weapons**, they are allowed to notify the **police** (Usually by dialing 911).

LAW ENFORCEMENT PROFESSIONALS

In all cases of **Workplace Violence** or calling the **Police** notify **Security** & your **Supervisor** without delay.

Notes

_____

_____

_____

_____

_____

Use-of-Force

A term that describes the right of an individual or authority to settle conflicts or prevent certain actions by applying measures to either:

1. **Dissuade another party from a particular course of action...or**
2. **Physically intervene to stop or control them.**

Reasonable Force: The degree of force which is not excessive and is appropriate in protecting one's self or one's property.

- **When such force is used, a person is justified and is not criminally liable nor liable in tort.** (A tort is an act that damages someone in some way and for which the injured person may sue the wrongdoer for damages.)

Reasonable Belief: The facts or circumstances that an individual knows, or should know, are such as to cause an ordinary and prudent person to act or think in a similar way under similar circumstances.

Deadly Force: Force that is likely or intended to cause death or great bodily harm. Deadly force may be reasonable or unreasonable, depending on the circumstances.

Excessive Force: That amount of force which is beyond the need and circumstances of the particular event, or which is not justified in the light of all the circumstances, for instance, in the case of deadly force to protect property as contrasted with protecting life.

Dangerous and Deadly Weapons

"Dangerous Weapon" is a device or instrument which, in the manner it is used, or intended to be used, is calculated or likely to produce death or great bodily harm.

"Deadly Weapons" includes any firearm, whether loaded or unloaded or a device designed as a weapon and capable of producing death or great bodily harm.

80

Levels of Force and Defense

The following chart is designed to give you a basic understanding of how your actions may apply to the actions of an aggressive subject. You may need to increase or decrease your action level, depending on the situation. Any Use-of-Force or Self-Defense MUST be lawful.

Subject's Actions | Your Actions

#	Subject's Actions	Your Actions	
9	DEADLY FORCE	DEADLY FORCE	+
8	ACTIVE ASSAULT	TASER™ | IMPACT WEAPONS	+
7	ACTIVE ASSAULT	CHEMICAL AGENT SPRAYS	+
6	ACTIVE ASSAULT	PERSONAL DEFENSIVE TECHNIQUES	+
5	INCREASED ACTIVE RESISTANCE	DEFENSIVE TACTICS	+
4	ACTIVE RESISTANCE	PEPPER SPRAYS	+
3	PASSIVE RESISTANCE	ESCORT TECHNIQUES	+
2	VERBALLY RESISTIVE | UNCOOPERATIVE	INTERPERSONAL COMMUNICATION SKILLS	+
1	SUBJECT | COMPLIANCE	OFFICER | YOUR PRESENCE	+

Lawful Use-of-Force & Defense is permissible:

1. When used to control an out-of-control individual
2. When used to overcome resistance of the out-of-control individual
3. When used to prevent escape from an individual who is under your control (hold)
4. When used in self-defense or in defense of others

Use-of-Force & Self-Defense <u>MUST</u> be Reasonable

YOU should always take into consideration the <u>facts</u> and the <u>circumstances</u> of the incident.

- Type of crime and severity of the crime
- The resistance of the subject when needing to control them
- The threat and safety to others in the area
- Aggressive Subject and Staff Factors

Every person must take into consideration their moral, legal, and ethical beliefs and rights and understandings when using any type of force to defend themselves or others. Personal Safety Training Inc. makes no legal declaration, representation or claim as to what force should be used or not used during a self-defense/assault incident or situation. Each individual must take into consideration their ability, agency policies and procedures and laws in their state and/or country.

Aggressive Subject and Staff Factors

Many factors may affect your selection of an appropriate level of use-of-force or self-defense. These factors should be articulated in your post-incident documentation.

Examples may include:

Age: In dealing with an aggressive subject who is agile, younger, faster, stronger, and has more stamina, an older staff person may have to use more force/control/defense. In contrast, a younger staff person might need to use less control/force/defense on an older person.

Size: In dealing with a larger aggressive subject, a smaller staff person may need to use more force/control/defense during the incident. A larger staff person would obviously, use less force/control/defense with an aggressive subject who is smaller.

Skill Level: In dealing with a subject skilled in mixed martial arts or an expert in karate, it may be more difficult to control or defend against them based on their skill level. A staff person who is skilled in defensive tactics may only need to use a minimum of force (with proper technique) to control/defend the subject. A staff person without current training and experience may need to use more force/defense to control or defend against the subject.

Relative Strength: The different body compositions of males and females may be a factor in controlling a member of the opposite gender. Females typically have less torso strength than their male counterparts. Male staff may have to use less force to control a female subject. In contrast, a female staff person may need to use more force to control a male subject.

Multiple Aggressors: A staff person who is being physically attacked by multiple aggressors is at a disadvantage. Even highly skilled staff involved in defensive tactics is likely to be harmed in a situation such as this. In order to survive multiple aggressor attacks, higher levels of force may be necessary.

Every person must take into consideration their moral, legal, and ethical beliefs and rights and understandings when using any type of force to defend themselves or others. Personal Safety Training Inc. makes no legal declaration, representation or claim as to what force should be used or not used during a self-defense/assault incident or situation. Each individual must take into consideration their ability, agency policies and procedures and laws in their state and/or country.

Post-Incident Response

It's vital for all employers to have a Post Incident Response protocol. The following points are guidelines for the proper and most efficient response to a violent incident.

- **Triage (Medical/Hazmat)**: Triage is the process of determining the priority of patients' or victims' treatments based on the severity of their condition. Initial first-aid treatment and protocols for hazardous materials and clean-up should be handled immediately.

- **Report the Incident: Police, Security, Risk Management, Human Resources, etc.:** Follow standard operating procedures in reporting incidents.

- **Consider all Involved—staff, guests, visitors**, patients, or anyone who was witness to the incident should be treated accordingly for medical and stress debriefing.

- **Provide for Incident Debriefing:** Debriefing allows those involved with the incident to process the event and reflect on its impact. Depending on the situation, a thorough debriefing may need to take place. Even those not specifically involved in an incident may suffer emotional and psychological trauma.

- **Critical Incident Stress Debriefing (CISD):** is a specific technique designed to assist others in dealing with physical or psychological symptoms that are generally associated with critical incident trauma exposure. Research on the effectiveness of critical incident debriefing techniques has demonstrated that individuals who are provided critical stress debriefing within a 24- to 72-hour window after experiencing the critical incident have lower levels of short- and long-term crisis reactions and psychological trauma.

- **Employee Assistance Programs (EAP):** EAPs are intended to help employees deal with work or personal problems that might adversely impact their work performance, health, and well-being. EAPs generally include assessment, short-term counseling, and referral services for employees and their household members. Employee benefit programs offered by many employers, typically in conjunction with health insurance plans, provide for payment for EAPs.

- **Document Incident to Include Any Follow-Up Investigations:** Post-incident documentation is absolutely critical for reducing liability risk, preventing recurrences, and assisting in follow-up investigations.

- **Initiate Corrective Actions to Prevent Incident Recurrences:** Preventing similar future incidents involves taking proactive corrective actions. Agency management, supervision, security, risk management, employee safety committees, the environment of care committee, etc., should initiate, track, and follow up on corrective actions.

Post-Incident Documentation

- **Who–What–Where–When–Why–How**
The first rule in post-incident documentation is the "who, what, where, when, why, and how" rule of reporting. After writing an incident narrative, double-check to see if you have included the first rule of reporting.

- **Witnesses (Who Was There?)**
Make sure to include anyone who was a witness to the incident. Staff, visitors, guests, and support services (police, fire, EMS, etc.) can be valuable witnesses should an incident be litigated.

- **Narrative Characteristics**
A proper narrative should describe in detail the characteristics of the violent offender/predator.

- **Before, During, and After**
A thorough incident report will describe what happened before, during, and after the incident. Details matter!

- **1st Person vs. 3rd Person**
The account of an incident can be described in the first person or the third person. This can be specific to your agency protocols or the preference of the person documenting the incident.

- **Post-Follow-Up (Track and Trend)**
Most agencies use electronic documentation, which allows for easy retrieval, tracking, and trending. Using technology assists agencies in following up and initiating proactive corrections.

- **Follow Standard Operating Procedures**
Whether handwriting incident reports or using electronic documentation and charting, staff should consistently and thoroughly document all incidents relating to violence in the workplace.

Module Six: Stress Management

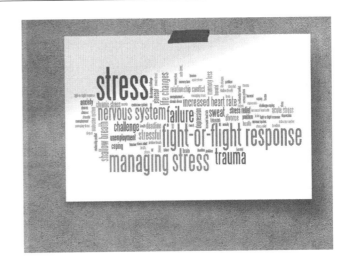

MANAGING STRESS

Stress is the **physical**, **emotional**, & **mental** strain or tension that is brought on by **internal** and **external** factors.

> *"If you are distressed by anything external, the pain is not due to the thing itself, but to your estimate of it; and this you have the power to revoke at any moment."*
> **– Marcus Aurelius Antoninus (121 AD - 180 AD)**

In 1975, Hans Selye, a doctor of medicine and chemistry, published a model that divides stress into distress and eustress. Persistent stress that is not resolved by a coping mechanism or adaptation is deemed distress. Distress may lead to anxiety, withdrawal, and depression. Stress that enhances functions (physical or mental, such as through strength training or challenging work) is considered eustress.

Types of Stress

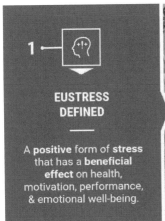

1

EUSTRESS DEFINED

A **positive** form of **stress** that has a **beneficial effect** on health, motivation, performance, & emotional well-being.

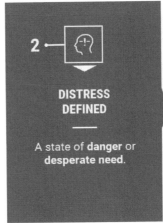

2

DISTRESS DEFINED

A state of **danger** or **desperate need**.

The difference between eustress and distress is the result of the stress determined by a person's experience (real or imagined), their expectations, and their resources to cope with the stress.

> *"Adopting the right attitude can convert a negative stress into a positive one."*
> **– Dr. Hans Selye**

Stress Management - FEAR

Fear is a distressing emotion aroused by a perceived threat. It is a basic survival mechanism that occurs in response to a specific stimulus, such as pain or the threat of danger. Some psychologists suggest that fear belongs to a small set of basic or innate emotions, along with other emotions such as joy, sadness, and anger. Fear should be distinguished from the related emotional state of anxiety, which typically occurs without any external threat.

Fear may be induced whether the threat is real or imagined.

Additionally, fear is related to the specific behaviors of escape and avoidance, whereas stress is the result of threats that are perceived to be uncontrollable or unavoidable. Worth noting is that fear almost always relates to future events, such as worsening of a situation or continuation of a situation that is unacceptable. Fear could also be an instant reaction to something happening in the present.

"Fight–Flight–Freeze"

You've heard of fight-or-flight, which is a reaction to a threat with a general discharge of the sympathetic nervous system, priming the organism for fighting or fleeing. If completely overwhelmed, a person may freeze.

The **fight-flight-freeze response** is a basic, primal, physiological urge to defend or to flee in times of danger. When faced with a situation that is frightening, your perception of it stimulates the part of the brain called the hypothalamus. The hypothalamus emits a hormone that stimulates the pituitary gland to release substances that excite the adrenal gland to release adrenaline (epinephrine) and cortisone.

- Blood pressure goes up as more blood is being pumped, but many vessels constrict to slow/shunt the blood flow.
- The breath may become faster and shallower, or you hold your breath.
- Adrenaline causes the heart to beat faster and vessels carrying blood to the muscles to open.
- Blood shunts systematically from the vegetative organs to muscles preparing you to fight or take flight.
- The vessels that run the digestive and eliminative organs constrict.

Strategies for Managing the Stress Continuum

Putting the Brakes on the Fight-Flight-Freeze (Stress Continuum)

Awareness Controlled Breathing and **Awareness Positive Thinking** are considered the best stress management techniques for immediate stressors (fight-flight) and for the ongoing stressors of life.

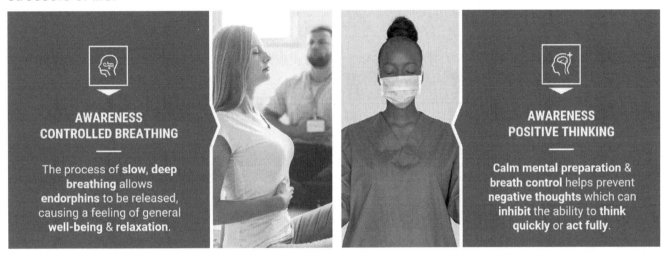

AWARENESS CONTROLLED BREATHING

The process of **slow, deep breathing** allows **endorphins** to be released, causing a feeling of general **well-being & relaxation**.

AWARENESS POSITIVE THINKING

Calm mental preparation & breath control helps prevent **negative thoughts** which can **inhibit** the ability to **think quickly** or **act fully**.

Awareness Controlled Breathing is a very useful tactic in lowering our blood pressure. Studies have shown that during the process of slow, deep breathing, endorphins are released, causing a feeling of general well-being and relaxation. Endorphins apply a brake to the hypothalamic fight-flight response in a situation of imminent danger. Try this: inhale slowly, about two-thirds of your lung capacity. Breathe in for a count of four seconds; breathe out slowly to a count of eight seconds. Notice you immediately feel calmer.

Awareness Positive Thinking and calm mental preparation were recognized to be highly valuable to the Samurai of feudal Japan. In fact, the Samurai spent as much time in mental training as they did preparing their bodies for battle. Samurai employed two techniques to prepare the mind to be tranquil, fearless, and energetic in combat: breath control and meditation. The Samurai knew that a warrior filled with fear (negative thoughts) was doomed. Fear inhibits the ability to think quickly or to act fully.

_____

_____

_____

_____

_____

_____

_____

_____

Caution! All strategies and methods for managing your stress should take into consideration your physical and mental health.
Consult your physician prior to any changes in your behavior.

Strategies for Managing Your Stress Before and After an Incident of Workplace Violence

1. **Healthy Eating:** Proper nutrition and healthy eating habits can help you get through stressful times. Eating well will increase your physical, mental, and emotional stamina. Fueling yourself with food high in nutrients can boost your immune system, help you maintain a healthy weight, and help you feel better about yourself.

2. **Regular Exercise:** Frequent exercise is one of the best physical stress-reduction techniques. Exercise not only improves your health and reduces stress; it also relaxes tense muscles and helps you to sleep better. Most importantly, there is evidence that suggests that physically fit people have less severe physiological responses when under stress than those who are not.

3. **Proper Hydration:** Stress can lead to dehydration. Dehydration affects thinking and causes headaches, nausea, constipation and irritability. Water is essential to your wellbeing.

4. **Time Management:** Planning your day can help you accomplish more and feel more in control of your life. Write a to-do list, putting the most important tasks at the top. Keep a schedule of your daily activities to minimize conflicts and last-minute rushes. Prioritize your tasks and say "no" to nonessential tasks.

5. **Positive Thoughts:** Negative thoughts and energy can affect you in many ways and cause you additional stress. Developing more positive thoughts is an important way to reduce stress in your life. You can help yourself maintain and increase positive thoughts by listening to uplifting music, reading inspirational books, spending time with positive people, and using positive affirmations.

Caution! All strategies and methods for managing your stress should take into consideration your physical and mental health.
Consult your physician prior to any changes in your behavior.

Strategies for Managing Your Stress Before and After an Incident of Workplace Violence

6. **Touch Therapy:** Touch is the first sense to develop in humans. It is essential to our health and wellbeing. Babies have been known to fail to thrive and even die without an adequate amount of physical contact. Adults, as well, can become depressed and ill if they are isolated from this most basic of human needs.

7. **Support System:** It doesn't take a scientific study to show that surrounding yourself with a supportive family, friends, and co-workers can have a positive effect on your mental well-being.
A strong social support network can be critical to helping you through the stress of tough times, whether you've had a bad day at work or a year filled with loss or chronic illness.

8. **Recreation:** Recreational activities are experiences in which you actively participate in an organized activity, generally with others, to have fun and enjoy life. They include participation in sports, arts and crafts, games, dancing, or any activity that takes involvement and participation.

9. **Nature:** Use nature to reduce stress. Go outside, hike in the woods, walk on the beach, anything that puts you in contact with the natural world. It is difficult to feel stressed when you are surrounded by nature's abundance of vitality and wonder.

10. **Sacred Space:** Sacred space is defined as any place where you're temporarily sealed off from the world. This can be a room, a special chair, even an activity, or just a state of mind. But the idea is that when you're in a sacred space, whatever you're doing becomes a meditation or a peaceful state for your mind and body. Creating and maintaining your sacred space is a great way to reduce stress.

Post-Incident Stress Debriefing

The methods described here will help manage your stress after an incident occurs. The goal of debriefing is to reduce the chance of Post-Traumatic Stress symptoms and Post-Traumatic Stress Disorder (PTSD).

- **Always debrief.** Staff should debrief after every workplace violence incident, regardless of the severity. Oftentimes a brief discussion of the events and outcome is enough. Other times, a more intensive debriefing is needed.

  - **The goal of debriefing is to reduce the chances of Post-Traumatic Stress Symptoms and Post Traumatic Stress Disorder (PTSD).**

- **Acknowledge humanness.** As humans, we are susceptible to the frailties of human nature. This acknowledgement creates an awareness that it is okay to seek and ask for help.

- **Talk to co-workers.** Almost all workers have experienced or witnessed some type of workplace violence incident. Your co-workers can be a great resource to vent your concerns about your feelings after an incident.

- **Be aware of post-event feelings.** Having the knowledge and awareness that you may experience strong feelings from an event can give you the confidence to seek help and discuss feelings with others.

- **Take advantage of your Employee Assistance Program (EAP).** Agencies realize that feelings may persist for longer than you might expect after an incident. Employee Assistance Programs can benefit employees and help them deal with post-incident stress or other work/personal problems. EAPs are intended to help employees deal with problems or issues that might adversely affect their work performance, health, and well-being. EAPs generally include assessment, short-term counseling, and referral services for employees and their household members.

- **Know the signs and symptoms of Post-Traumatic Stress Disorder (PTSD).** PTSD is a psychological reaction occurring after experiencing a highly stressful event (such as wartime combat, physical violence, or a natural disaster). It's usually characterized by depression, anxiety, flashbacks, recurrent nightmares, and avoidance of reminders of the event.

- **Take the time to follow-up with other staff.** As human beings, we often focus on the needs of others and not ourselves. Take the time to discuss workplace incidents, your feelings about the incidents, and how incidents in the workplace could improve.

Critical Incident Stress Debriefing (CISD)

Debriefing is a specific technique designed to **assist others** in dealing with the **physical** or **psychological symptoms** that are generally associated with **trauma exposure**.

Debriefing allows those involved with the incident to **process the event** and **reflect** on its **impact**.

Individuals who are exposed to an assault situation (as a witness or a victim) should consider some level of critical incident debriefing or counseling. The final extent of any traumatic situation may never be known or realistically estimated in terms of trauma, loss, and grief. In the aftermath of any critical incident, psychological reactions are quite common and are fairly predictable. CISD can be a valuable tool following a traumatic event.

Research on the effectiveness of critical incident debriefing techniques has demonstrated that individuals who are provided CISD within a 24- to 72-hour period after the critical incident experience lower levels of short- and long-term crisis reactions, psychological trauma, and PTSD.

Conducting an Incident Debrief

Staff should debrief after every workplace violence incident, regardless of the severity. Oftentimes a brief discussion of the events and outcome is enough. Other times, a more intensive debriefing is needed. **Debriefs are always POSITIVE!** After action, corrections should be done at a later date.

There are four primary steps for conducting an Incident Debrief:
1. **Wellness Check:** the facilitator conducting the debrief asks each person involved and gets a verbal acknowledgement of their mental and physical wellness.
2. **What Happened:** the facilitator conducting the debrief asks each person to briefly describe what they saw, heard, and experienced during the incident.
3. **What did WE do well:** the facilitator conducting the debrief will ask each person to briefly describe what the team (we) did well in responding and dealing with the incident.
4. **What can WE Improve Upon:** the facilitator conducting the debrief will ask each person to briefly describe what they believe the team (we) can improve upon in future incidents. Positive!!

Remember: **The goal of debriefing is to reduce the chances of Post-Traumatic Stress Disorder (PTSD) and Post-Traumatic Stress Symptoms.**

AVADE® DEBRIEF PROCESS FORM

▸ Conducting an Incident Debrief

☑ After a violent incident, it is important that **all personnel involved in the incident meet immediately following the incident to debrief.**

☑ The debrief should be **led and documented by the supervisor and/or person in charge on duty** at the time of the incident, in coordination with security personnel.

FOUR PRIMARY STEPS TO CONDUCTING AN INCIDENT DEBRIEF:

1. **Wellness Check:** The facilitator conducting the debrief *asks each person* involved and gets a *verbal acknowledgement* of their **mental** and **physical wellness.**

   - The debrief leader will **assist in determining if anyone requires immediate or follow up medical treatment** as a result of *injury sustained* as a *result of the incident.*

   - If any personnel are identified as *sustaining injury* or *experiencing extensive stress* as a result of the incident, the agency will need to **follow up and provide further support and resources**, in line with the facilities policy & procedures.

2. **What Happened:** The facilitator conducting the debrief *ask each person* to briefly **describe what they saw, heard and experienced** during the incident.

   - It is important to assist in creating an environment within the debrief that allows **ALL individuals involved** to appropriately decompress and gain their composure prior to returning to regular job duties.

3. **What Did We Do Well:** The facilitator conducting the debrief will a*sk each person* to briefly **describe what the team (we) did well** in responding and dealing with the incident?

   - Often, individuals *immediately following an event* will still be experiencing a **high level of adrenaline**. This is especially true for those who may have not experienced a violent event very often.

4. **What Can we Improve Upon:** The facilitator conducting the debrief will ask each person to briefly describe what they believe the team (we) can improve upon in future incidents? Positive!!

   - An individual still experiencing an *adrenaline rush,* may not be aware of their need to decompress or how the incident may have impacted them emotionally and/or mentally. Because of this, as a **TEAM**, ensure that you encourage each other to take a moment and *assess your ability to return to your regular job duties.*

Staff should debrief after every workplace violence incident, *regardless of the severity*. Often times a brief discussion of the events and outcome is enough. Other times, a more intensive debriefing is needed. Debriefs are **always POSITIVE!** After action corrections should be *done at a later date.*

Remember: The goal of debriefing is to **reduce the chances of Post-Traumatic Stress Disorder** (PTSD) and **Post-Traumatic Stress Symptoms.**

A) **Wellness Check:** _____

_____

B) **What Happened:** _____

_____

C) **What Did We Do Well:** _____

_____

D) **What Can We Improve Upon:** _____

_____

Education, Prevention, and Mitigation for *Violence in the Workplace*

© Personal Safety Training Inc. | AVADE® Training

Exercise – Testing our Thoughts (Awareness Positive Thinking)

_____

_____

_____

_____

_____

_____

_____

_____

_____

_____

_____

_____

_____

_____

_____

Do our thoughts influence our stress and overall wellbeing?

Module Seven: Time and Distance

Time and Distance = Safety

The concept of time or distance illustrates that having time or distance can give us distance or time from a violent person, place, event, or thing. What we do with our time can be the most precious investment we ever make. Imagine that you have the ability to use time and distance to your advantage. And remember:

Reaction Time (OODA Loop)

Air Force Colonel John Boyd coined the term "OODA Loop" to describe a form of reaction time and decision-making. OODA stands for **O**bserve-**O**rient-**D**ecide-**A**ct.

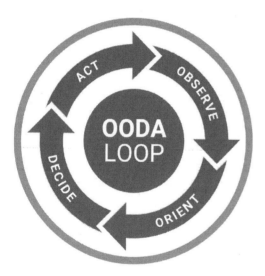

Boyd's key concept is that the decision cycle is the process by which an individual reacts to an event. Accordingly, the key to victory is to be able to create situations wherein one can make appropriate decisions more quickly than one's opponent. This was originally a theory of achieving success in air-to-air combat.

Time is the dominant parameter in the OODA Loop. The individual who goes through the OODA Loop in the shortest time prevails because his opponent is caught responding to situations that have already changed.

☑ **Observation:** The collection of **relevant data** through your **senses**

☑ **Orientation:** The analysis of **observed data** to form your **current mental perspective** of what is happening

☑ **Decision:** Determining a **course of action** based on one's **current mental perspective**

☑ **Action:** Physically **acting out** your **decisions**

Weapons and Time/Distance

Being faced with a weapon is terrifying. Know what to do ahead of time, and use the OODA Loop to your advantage.

Unarmed Attacks = 4-6 Feet (minimum): You need a distance of at least four to six feet to give you time to escape from an attack. Variables that can affect this are environment, distractions, and physical ability.

Clubs and Sticks: When encountering an individual with a club, stick, or any type of impact weapon, the best defense is to create as much distance as you can between you and that individual.

Knives—Edged or Sharpened Weapons: Twenty-one feet is the minimum distance you need from a person with any type of edged weapon. Your ability to defend yourself will need to increase to match the type of weapon being used against you. Again, your best defense is always to escape when possible. -*Studies have shown that individuals with weapons can cover a distance of twenty-one feet in approximately 1.5 seconds.*

Thrown Objects Like the above weapons, a thrown object (chair, table, computer, etc.) can seriously injure an individual. Putting as much distance as possible between you and the aggressor is recommended.

Guns In an active shooter situation, the best defense is to escape or seek cover.
Examples of cover: locations such as a safe room, behind a large barrier that is impenetrable, away from the area in stairwells, elevators, etc.

- Without the ability to seek cover immediately, your best defense is to **RUN!**
- Run, zigzag, jump and keep moving away until you are in a covered position.
- It is very difficult for a person to hit a moving target.
- Most experienced law enforcement officers and trainers will tell you that a moving target is far harder to hit than a fixed target. Couple that with creating distance, and you have a better chance of surviving.
- Active Shooter awareness, preparedness, and responses will be covered in-depth in module ten.
- "Gun Threat Response Defense" is covered in AVADE® Level II Self-Defense Tactics.

Dangerous Weapons in YOUR Workplace

Be aware and vigilant while using time and distance to protect yourself from any use of a regular item that suddenly becomes a weapon.

Pens: Carry your pens so that they cannot be grabbed off of your person and used against you. A pen can easily impale the human body. Pens are a common tool that we all use. Increase your awareness by knowing that they can also harm you when in the hands of an out-of-control, combative individual.

Chairs: Escape immediately if a person has grabbed a chair and is preparing to throw it at you.

Glass/Beverages: Glass and other hard items that hold beverages and food can be thrown or used to strike at you. The contents in these can also be used to assault you—hot beverages such as coffee/tea.

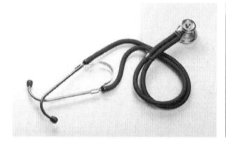

Name Badges/Lanyards – Stethoscopes: Use caution with anything that is around your neck.

Items that can be moved or picked up: Anything that can be picked up can be used as a weapon—staplers, heavy binders, small copiers, etc.

Edge Weapons: scissors, utensils, etc. Be cautious and aware that edged weapons are almost everywhere in the workplace environment. Kitchen utensils and office items are found in most work environments and may pose a threat in the hands of an aggressor.

The Art of Distraction

The Art of Distraction **is a process by which you can buy valuable time to Escape, Control, or Defend.**

Distractions affect the senses, and it takes time for the mind to process the new information. They mainly affect a person's sight and sense of hearing; however, psychological distractions, such as asking a person something completely out of the ordinary, can cause a mental delay as well. Distractions have been used since ancient times and are a valuable advantage you should always use.

Sounds: Using a loud scream or yell can cause a momentary delay.
Movements: Using your hands, eyes, and body can distract and cause a momentary delay.
Psychological: Asking a person something completely out of the ordinary can cause them to have a mental delay (e.g., "What color socks are you wearing?")
Lights: Flashlights, the sun, emergency lights, etc., can cause a delay.

Examples of Sound to distract a person: Loud Scream of *NO! - STOP! - FIRE!*

Examples of Movements that would distract a person:

- Placing your hand in front of someone's face
- Covering their eyes
- Bobbing, weaving, running or jumping
- Looking behind a person
- Stomping your foot on the ground

Examples of a Psychological distraction: Asking a random question:
- "Do you know how to bake chocolate chip cookies?"
- "When was the last time you bought socks?"

4. Examples of Light that would distract a person:

- Moving to a position where the sun or any type of light is in their eyes
- Shining a high-powered flashlight into a person's eyes
- Emergency vehicle lights

Learning to use time (distractions) and distance can keep you safe, unhurt, and alive in instances of workplace violence.

"Reactionary Gap" Exercise - Part 1

The distance between YOU and an aggressor in which your ability to react/respond is impaired due to the close proximity of the aggressor.

Reactionary Gap |

"**Reactionary Gap**" is the distance between and individual and an aggressor in which the ability to react is impaired due to the close proximity of the aggressor.

#	(Reactionary Gap Exercise)
1.	**Form two Lines** with participants facing each other at approximately **10' apart**.
2.	Have **Line A** approach **Line B** until they are arms length away from them and able to touch their shoulder. **a)** Ask participants how many of you got your shoulder touched in the **Part 1 exercise**?
3.	Have both **Line A** and **Line B** place their hands in the prayer position.
4.	**Line A** will begin by quickly touching **Line B**'s shoulder with either hand. (Always coming back to the prayer position | The touching of the shoulder is *simulating an unarmed attack*)
5.	**Line B** will try to defend against the shoulder attack by blocking with either hand or moving out of the way.
6.	**Reverse the roles** of attacker and defender.
7.	How did it go? Who didn't get hit? "Action beats Reaction within the **Reactionary Gap**"

Student Exercise Diagram: Reverse Roles

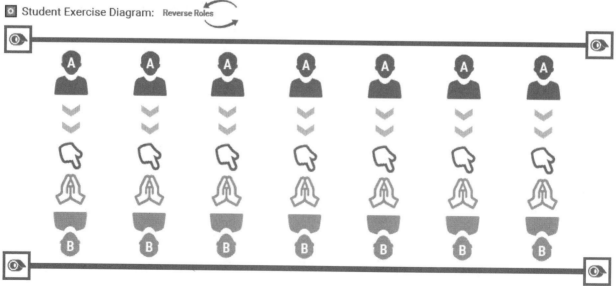

"Reactionary Gap" Exercise - Part 2

The distance between YOU and an aggressor in which your ability to react/respond is impaired due to the close proximity of the aggressor.

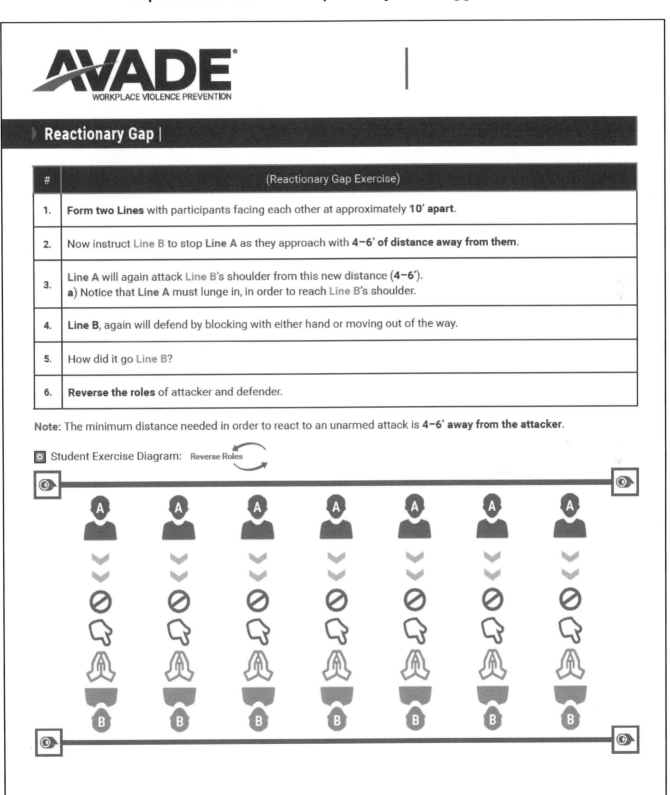

#	(Reactionary Gap Exercise)
1.	**Form two Lines** with participants facing each other at approximately **10' apart**.
2.	Now instruct Line B to stop Line A as they approach with **4–6' of distance away from them**.
3.	Line A will again attack Line B's shoulder from this new distance (**4–6'**). **a)** Notice that Line A must lunge in, in order to reach Line B's shoulder.
4.	**Line B**, again will defend by blocking with either hand or moving out of the way.
5.	How did it go Line B?
6.	**Reverse the roles** of attacker and defender.

Note: The minimum distance needed in order to react to an unarmed attack is **4–6' away from the attacker**.

Student Exercise Diagram: Reverse Roles

Module Eight: Escape Planning

The Fifth Principle of the AVADE® Training Program

Developing escape plans for the environments you are in prepares you in advance for an unfortunate situation where you need to escape from an aggressive or violent incident.
This preparation is not intended to make you scared; it's intended to prepare you for the unexpected.

Escape planning begins with an awareness of where all of your exits are in all of your environments. Developing this habit could literally save your life.

> *"Prepare for the worst, hope for the best, and expect some surprises along the way."*
>
> **- David Fowler, author and founder of AVADE® Training**

The first thing is to learn where all the exits are in all your environments. It's a habit that could save your life. But not only are physical escapes needed, so are quick verbal responses. These can detach you from potential situations that can be negative, threatening, and potentially embarrassing or dangerous.

> *"He who fails to plan, plans to fail."*
> *- Proverb Quote*
>
> ---
>
> *"Planning is bringing the future into the present so that you can do something about it now."*
>
> – Alan Lakein, author of *How to Get Control of Your Time and Your Life*

Developing Escape Plans

1. Own the **door**
2. Dominant **hand**
3. Proper **positioning**
4. Approach at a **45° angle**
5. Spatial **empathy**
6. Proper **escorts**
7. **Relationships**

Having an awareness of your exits in all environments is a highly useful habit that should be developed.

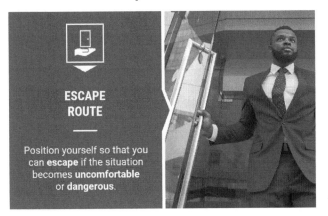

ESCAPE ROUTE

Position yourself so that you can **escape** if the situation becomes **uncomfortable** or **dangerous**.

OWN THE **DOOR**

The concept of **"Own the Door"** means not allowing others to get **between you** and the **door** (Your escape route) in any environment.

The concept of "own the door" means not allowing others to get between you and the door (your escape route) when giving care in the healthcare environment (or any environment). Position yourself so that you can escape if the situation becomes uncomfortable or dangerous. The environmental design of the location can be limiting, but your awareness of your escape routes is the most important factor. What would you do if you needed to perform patient care on someone who might try to harm you, and the environmental design of the room does not allow you to own the door? The answer is to have a backup! Bring additional staff with you while treating aggressive patients.

Always position yourself with an escape route in mind:
When multiple individuals are in a room (visitors, guests, family members), politely ask them to all move to the furthest side of the room away from the doorway. If the environmental design is such that you cannot own the door and you are concerned about being trapped, plan to have an additional person in the room with you.

Having a second person: Provides ready assistance gives you confidence and changes the dynamics of the situation from the aggressive person's perspective.

Improper Positioning

The best self-defense is to not be there when the attack takes place (avoidance), but if your escape route is compromised, your last resort may be to defend yourself from an imminent attack. Always position yourself with an escape route in mind.

POSITION IS KEY

The best **self-defense** is to **not be there** when the attack takes place (Avoidance). If your **escape route** is **compromised**, your last resort may be to **defend yourself** from an imminent attack.

Always **position yourself** with an **escape route** in mind.

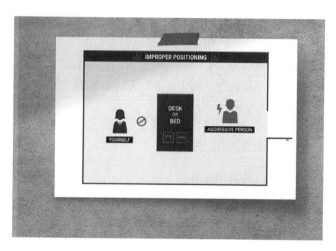

Staff whose work area is structured in such a way as this picture should:

1. Avoid dealing with difficult situations/people in your workspace.
2. If unavoidable (upset person just walks in), have a plan-use distraction technique to get out of your office and then confront the individual in the hallway or open space where available escape routes exist. For healthcare staff, if possible have another person in the room with you.

Dominant Hand / Proper Positioning

If a person becomes combative, they will more than likely strike you with their dominant hand. Positioning yourself on their dominant side makes it more difficult for them to strike at you, so when dealing with at-risk individuals, position yourself on their dominant side.

Proper Positioning

You are always safer when you're at a 45-degree angle to a person who is upset. When standing, approaching, providing service to upset individuals, and escorting individuals, use a 45-degree angle. This position is less threatening than a face-to-face position; it's a de-escalation technique, and it's the safest position for you to be in.

- Safe = 45 degrees in front of individual
- Safest = 45 degrees behind individual
- Unsafe = directly in front of an individual

Distance from the individual is also a major component of proper positioning.

"Spatial Empathy" is an informal term used to describe our awareness of the proximity, activities, and comfort of the people around us. Having spatial empathy means that you are aware of your personal zones and the personal zones of other people. It's important to realize that being in other people's personal zones may make them uncomfortable. Being aware of that allows you to better help them and to be safer yourself.

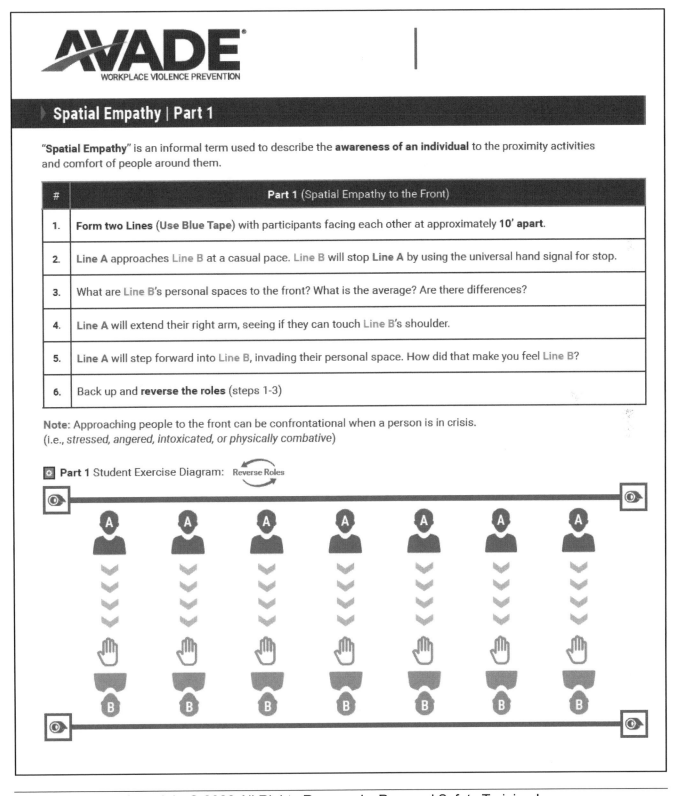

AVADE®
WORKPLACE VIOLENCE PREVENTION

Spatial Empathy | Part 1

"Spatial Empathy" is an informal term used to describe the **awareness of an individual** to the proximity activities and comfort of people around them.

#	Part 1 (Spatial Empathy to the Front)
1.	**Form two Lines (Use Blue Tape)** with participants facing each other at approximately **10' apart**.
2.	**Line A** approaches **Line B** at a casual pace. **Line B** will stop **Line A** by using the universal hand signal for stop.
3.	What are **Line B**'s personal spaces to the front? What is the average? Are there differences?
4.	**Line A** will extend their right arm, seeing if they can touch **Line B**'s shoulder.
5.	**Line A** will step forward into **Line B**, invading their personal space. How did that make you feel **Line B**?
6.	Back up and **reverse the roles** (steps 1-3)

Note: Approaching people to the front can be confrontational when a person is in crisis.
(i.e., *stressed, angered, intoxicated, or physically combative*)

Part 1 Student Exercise Diagram: Reverse Roles

Spatial Empathy | Part 2

#	Part 2 (Spatial Empathy to the Side)
1.	**Form two Lines** and have participants turn and face the same direction at approximately **10' apart**.
2.	Line B approaches **Line A** with a side step. One at a time.
3.	As Line B approaches **Line A**, ask **Line A** how they feel in regard to their space to the side.
4.	Have Line B approach up to the point where they are shoulder to shoulder with **Line A**.
5.	How does that feel? Then have them go face-to-face. How does that feel!?! Go back side to side.

Note: When approaching people who are in crisis (i.e., *stressed, angered, intoxicated, or physically combative*) we recommend you **approach them at a 45° angle**. This exercise illustrates that we feel more comfortable to have someone beside us, versus face to face.

⚙ **Part 2** Student Exercise Diagram:

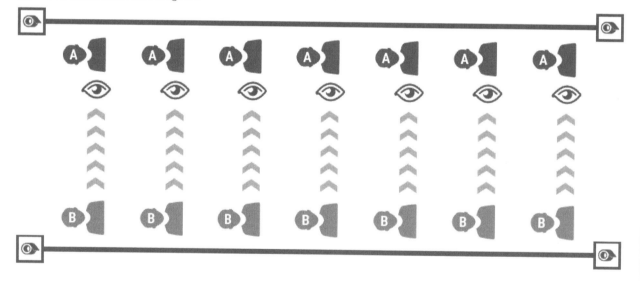

Spatial Empathy | Part 3

#	Part 3 (Spatial Empathy to the Rear)
1.	**Form two Lines** with Line B facing the opposite direction as **Line A** at approximately **10' apart**.
2.	Line B turns their head to see their partner in **Line A** behind them.
3.	Make sure Line B keeps their eyes forward and motion to **Line A** to quietly move in behind their partner in Line B.
4.	Ask Line B, did you feel anything?
5.	Now have Line B turn their head to see that their **Line A** partner is right behind them.

Note: Most people do not like others directly behind them. It gives people a feeling of discomfort and uneasiness.

⚙ **Part 3** Student Exercise Diagram:

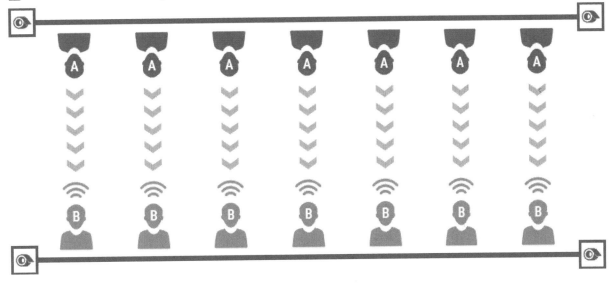

Proper Escort is used for individuals in crisis.

The ABCs of proper escort are:

A Have the individual **walk in front** of you

B Maintain a **45° angle** to them with proper **distance**

C Use your **verbal** & **non-verbal skills** to **direct them** where you want them to go

D Avoid **pointing** | Use **open hand**

E Maintain your **awareness**

Escape Plans refer to determining your escape route ahead of time in relation to the people/environment you are around or come in contact with.

The following scenarios are for uncomfortable and emergent situations. As you read through these scenarios, take a moment and pre-plan your escape/response mentally. Mental movies and impressing the unconscious mind build automatic responses during crisis times.

Scenario (1) What would you do?
An acquaintance calls one evening in an attempt to have you meet him at a local nightclub. The nightclub is known for its loud heavy music and occasional disturbances and incidents with the police. **What's your escape plan?**

Scenario (2) What would you do?
It's 3 am, and you awaken in the middle of the night from a disturbing sound in your front living room. Your kids are across the hall in two separate rooms. You hear footsteps.
What's your escape plan?

Scenario (3) What would you do?
You are walking through the parking lot work and see two kids crouched down by a car, a few cars from where you are parked. No one else is in the parking lot. It is 7 pm on a Monday evening. **What's your escape plan?**

Scenario (4) What would you do? You are at a friend's BBQ party, and one of his guests (his brother-in-law) starts to become verbally assaultive towards you. He has been drinking prior to you arriving there. **What's your escape plan?**

Scenario (5) What would you do?

You are driving home from work, and another driver becomes enraged as they believe you've cut them off. The driver gets right behind you and continues to follow you for miles. **What's your escape plan?**

Scenario (6) What would you do?

You are at the mall shopping with your family (two small children and an older aunt) when you hear what you believe to be gunshots coming from the west end of the mall. You are in a hallway a few hundred feet from the food court with three retail stores in between. The nearest exit is in the direction of where the gunshots are coming from. **What's your escape plan?**

Scenario (7) What would you do?

You are sitting at your desk working on a project when the receptionist dials your extension and asks if you are available. You then hear crashing glass and loud commotion coming from the front entrance where the receptionist is located. **What's your escape plan?**

Scenario (8) What would you do?

You arrive early one morning to the office ready to meet other employees for a local seminar you are all attending. No one else has arrived yet. While waiting in your car, two young men approach each side of your car. One is knocking on your window, wanting to speak to you. **What's your escape plan?**

Scenario (9) What would you do?

You've responded to a first aid emergency in the parking lot at Wal-Mart. An older woman has fallen and hurt her leg. The woman's significant other appears angry and is yelling at her to get up and get into the car. **What's your escape plan?**

Scenario (10) What would you do?

You're attending a work conference, and a fellow conference attendee befriends you. Prior to the lunch break, he asks if he can go with you. You politely agree. He appears to really like you. The conference is just about over, and you want nothing to do with him. **What's your escape plan?**

Scenario (11) What would you do?

You're at work in your office when a supervisor and an employee ask for your assistance. The employee hesitantly explains that she is the victim of domestic violence. She believes her estranged boyfriend is escalating. He has been physically aggressive towards her.

Scenario (12) What would you do?

Your child comes home from school one afternoon and seems to be withdrawn. You ask about his day, and he breaks down and explains that he has been the victim of being bullied for weeks.

Developing Escape Plans

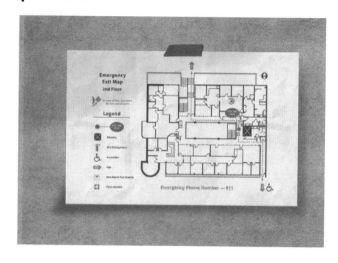

WHAT'S YOUR **PLAN?**

Determining your **escape route** ahead of time in relation to the people you are **around** or come in **contact** with is **very important** for your **safety**.

When it comes to developing escape plans, keep in mind the following:

- **Commitment:** Look at all your environments and pre-plan your escape routes. Saying you'll do it tomorrow turns into someday, which turns into no follow-through.

- **Involvement:** Management should ensure that all staff knows the plan. When discussing plans with staff, management should be serious and matter-of-fact. The leadership role when advising departmental staff members should be confident and free of emotional fear.

- **Practice:** Just like your kids do fire drills at school; you should physically and mentally run through the events of your escape. Have a schedule and practice routinely.

- **"What if?" Game:** The "What if?" Game means playing mental scenarios of situations that may arise and force us to take action. The best emergency responders and police officers play the "What if?" game regularly.

- **Changes:** Realize now that things are going to change. You are going to change, and so are most things in life. With this said, doesn't it make sense to update your escape plans as your life changes?

- **Environments:** Environmental Awareness means that you have an understanding of the different types of vulnerabilities and resources in your surroundings.

- **Relationships:** Escape planning always involves more than its physical nature. Successful personal safety involves communication skills that enable us to escape situations involving interpersonal relationships. A sharp awareness is keen to having a sharp tongue.

Module Nine: Environmental Factors

"You are a product of your environment. So choose the environment that will best develop you toward your objective. Analyze your life in terms of its environment. Are the things around you helping you toward success—or are they holding you back?"

- W. Clement Stone, Successful American Entrepreneur and Best-Selling Author (1902-2002)

Environments are a combination of external physical conditions that affect and influence the growth, development, and survival of organisms.

Workers move through many environments, even if they only work in one department. From parking lots to cafeterias, corridors, and lobbies, environments are unique in their associated risks. Environmental safety measures are put in place in workplaces to assist staff in protecting their environments, limiting access to their environments, and alerting others to assist them.

The following environmental safety measures are in place in multiple areas of the corporate and healthcare environment. Obviously, being in higher-risk areas require additional safety measures. All staff, regardless of their position, may need and do have access to many of these safety measures.

The following environmental safety measures are in place to create a safer workplace environment. These measures assist staff in protecting their environments, limiting access to their environments, and alerting others to assist them.

"Environment is Always a Factor"

- David Fowler, author and founder of the AVADE® training programs

Environmental Safety Measures

1. Safety Mirrors
2. Lighting
3. Cameras – CCTV
4. Panic Alarms
5. Private Places

6. Access Controls
7. Staff Identification
8. Parking Lot Safety
9. Obstacles Around You
10. Telephone Safety

Safety Measure # 1 - Safety Mirrors

You use mirrors every day in your vehicle to keep yourself safe and aware of what's around you. If available, use the safety mirrors in your environment to alert you of obstacles and threats so that you can yield to guests and visitors.

Safety Measure # 2 – Lighting

"Criminals don't like lights." It's an age-old axiom. Good lighting can discourage prowling or loitering. Always park and walk in areas with adequate lighting: entryways, pathways, and stairwells.

Safety Measure # 3 – Cameras—CCTV

Closed-circuit television allows you to see what is happening in different areas of your department or in the entire workplace. It also helps the security/surveillance department to monitor from a remote location. CCTV is a great deterrent against criminals; however, if no one is watching at the moment an incident happens, no responders will be alerted. CCTV then becomes a tool for retrieving video after the fact.

Safety Measure # 4 – Panic Alarms A panic or monitored alarm sends a signal to a remote location, alerting them (usually security) to a breach in your security. These devices are mainly silent and are mounted in inconspicuous areas (under desktops, etc.). Proper training and education on using alarms are essential to their use. Alarms should be regularly tested for efficiency. Many key chains and key fobs have a remote panic button that activates an audible alarm in the vehicle. This can be beneficial in parking lots and residences. Criminals are distracted by loud noises that alert others and draw attention.

Safety Measure # 5 - Private Places to Avoid: Stairwells & Elevators, Restrooms, etc. Avoid using isolated, unused stairways in your environment. When using elevators, stand near the control panel by the door so you can easily press the alarm button in an emergency. If a suspicious-looking person follows you into an elevator, step out of the elevator immediately. If you see a suspicious-looking person inside an elevator you are about to enter, do not get in. If you are in an elevator and another person makes you feel uncomfortable, get off as soon as possible. Trust your instincts! Restrooms can isolate a person and compromise their escape route. If private restrooms are unavailable, lock doors, check stalls before entering, lock stall doors, and trust your instincts.

Safety Measure # 6 – Access Controls (door locks)
Access controls are designed to keep people out of specific areas. Memorize codes, be aware of who is around you when entering a locked area, and do not give codes or access to anyone who is unauthorized to be in the particular area. Be cautious of "piggybacking"— when someone enters an accessed area right after an authorized person has entered, following them in without approved access. **Security systems are only as good as the people using them.**

Safety Measure # 7 – Staff Identification
To promote overall security and support the specific protocols for entry into sensitive areas, it's important for staff to wear their IDs. This ensures that access control is maintained as well as specific protocols for areas that are at a higher risk (ED, pediatrics, cash vaults, administrative areas, staff-only restrooms, etc.).

Safety Measure # 8 – Parking Lot Safety

Parking lots, loading docks, blind alleys, and trash container areas are prime crime points.

Most common crimes in these areas:

- Theft and Physical Assault

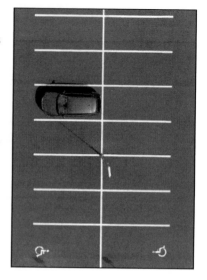

If possible, travel to and from work and parking areas with other people. Always park in areas that are patrolled and well-lit after dark and use security escorts during off-hours when others are not around.

Also, keep in mind:

- **Lighting:** Always choose well-lit parking areas. Be aware of your surroundings!

- **Don't Sit:** Don't loiter in the parking lot. Take care of phone calls and other matters inside the location, you're going to or from. Always turn off the ignition, remove the key, and lock your car doors, no matter how soon you plan on returning.

- **Valuables:** Keep valuables and packages locked in the trunk. If you are carrying packages, try to keep one hand free, even if it means making an extra trip.

- **Approaching:** Be alert as you approach your car in the parking area. Pay attention to nearby vehicles, individuals, and hiding areas that criminals might use, such as under the car or in the back seat. Your keys and cell phone should be in hand or in your reach. Always look around before you get in or out of your car.

- **Buddy System:** Always walk in groups when possible. Safety in numbers!

- **Security Escort:** Get a security escort if available.

- **Who's next to you?** Assess who you are next to when parking your car and when coming back to your vehicle. If possible, do not park next to vans, trucks with campers, or other vehicles whose size and structure can provide concealment for a potential assailant.

- **Parking Garages:** Exercise caution and be extra alert when using underground or enclosed parking garages. Walk in the center aisle rather than close to parked cars. If you have a choice, park in areas that have an attendant or in locations that have heavy pedestrian traffic. Have your key in hand before you get to your car and be aware of the occupied cars around you.

Safety Measure # 9 – Obstacles Around You

The workplace environment is filled with numerous obstacles that can inhibit your ability to escape a situation. Some common obstacles that can be trip hazards are chairs, beds, people, walls, tables, cars, curbs, trees, inclement weather, machines, desks, spills on the floor, etc.

Some common obstacles that can be trip or escape hazards are:

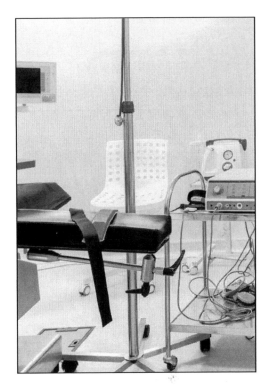

- Desks

- Chairs

- Beds

- Walls

- Intravenous (IV) poles

- Stairs—inclines/declines

- Blood or liquid on the floor

- Medical equipment

- Inclement weather

- Curbs, Cars, Trees, and People

Safety Measure # 10 – Telephone Safety—Telephones & Emergency Number's

In case of an emergency situation:

- Alert people using cell phones.

- Report the threatening, harassing, or obscene calls.

- Keep records of such calls.

- Have access to your emergency numbers.

- Practice emergency drill calls.

- Use emergency phones.

Cell Phones: Cell phones are a great tool for alerting others in almost every environment. Program numbers into your cell phone so that they are easily found and used. Some agencies use mass alert text messaging.

Threatening Calls: If you receive a threatening, harassing, or obscene telephone call, notify security or police, your supervisor, and the telephone company.

Keep Records: Keep a record of the date, time, and the content of each threatening, harassing, or obscene telephone call for security or police and the telephone company. In some cases, cell phone companies can block callers who are threatening and harassing.

Emergency Numbers (What are yours?): Memorize numbers for emergency codes, police, security, fire, etc. Post the numbers near every telephone or on your person. Follow "Emergency Codes" response protocols.

Practice Emergency Numbers: Rehearse mentally and physically (turn the phone off when practicing) calls you would make to police, fire, emergency personnel, or anyone who would respond to your situation. Considering your stress level response, this skill could save your life.

ICE = In Case of Emergency: Program your cell phone with ICE numbers should you be unable to make a call yourself. Multiple ICE numbers can be added to your cell phone address book. Label them as ICE-1, ICE-2, etc.

Emergency Phones: Emergency phones can alert security personnel to your situation. Blue emergency phones are commonly found in parking structures and lots.

Consider all these factors when thinking about how your work environment will contribute to your safety—or not. Be aware of changes in your environment that might inhibit your ability to escape a potentially violent incident.

_____
_____
_____
_____
_____
_____
_____
_____
_____
_____
_____

Module Ten: Emergency Codes & Procedures

The use of **codes** is intended to convey **essential information** quickly and with a **minimum** of **misunderstanding** to staff, while preventing **stress** or **panic** among patients and visitors to the workplace.

Note: **Emergency Codes** are frequently **coded** by **color**, and the color codes denote **different events** at **different corporations** and are **not always universal**.

> *"Be Prepared... the meaning of the motto is that a scout must prepare himself by previously thinking out and practicing how to act on any accident or emergency so that he is never taken by surprise."*
>
> **- Sir Robert Baden-Powell, British Army Officer, founder of the Boy Scouts (1857-1941)**

The use of codes is intended to convey essential information quickly, with a minimum of misunderstanding to staff, while preventing stress or panic among guests and visitors to the workplace. Emergency codes are frequently coded by color. The color codes signify different events at different corporations and are not always universal. **Plain language is also used to denote different types of emergencies. Know your emergency codes and responses!**

This module is presented with the intent to prepare individuals in the workplace for emergent situations. The common emergent situations may include but are not limited to Fire, Medical, Hazmat, Bomb Threat, Lost Person, Robbery, Combative Person, Active Shooter, and Personal Codes for Alerting Others.

Your policies and procedures should be adhered to when responding to the following emergency situations.

FIRE CODE

Provides an appropriate response in the event of an **actual** or **suspected fire** in order to **protect life, property**, & **vital** services.

MEDICAL CODE

Provides an appropriate response to a **suspected** or **imminent medical emergency** for a **guest** or **staff** person.

HAZMAT CODE

Provides an appropriate response to an **actual** or **suspected hazardous material spill** or **release** in a manner that is **safe** for **staff, guests**, & **visitors**.

Characteristics of an Abductor (Risk Factors)

National Center for Missing and Exploited Children (NCMEC). NCMEC has developed a list of characteristics from an analysis of 327 missing infants under six months of age related to healthcare occurring from 1964 through October 2019 in the United States. However, there is no guarantee an infant abductor will fit this description.

Usually, a female of childbearing age who appears to be pregnant.
- Most likely compulsive; most often relies on manipulation, lying, and deception.
- Frequently indicates she has lost a baby or is incapable of having one.
- Often married or cohabitating, the companion's desire for a baby or the abductor's desire to provide her companion with "his" baby may be the motivation for the abduction.
- Usually lives in the community where the abduction takes place.
- Frequently initially visits nursery and maternity units at more than one health care facility prior to the abduction; asks detailed questions about procedures and the maternity floor layout; frequently uses a fire exit stairwell for her escape, and may also try to abduct from the home setting.
- Usually plans the abduction but does not necessarily target a specific infant; frequently seizes any opportunity present to abduct a baby.
- Frequently impersonates a nurse or other allied health care personnel.
- Often becomes familiar with health care staff members, staff member work routines, and victim parents.
- Often demonstrates the capability to provide care to the baby once the abduction occurs, within her emotional and physical abilities.

In addition, an abductor who abducts from the home setting (is):
- More likely to be single while claiming to have a partner
- Often targets a mother whom she may find by visiting health care facilities and tries to meet the target family.
- Often plans the abduction and brings a weapon, although the weapon may not be used.
- Often impersonates a health care or social services professional when visiting the home.

http://www.missingkids.com/theissues/infantabductions

Robbery Code provides an appropriate response in the event of an armed or unarmed robbery. Businesses that handle money and deal with prescription pharmaceuticals or sell high-end items are at risk of robbery.

AVADE® Robbery Prevention & Response Guidelines

Robbery is the crime of seizing property through violence or intimidation. A perpetrator of a robbery is a robber. Because violence is an ingredient of most robberies, it may result in the harm or murder of their victims.

Robbers want your money or property, and they want it quickly. Robbery is a risky business, and robbers are usually nervous. You do not want to delay a robbery in any way—it increases the potential for violence. Give the robber what he or she wants and do it quickly. Do not risk your life, or another person's life, for the property.

Robberies occur at predictable times. Opening and closing periods are particularly vulnerable times due to low staffing and large amounts of cash on hand. Robberies increase during the holiday season due to the increased cash volume and the presence of large crowds that distract and preoccupy store and company personnel.

Report suspicious activity. If you observe an individual(s), or occupied vehicle, lingering around your business for a time, or in a manner that makes you suspicious or uncomfortable, write down the license number, color and make of the car, description of the individual(s) and call police or security. Many robbers like to watch and wait for the right opportunity.

PREVENTION - Security Devices *(See module 9: Environmental Factors)*

- Control access to areas where cash or other valuable items are stored.

- CCTV is a great deterrent against criminals.

- Signage inside and outside will emphasize your security policy on limited cash on hand and/or employee inaccessibility to the safe.

- Silent "hold-up" or "panic" alarms should be considered.

PREVENTION - Identification

- Greet each customer. Establish eye contact and remember their general appearance. Good customer service discourages hesitant robbers as well as other thieves. This attention to detail conveys control and puts people on notice they have been observed and can be identified later.

- Place height markings along the vertical frame at the entrance. This gives employees the ability to tell how tall the robber is at a glance, so they can tell the authorities.

PREVENTION - Policy Considerations

Recognize your potential for being held up. Work with local police and crime prevention specialists. Preventive strategies are as much their concern and responsibility as apprehension of criminals.

- Check references of prospective employees. Do a background check of their previous employers.

- Keep a file on all employees, including their pictures. Past employees know the store procedures and where the money is kept.

- Re-key locks and reset codes and combinations when affected employees are dismissed for cause.

- Establish clear and consistent policies regarding money in the till. Establish how much money will be kept in the till, what bill denominations employees will accept, how to respond to "suspicious" inquiries, and how to handle loiterers. All employees should be trained and given a written description of the store policy.

- Maintain adequate staff levels. Be especially careful during opening and closing periods, lunch hours, and holiday seasons when there is more money on-site and more distractions.

- As an employee, your commitment to security procedures will reduce the risk of criminal confrontation and physical harm.

PREVENTION - Design Considerations

- Use gates and counters to separate clients from employees when appropriate.

- Post signs to designate restricted areas: "Private" or "Employees Only."

- Install an information desk and staff it during business hours. It will provide some surveillance of the main entrance of the building.

- Create transition zones. These can be steps up or down, screened or partitioned off areas, different levels of lighting, or carpeting in a given space. These methods subtly indicate a change in usage from public to private.

- Report any broken lights, flickering lights, broken locks or doors, dimly lit corridors, doors that don't lock properly, broken windows, or lock devices to management or security immediately. Not attending to these items can create an environment conducive to crime. The faster they are repaired, the safer the environment will be.

PREVENTION - Business Security Procedures

Develop company security procedures. The procedures should state the company's policy and dedication to a crime-and-violence-free workplace. Including procedures for the following will help empower employees to make their workplace safe and crime-free.

- Dealing with trespassers and/or difficult people
- Opening and closing the office
- Using the office during off-hours
- Recommendations for personal property security
- Who to report crimes and suspicious activities to
- Emergency exit plan

Robbery Prevention

When to Call Emergency Numbers:
- A crime is in progress
- A situation is about to escalate into an emergency (endangering life or major property)
- A crime has just occurred (remember the description of the suspect and direction in which he or she fled)

Be Alert Pay attention to who is in your work area, and know who belongs in your work area. Become familiar with the faces of people who belong in your building. Pay attention to people who behave suspiciously, i.e., someone who loiters in the area with no apparent purpose. Be particularly aware of a person you have seen loitering more than once.

Response During the Robbery

- Remain calm. Most robbers do not wish to harm their victims. They are only interested in getting money or property. The calmer you are, the less chance that the robber becomes agitated or dangerous. This also increases your chances of getting a more accurate description of the robber, which may aid in the robber's apprehension.

- Do not argue, fight, surprise, or attempt to use weapons against a robber. He has already taken a major risk by entering your business and is usually as frightened as you are. Because of this, additional provocation on your part could make the situation worse. Therefore, give the robber exactly what he or she wants and do it quickly. Don't take unnecessary chances with your life!

- While you should cooperate with robbers, don't volunteer any assistance. Don't give all the money if the robber only asks for twenty-dollar bills.

- Activate silent alarms/security devices if you can do this without detection.

- Watch the robber's hands. If the robber is not wearing any gloves, anything he touches might leave good fingerprints.

- Give the robber your "bait" money. Be sure to inform the investigating officer that you did so.

- Be systematic in your observations. Look the robber over carefully. Mentally note as many details as possible until you can write them down. Compare the robber with yourself. Is he taller, heavier, older, etc.

- Notice the type and description of any weapons used. Glance at the weapon only long enough to identify it. Look at the robber from then on. Make no sudden movements, and don't be heroic!

- Observe the direction the robber takes in leaving the scene. If a vehicle is involved, make a note of the make, model, year, color, license plate number, and issuing state.

Response After the Robbery

- Telephone police immediately. If you act quickly, the police might be able to catch the suspect and recover your money. When you dial 9-1-1, the procedure is always the same. You will be asked if your emergency involves police, fire, or medical—request police response.

- Lock all doors and allow no one in. Ask witnesses to remain on the premises until police arrive. Do not touch anything the robber may have touched. Do not discuss what happened with any other witnesses. Your own impressions should be kept untainted until you have talked with authorities.

- Complete your post-incident documentation. Be as complete as possible. Police may want a copy of your report. (See module 5 for post-incident documentation procedures.)

- Provide incident debriefing. (See module 6 for critical incident stress debriefing.)

Robbery response strategies require planning and coordination between employees and management. Give some thought to how you might react in a robbery situation and discuss your concerns with co-workers and employers. Common sense, caution, and adherence to established policies and procedures can reduce the amount of money stolen and minimize the chance for injury and loss of life.

Combative Person Code Provides an appropriate response to situations involving an aggressive/hostile/combative or potentially combative person.

Note: *Early Warning Signs*
(See module 4 Combative Person Signs & Symptoms)

To avoid a threatening or escalated response by the aggressive individual proper positioning of the team is crucial. Team cornering of an aggressive individual may escalate the situation.

Contact and Cover Positioning

Level III Defensive Control Tactics and Techniques covers team response to a combative person known as "Contact and Cover."

It is critically important when having to confront and control a combative person that you **DO NOT** surround or corner them. Proper positioning is crucial. Contact and Cover is the main strategy in defensive control tactics and techniques.

Combative Person Contact & Cover Team Positioning

CONTACT & COVER

In order to avoid a threatening or escalated response by the aggressive individual, **proper positioning of the team is crucial**. Team cornering may **escalate** the situation.

It is critically important when having to confront and control a combative person that you **DO NOT** surround or **corner** them.

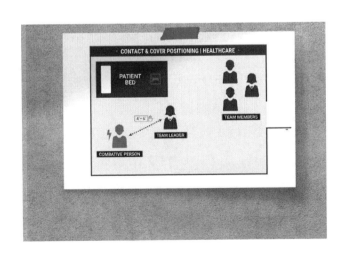

Active Shooter Code Provides an appropriate response in the event of an incident involving a person brandishing or using a weapon.

Active Shooter (Awareness-Preparedness & Response)

PROPER **RESPONSE**

An **Active Shooter** is an individual actively engaged in **killing** or **attempting to kill** people in a **confined space** and other **populated areas**.

In most cases, **Active Shooters** use **firearms** and there is no pattern or method to their selection of victims.

- **Armed Response:** Law Enforcement & Armed Security
- **Unarmed Response:** Escape!

The most extreme incidence of violence in today's society is an active shooter event.

Active Shooter incidents take place in a variety of environments. Environmental Awareness for Active Shooter Incidents is critical.

Incidents happen in many environments, such as:

- Malls
- Schools
- Hospitals
- Churches
- Restaurants
- Medical Clinics
- Movie Theatres
- Sporting Events
- Military Installations
- Government Buildings
- Retail Shops and Stores

Active Shooter Situations are unpredictable, evolve quickly, and continue until stopped by law enforcement, suicide, or intervention.

What We Know about Active Shooters

- The active shooter is acting alone most of the time.

- He is suicidal most of the time and usually commits suicide onsite.

- He almost never takes hostages nor has any interest in negotiating.

- He is preoccupied with a high body count, which is almost always his one and only goal.

- Active shooters race to murder everybody they can reach in an effort to avoid contact with police. Most incidents are over within 4-8 minutes or less!

- The shooter usually has multiple weapons and the ability to reload his weapons several times.

- Long arms (rifles/shotguns) are involved over half of the time. Handguns are most often used.

- High likelihood of serious injury to the innocent and unarmed.

- At least 50% of the time, the person stopping the incident is non-police.

Active Shooter Characteristics

Active Shooters are motivated by:
- EVIL
- Anger
- Ideology
- Religion
- Revenge
- Retaliation
- Mental Illness
- Media Stardom

Rules for Surviving an Active Shooter

1. **Escape**, if safe to do so!
2. **Hide** & **cover** in place, if you cannot escape. (Safe Room)
3. **Alert** authorities | Police, Security
4. **Lock doors** in your immediate area
5. **Place barriers** & remain absolutely **quiet**
6. **Attack** the **attacker**, if escape is not possible
7. When law enforcement arrives, **be submissive, expose palms**, & **do what they tell you to do**

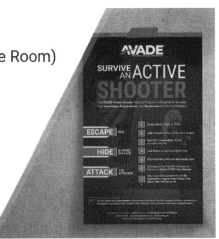

1 - Escape if safe to do so!

- Have an escape route & plan in mind
- Leave your belongings behind
- Help others escape, if possible
- Evacuate regardless of others
- Warn/prevent individuals from entering
- Do not attempt to move wounded people

#2 - Hide and cover in place if you cannot escape. (SAFE ROOM)

Your hiding spot should:
- Be out of the active shooter's view
- Provide protection if shots are fired
- Not restrict options for movement

#3 - Alert authorities—police, armed security.
Provide Law Enforcement or 911 operators with:

- Location of shooter(s)
- Number of shooters
- Physical description of shooter(s)
- Number and types of weapons
- Number of potential victims

#4 - Lock doors in your immediate area.
If the shooter is nearby:

- Lock the door
- Hide behind large item (cabinet, desk)
- Silence your cell phone/pager
- Remain quiet

#5 - Place barriers and remain absolutely quiet. #5

Use items in your environment:

- Stack chairs to block the door
- Place tables and large items in the doorway
- Use belts, rope, and wire around door hardware
- Remain quiet and wait for law enforcement to arrive

#6 - If escape is not possible and danger is imminent, attack the attacker.

As an absolute last resort:

- Act as aggressively as possible
- Improvise weapons/throw items
- Swarm if more than one of you
- Yell and Scream!
- Commit to your actions
- Strike to High-Risk Target Areas

Awareness and vigilance play the most important role in overall prevention and intervention of violence. If you are faced with imminent danger, realize that mental strength will be absolutely necessary to stay alive.

#7 - When law enforcement arrives, be submissive, expose your palms, and do what they tell you to do.

- Remain calm and DO what they tell YOU!
- Put down any items in your hands
- Raise hands and spread fingers
- Avoid quick or sudden movements
- Avoid pointing, screaming, or yelling
- Proceed in the direction from which officers are entering

Law Enforcement Role in an Active Shooter Situation

Law Enforcements Immediate Purpose:
- Stop the active shooter!
- Proceed to the area where the last shots were heard
- The first priority is to eliminate the threat

Police Entry Teams May:
- Wear bulletproof vests, helmets, and other tactical equipment
- Be armed with rifles, shotguns, and/or handguns
- Shout verbal commands!
- Push individuals to the ground for their safety

Go to a Safe Location!
Area controlled by law enforcement until:
- The situation is under control
- All witnesses are identified and questioned
- They release you to leave the area

See Run-Hide-Fight Video:
https://www.fbi.gov/about-us/office-of-partner-engagement/active-shooter-incidents/run-hide-fight-video

Armed! Are you ready- Hospital Training
https://www.youtube.com/watch?v=ceCiP4yvYPs

For more information on AVADE® Active Shooter Training:
https://personalsafetytraining.com/avade-active-shooter/

PERSONAL SAFETY TRAINING INC.

AVADE®
WORKPLACE VIOLENCE PREVENTION

SURVIVE AN ACTIVE SHOOTER

The **AVADE®** Active Shooter Training Program Is Designed to Increase Your **Awareness, Preparedness,** and **Responses** for Extreme Violence

ESCAPE | RUN

1 Escape (Run) if Safe to Do So!

2 **Hide & Cover** in Place if You Can't Escape

3 **Alert (911) Authorities** | Police & Armed Security

HIDE | & COVER IN PLACE

4 **Lock Doors** in Your Immediate Area

5 Place Barriers & Remain **Absolutely Quiet**

ATTACK | THE ATTACKER

6 If Escape is Not Possible & Danger is Imminent, **Attack (FIGHT) the Attacker**

7 When Law Enforcement Arrives, **Be Submissive, Expose Your Palms,** & Do What They Tell You to Do

Active Shooter Defined:
The FBI defines an **Active Shooter** as *one or more individuals actively engaged in killing or attempting to kill people in a populated area.* Implicit in this definition is the shooter's use of **one** or **more firearms.**

Education, Prevention, and **Mitigation** for *Violence in the Workplace*
1.866.773.7763 · personalsafetytraining.com · avadetraining.com
© Personal Safety Training Inc. | AVADE® Training

Stop the Bleed

The **'Stop the Bleed' campaign** was initiated by a federal interagency workgroup convened by the National Security Council Staff, The White House. The **purpose** of the campaign is to **build national resilience** by better preparing the public to save lives by **raising awareness** of basic actions to stop **life-threatening bleeding** following everyday emergencies and man-made and natural disasters. Advances made by military medicine and research in hemorrhage control during the wars in Afghanistan and Iraq have informed the work of this initiative, which exemplifies the translation of knowledge back to the homeland for the benefit of the general public.

The Department of Defense owns the 'Stop the Bleed' logo and phrase – trademark pending. AVADE® WPV Training supports the efforts of this campaign and is committed to equipping YOU to save your own life and possibly the lives of others.

How to Stop the Bleed - Call 9-1-1

- Call 9-1-1 yourself
    OR
- Tell someone to call 9-1-1

Ensure Your Safety

- Before you offer any help, you must ensure your own safety!

- If you become injured, you will not be able to help the victim.

- Provide care to the injured person if the scene is safe for you to do so. If, at any time, your safety is threatened, attempt to remove yourself (and the victim if possible) from danger and find a safe location.

- Protect yourself from blood-borne infections by wearing gloves, if available.

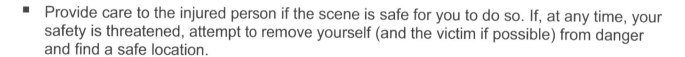

Look for Life-Threatening Bleeding

- Find the source of bleeding

- Open or remove the clothing over the wound so you can clearly see it. By removing clothing, you will be able to see injuries that may have been hidden or covered.

- Look for and identify "life-threatening" bleeding.

  - Examples include:
    - Blood that is spurting out of the wound.
    - Blood that won't stop coming out of the wound.
    - Blood that is pooling on the ground.
    - Clothing that is soaked with blood.
    - Bandages that are soaked with blood.
    - Loss of all or part of an arm or leg.
    - Bleeding in a victim who is now confused or unconscious.

Compress and Control

There are a number of methods that can be used to stop bleeding, and they all have one thing in common—compressing a bleeding blood vessel in order to stop the bleeding.

If you DON'T have a trauma first aid kit:
Apply direct pressure on the wound. (Cover the wound with a clean cloth and apply pressure by pushing directly on it with both hands.)

1. Take any clean cloth (for example, a shirt) and cover the wound.

2. If the wound is large and deep, try to "stuff" the cloth down into the wound.

3. Apply continuous pressure with both hands directly on top of the bleeding wound.

4. Push down as hard as you can.

5. Hold pressure to stop bleeding. Continue pressure until relieved by medical responders.

If you DO have a trauma first aid kit:
For life-threatening bleeding from an arm or leg when a tourniquet is NOT available OR for bleeding from the neck, shoulder, or groin:

- Pack (stuff) the wound with a bleeding control (also called a hemostatic) gauze, plain gauze, or a clean cloth, and then apply pressure with both hands

1. Open the clothing over the bleeding wound.

2. Wipe away any pooled blood.

3. Pack (stuff) the wound with bleeding control gauze (preferred), plain gauze, or clean cloth.

4. Apply steady pressure with both hands directly on top of the bleeding wound.

5. Push down as hard as you can.

6. Hold pressure to stop bleeding. Continue pressure until relieved by medical responders.

Uncontrolled bleeding is a major cause of preventable deaths. Approximately 40% of trauma-related deaths worldwide are due to bleeding or its consequences, establishing hemorrhage as the most common cause of preventable death in trauma.* [14]

Tourniquets

For life-threatening bleeding from an arm or leg when a tourniquet is available:

1. Applying the tourniquet[15]

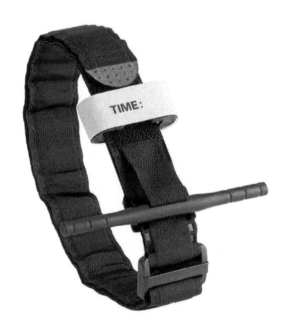

1. Wrap the tourniquet around the bleeding arm or leg about 2 to 3 inches above the bleeding site (be sure NOT to place the tourniquet onto a joint—go above the joint if necessary).

2. Pull the free end of the tourniquet to make it as tight as possible and secure the free end.

3. Twist or wind the windlass until bleeding stops.

4. Secure the windlass to keep the tourniquet tight.

5. Note the time the tourniquet was applied.

Note: A tourniquet will cause pain, but it is necessary to stop life-threatening bleeding.

---

[14] * Curry N, Hopewell S, Doree C, Hyde C, Brohi K, Stanworth S. The acute management of trauma hemorrhage: a systematic review of randomized controlled trials. Crit Care. 2011;15(2):R92.
[15] Pons PT, Jacobs L. Save a life: What everyone should know to stop bleeding after an injury. Chicago, IL: American College of Surgeons; 2016.

Personal Codes for Alerting Others

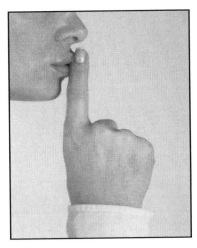

Personal Codes for Alerting Others provide quick, non-attention-getting communication to security or other responders of a possible threatening, emergent or imminent situation. Using personal codes between team members can alert help without alerting the assailant that you are requesting assistance/help.

AVADE® Level I Education, Prevention, and Mitigation of WPV

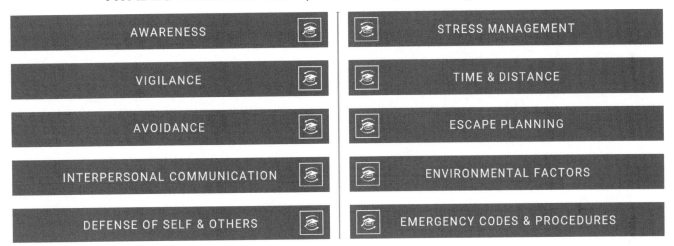

AWARENESS		STRESS MANAGEMENT
VIGILANCE		TIME & DISTANCE
AVOIDANCE		ESCAPE PLANNING
INTERPERSONAL COMMUNICATION		ENVIRONMENTAL FACTORS
DEFENSE OF SELF & OTHERS		EMERGENCY CODES & PROCEDURES

Conclusion

Workplace violence unfortunately, is on the rise. By learning and studying the AVADE® strategies, integrating them, teaching them, and modeling them to your co-workers, you can lessen your chances of being a victim of workplace violence.

Integrate the AVADE® safety principles into your workplace/life-place for defusing tense situations. Learn to identify the signs and symptoms of potential violence. Above all, learn to trust your instincts and listen to your intuition. Remember: your best tool for keeping yourself safe is your own mind and personal safety habits.

AVADE® WPV PREVENTION
NOTEPAD

AVADE® Level II
Self-Defense Tactics and Techniques

The Goal of Self-Defense

The goal of this section is to teach self-defense intervention tactics and techniques. Most incidents can be prevented using your awareness, vigilance, and avoidance. However, there may be times when you need to physically intervene to protect yourself or another person. **After any self-defense intervention, always escape and report immediately.** Before conducting any physical training, be sure to cover the following safety rules with your class. Safety is the most important rule in physical training.

In today's society, corporations, healthcare, schools, gaming, law enforcement, security, corrections, the military, and protective services agencies realize that self-defense tactics and techniques are essential for protecting themselves and the public they serve. These agencies also understand that mitigating liability begins with proper training and education in self-defense tactics and techniques.

The AVADE® training program is designed for agencies to reduce the potential for injury and liability risk when employees are lawfully defending themselves or controlling an aggressive individual. The tactics and techniques in this training curriculum are for incidents where the aggressor is physically combative, resistive, and unarmed.

This training manual provides training and education that is designed to empower individuals and to increase awareness, knowledge, skills, and actions with regard to the use of force, control and restraint, self-defense, and defending others with self-defense tactics and techniques.

This course stresses the importance of knowing your agency's policies and procedures in regard to using force and defending yourself or another person. The **AVADE®** training is intended to give the trainee the basic understanding of self-defense, use of force, control and restraint, reasonable force, and basic legal definitions of force. **Personal Safety Training Inc.** makes no legal declaration, representation, or claim as to what force should be used or not used during self-defense, use of force incident, or assault incident or situation. Each trainee must take into consideration their ability, agency policies and procedures, and laws in the state and country in which they reside.

Most individuals can learn and develop proficiency in the techniques taught in this training course. Basic self-defense fundamentals are followed by defensive blocking techniques, personal defensive techniques, vulnerable areas of the body, specific responses to holds–assaults, and post-incident response and documentation procedures.

AVADE® FIRST RULE OF TRAINING = SAFETY

▶ AVADE® Training Safety Rules

1 **SAFETY & WAIVER AGREEMENT**
Each individual trained **MUST** complete the **Student Registration & Recertification Form**. The instructor will advise the student how to fill it out and answer any questions pertaining to it.

2 **WEAPONS FREE ENVIRONMENT**
NO WEAPONS are allowed anywhere in the training area. Instructor will advise participants in proper procedures in securing weapons and ammunition. Follow agency policy and procedures.

3 **REMOVE JEWELRY, ETC.**
The following should not be worn during a class which involves hands-on training: all jewelry with sharp edges, pins or raised surfaces, or jewelry that encircles the neck.

4 **NO HORSEPLAY RULE**
Any participant who displays a disregard for **SAFETY** to anyone in class will be asked to leave the class. Please practice only the technique currently being taught. **DO NOT PRACTICE UNAUTHORIZED TECHNIQUES.**

5 **PAT OUT RULE** (USED FOR PARTNER TECHNIQUES)
Upon hearing/feeling/seeing the "**PAT**," your partner applying the technique will immediately release the pressure of the technique to reduce discomfort/pain. The technique will be immediately and totally released on instructions from the instructor or when a safety monitor says "**RELEASE**," "**STOP**," or words similar to them.

6 **BE A GOOD "DEFENDER" AND A GOOD "AGGRESSOR"**
Essentially this means working together with your partner when practicing the techniques. Without cooperation while practicing self-defense or defensive control tactics techniques, time is wasted and injury potential is increased.

7 **PRACTICE TECHNIQUES SLOWLY AT FIRST**
Gain balance and correctness slowly before practicing for speed. Proceed at the pace directed by your trainer.

8 **CHECK EQUIPMENT FOR ADDED SAFETY**
The instructor will check **ALL** equipment used during the training to ensure proper function, working order and safety.

9 **ADVISE INSTRUCTOR OF ANY PRE-EXISTING INJURIES**
Any injury or condition that could be further injured or aggravated should be brought to the **immediate attention** of your instructor, and your partner, prior to participating in any hands-on training.

10 **ADVISE INSTRUCTOR OF ANY INJURY DURING CLASS**
Any injury, regardless of what it is, **needs to be reported** to the primary instructor.

11 **SAFETY IS EVERYONE'S RESPONSIBILITY!**
Safety is everyone's responsibility and everyone is empowered to **immediately report** or **YELL OUT** any safety violation.

12 **TRAINING HAZARDS**
Always keep any items or training equipment and batons off the floor/ground and out of the way when not in use.

13 **SAFETY MARKINGS**
Colored wrist bands or blue tape marking is a visual aid for pre-existing injury. Use **CAUTION**.

14 **LEAVING TRAINING AREA**
If you must leave the training area for any reason, please **advise your instructor** prior to doing so.

Education, Prevention, and Mitigation for Violence in the Workplace

© Personal Safety Training Inc. | AVADE® Training

AVADE® Level II Self-Defense Tactics & Techniques Modules

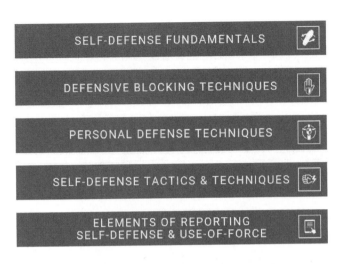

- SELF-DEFENSE FUNDAMENTALS
- DEFENSIVE BLOCKING TECHNIQUES
- PERSONAL DEFENSE TECHNIQUES
- SELF-DEFENSE TACTICS & TECHNIQUES
- ELEMENTS OF REPORTING SELF-DEFENSE & USE-OF-FORCE

Personal Safety Training Inc. makes no legal declaration, representation or claim as to what force should be used or not used during a self-defense, use of force incident, or assault incident or situation. Each trainee must take into consideration their ability, agency policies and procedures and laws in the state and country in which they reside.

Self-defense is the right to use *reasonable* force to protect oneself or members of one's staff/family from bodily harm from the attack of an aggressor if you have reason to believe that you or they are in danger. Self-defense must always be your last resort. When it is used, the force used must be considered "reasonable,"; e.g., striking someone who yells an obscenity at you is not considered "reasonable force."

Individuals do have the right to self-defense. The application of force must follow any agency policy and procedure as well as state and federal law. The best self-defense is to avoid the situation and getaway. If avoidance and escape are not possible, a reasonable defense would be lawful as a last resort.

The best self-defense is to avoid the situation and getaway. If avoidance and escape are not possible, a reasonable defense would be lawful as a last resort. You have the right to defend yourself; however, any use of self-defense must follow any agency policy and procedure, as well as state and federal law.

The following information will provide a general understanding of what self-defense and use of force are, how you can legally protect yourself against assault, as well as the risk of liability associated with any type of self-defense or force.

Module One –Self-Defense Fundamentals

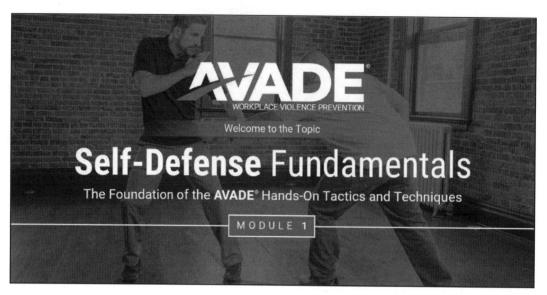

Every tactic and technique requires the use of fundamental laws. If you don't understand the fundamental rules of self-defense, your ability to defend yourself is compromised. A basic understanding and use of these laws will give you an advantage in a situation where you might need to use force to defend yourself or another person.

Fundamentals

Fun·da·men·tal (from the Latin medieval: *fundāmentālis*: late Middle English)
—*Synonyms* 1. Indispensable, primary.
–*adjective* 1. Serving as, or being an essential part of, a foundation or basis; basic; underlying: *fundamental principles; the fundamental structure.*
2. Of, pertaining to, or affecting the foundation or basis: *a fundamental revision.*
3. Being an original or primary source: *a fundamental idea.*
–*noun* 1. A basic principle, rule, law, or the like, that serves as the groundwork of a system; essential part: *to master the fundamentals of a trade.*

Self-Defensive Fundamentals

Stance | Balance | Stability | Bladed Defensive Stance

The Bladed (defensive) Stance
All techniques in the defense tactics training are performed from the bladed stance.

Objective—Demonstrate how to correctly position your body to protect your vulnerable line and maintain stance, balance, and stability.

Performance—Bladed Stance
Face the clock (diagram on PowerPoint or imagine of a clock front of you) with your feet shoulder-width apart.

1. Step straight back with either left or right foot. Usually, individuals prefer to have their dominant foot to the rear.

2. If you step back with your right foot, turn your feet and body to the one o'clock position.

3. If you step back with your left foot, turn your feet and body to the eleven o'clock position.

4. Keep your weight equal on both feet and your knees slightly bent.

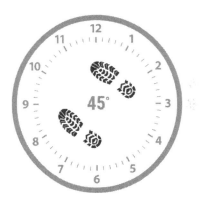

Performance Stability Test (Bladed Stance)

1. Partner exercise (A & B)

2. Partner A places his/her feet together. Partner B gently pushes partner A to the front, back, left side, and right side. Reverse roles.

3. Partner A stands with his/her feet should width apart. Partner B gently pushes partner A to the front, back, left side, and right side. Reverse roles.

4. Partner A now assumes the bladed stance. Partner B gently pushes partner A to the front, back, left side, and right side. Reverse roles.

The Bladed Stance protects your "Vulnerable Line" away from the subject.

ON TARGET TRAINING

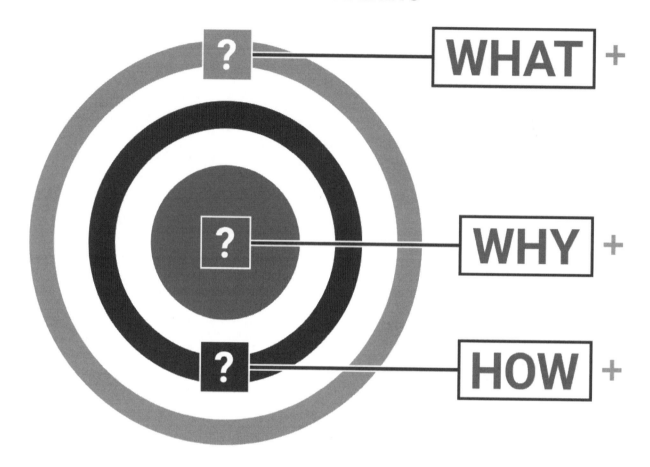

The WHAT describes a technique or tactic.
The first step in teaching a hands-on technique is to explain what the technique is by the name of it. For example, we will be learning about defensive movement, and the first defensive movement technique is forward shuffle.

While the HOW is the manner or method, the technique or tactic is performed.
The second step in teaching a hands-on technique is to explain and demonstrate how to do it. This step should be done a couple of times so that students can see it fully and completely.

And most importantly is the WHY. It's the purpose, reason, intention, justification, or motive of a technique or tactic.
The third step and most important step in teaching hands-on techniques are to explain why the technique is done a certain way and why you should have this technique in your arsenal of defenses. Without this understanding, the student is not bought into believing that the technique is needed or effective.

To really understand a technique or tactic, you must know the WHY (Bullseye).

Defensive Movements: Forward Shuffle

Forward movement is used to engage a subject for control or defense.

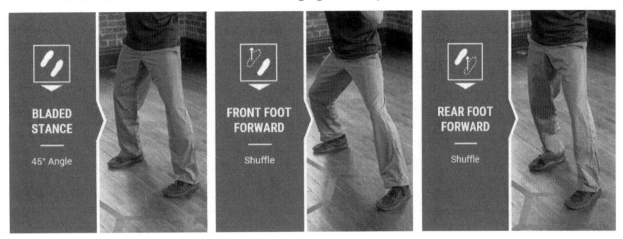

Forward Shuffle

This Defensive movement involves being able to move forward while maintaining balance and stability. All defensive tactics techniques are enhanced with defensive movement.

Objective—Demonstrate how to move forward correctly.

Performance—Forward Movement

1. Assume the bladed stance.

2. Take a short step forward with your front foot (shuffle).

3. Follow up with a short step forward using your rear foot.

4. Continue forward, using forward shuffling movement.

Caution: If the feet come together, balance and stability are compromised (common mistake).

The rule of defensive movement is: The foot that is closest to the direction you want to go always moves first.

Defensive Movements: Rear Shuffle

Rear movement is used to disengage from an aggressor.

BLADED STANCE — 45° Angle

REAR FOOT BACK — Shuffle

FRONT FOOT BACK — Shuffle

Rear Shuffle

This Defensive movement involves being able to move to the rear (backward) while maintaining balance and stability. All defensive tactics techniques are enhanced with defensive movement.

Objective—Demonstrate how to correctly move to the rear.

Performance—Rear Movement

1. Assume the bladed stance.

2. Take a short step back with the rear foot (shuffle).

3. Follow up with a short step back using your front foot.

4. Continue backward, using the rear shuffling movement.

Caution: If the feet come together, balance and stability are compromised (common mistake).

Caution: Backpedaling is another common mistake.

Caution: Obstacles in your environment.

The rule of defensive movement is: The foot that is closest to the direction you want to go always moves first.

Defensive Movements: Side to Side Shuffle

Side-to-side movement is used to avoid an attack from an aggressor.

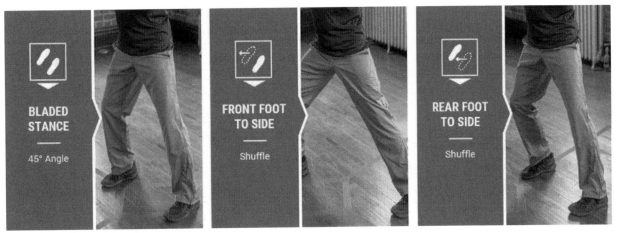

Side to Side Shuffle

This Defensive movement involves being able to move side to side while maintaining balance and stability. All defensive tactics techniques are enhanced with defensive movement.

Objective—Demonstrate how to correctly move side to side

Performance—Side-to-Side Movement

1. Assume the bladed stance.

2. Take a short step to the right using your right foot.

3. Follow up with a short step to the right using your left foot.

4. Take a short step to the left using your left.

5. Follow up with a short step to the left using your right foot.

Caution: If the feet come together, balance and stability are compromised (common mistake).

Caution: Crossing feet up is another common mistake.

Caution: Obstacles in your environment.

The rule of defensive movement is: The foot that is closest to the direction you want to go always moves first.

Defensive Movements: Forward and Rear Pivoting

Pivoting is used to reposition or to enhance your energy when using personal defensive techniques or defensive control tactics

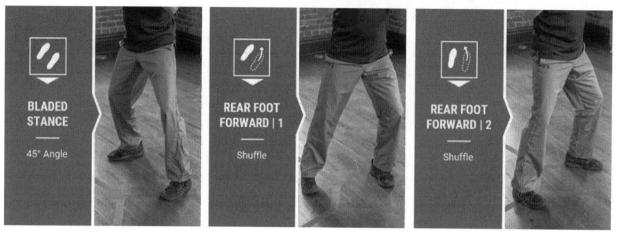

BLADED STANCE — 45° Angle

REAR FOOT FORWARD | 1 — Shuffle

REAR FOOT FORWARD | 2 — Shuffle

Forward & Rear Pivoting

This Defensive movement involves being able to pivot forward or back while maintaining balance and stability. All defensive tactics techniques are enhanced with defensive movement.

Objective—Demonstrate how to correctly pivot forward and backward.

Performance—Pivoting (forward and back)

1. Assume the bladed stance.

2. Take an arcing step forward with your rear foot (forward pivot).

3. Take an arcing step backward with your front foot (rear pivot).

4. When pivoting forward or backward, always remain balanced and stable.

5. Pivots can be small movements or up to a 360-degree pivot.

Caution: If the feet come together, balance and stability are compromised (common mistake).

Caution: Crossing feet up is another common mistake.

Caution: Obstacles in your environment.

Robot Exercise (The Best Self-Defense Technique!)

Defensive Movement "Robot Exercise"

The robot exercise involves being able to move in a lateral motion (side to side) to avoid an attack that is coming at you from a distance of 4' away or greater.

Objective—Demonstrate how to correctively avoid a forward attack by moving out of the way.

Performance—Robot Exercise

1. The defender assumes a bladed defensive stance.

2. From 4-6" away, the attacker places hands out directly toward the defender.

3. Attacker moves forward toward the defender, attempting to gently touch either shoulder of the defender.

4. The defender waits for the last moment to move to either side, away from the attack.

5. Using sounds and/or movements will assist the defender in distracting the attacker.

6. Once out of the attack zone, defender can proceed to keep moving away from the attacker.

Caution: Do not move too late!

Caution: Do not move too soon, or the attacker will have time to adjust (reaction time) and follow/track you.

Caution: Crossing feet up is another common mistake.

Caution: Beware of obstacles in your environment.

Core Energy Principle

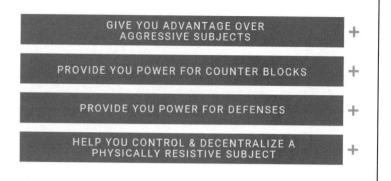

CORE ENERGY

Energy and **power** are generated and developed from the **core** of the human body, even though a lot of emphasis is placed on the body's extremities.

The **Core Energy Principle** will:

GIVE YOU ADVANTAGE OVER AGGRESSIVE SUBJECTS	+
PROVIDE YOU POWER FOR COUNTER BLOCKS	+
PROVIDE YOU POWER FOR DEFENSES	+
HELP YOU CONTROL & DECENTRALIZE A PHYSICALLY RESISTIVE SUBJECT	+

Core Energy: Our central and most essential part of our strength and power is our core energy. Without core energy, we rely on our extremities, which are not as strong as our central core. All defensive tactics techniques utilize this essential principle.

INEFFICIENT CORE ENERGY

Partner A faces Partner B with their **elbows away** from their core.

Partner A pushes Partner B back by pushing at their **shoulders**.

Reverse Roles

EFFICIENT CORE ENERGY

Partner A faces Partner B with their **elbows down** towards their core.

Partner A pushes Partner B back by pushing at their **shoulders**.

Reverse Roles

Objective—Demonstrate how to correctly use your core energy.

Performance—Core Energy

1. Partner exercise (A & B)

2. Partner A faces partner B with his/her elbows away from their core.

3. Partner B moves forward toward partner A. Partner A pushes partner B back by pushing at their shoulders. How did it go? Reverse roles.

4. Partner A again faces partner B with his/her elbows down towards their core. Partner B moves forward toward partner A. Partner A pushes partner B back by pushing at their shoulders. How did it go? Reverse roles

Defensive Verbalization

During all Defenses: Use loud, repetitive Defensive Verbalizations

NO!

STOP!

GET BACK!

LET ME GO!

LEAVE ME ALONE!

Defensive Verbalization | Why?
1. **Creates Witnesses**
2. **Establishes authority**
3. **Keeps you breathing**
4. **May be used as a distraction**
5. **Alerts others of a confrontation**
6. **Provides direction to the aggressor**
7. **Mitigates liability risk | You & Agency**

The Art of Distraction

It is a process by which we buy valuable time to Escape, Defend, or Control.

Sounds (Loud Scream/Yell) - Movements – Psychological - Lights

Distractions affect the senses, which take time for the mind to process the new information. Distractions have been used since ancient times. A valuable advantage!

Sounds: Using a loud scream or yell can cause a momentary delay.
Movements: Using your hands, eyes, and body can distract and cause a momentary delay.
Psychological: Asking a question that is out of the ordinary can cause them a mental delay.
Lights: Flashlights, the sun, emergency lights, etc., can cause a delay.

Escape Strategies

- Escape is the act or instance of breaking free from danger or threat or from being trapped, restrained, confined, or isolated against your will.
- Planning is the cognitive process of thinking about what you will do in the event of something happening.

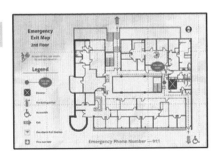

Reactionary Gap

The Reactionary Gap is 4-6 Feet. "Action beats Reaction with-in the Reactionary Gap"
The distance between an individual and an aggressor in which the ability to react is impaired due to the close proximity of the aggressor.

Hand Positions

There are six basic hand positions

Objective—Demonstrate how to correctly use your hands in the open, authority, stop, caution, and directive.

Performance—<u>Open or Authority</u> Hand Positions

1. Assume the bladed stance

2. Position your arms with your elbows down and your palms facing upward (Open).

3. Position your arms with your elbows down and your palms down (Authority).

Performance—<u>Stop or Caution</u> Hand Positions

1. Assume the bladed stance

2. Position your arms with your elbows down and your palms facing outward (Stop).

3. The non-verbal message says, "don't come close to me," or a non-threatening message if you are moving forward (Caution).

Performance—<u>Directive</u> Hand Positions

1. Assume the bladed Stance

2. Position your arms/hands, pointing with your open hand in the direction you want them to go (Directive).

- **Caution:** Do not point when giving, as pointing is perceived as a derogatory gesture.

- **Caution:** Closing your hands into a fist position may send a message of aggression.

Module Two –Defensive Blocking Techniques

During & After All Defenses

During all defenses use loud and repetitive defensive verbalizations (NO, STOP, GET BACK, STOP RESISTING, etc.) to direct the aggressor to stop attacking you, as well as using defensive movements - Escape!

After all defenses be sure to follow agency policies and procedures in regard to self-defense. Report and document immediately.

Defensive Blocking Techniques

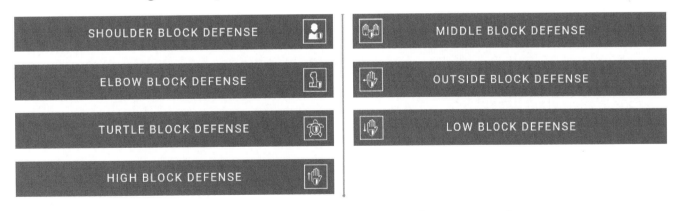

SHOULDER BLOCK DEFENSE

ELBOW BLOCK DEFENSE

TURTLE BLOCK DEFENSE

HIGH BLOCK DEFENSE

MIDDLE BLOCK DEFENSE

OUTSIDE BLOCK DEFENSE

LOW BLOCK DEFENSE

Empower yourself & your staff by being able to correctly **prevent** and **mitigate** against an **imminent assault** from an aggressor.

Shoulder Block Defense

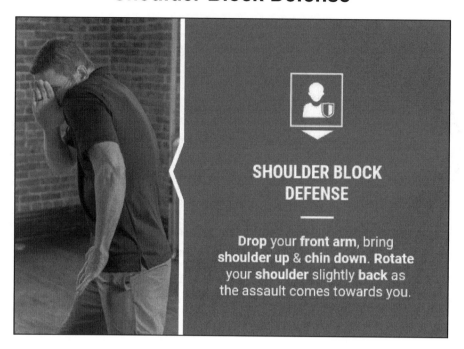

Shoulder Block Defense

It is a technique that teaches individuals how to deflect an imminent assault.

Objective—Demonstrate how to properly use a defensive shoulder block against a physical assault to your head.

Performance—Shoulder Block Defense

1. Assume the bladed stance.

2. Bring your chin down.

3. Drop the arm that is in front of you while bringing your shoulder up to your chin.

4. You can slightly rotate your body towards your backside as the assault comes towards you, further deflecting the attack.

During all Defenses:

- Use loud, repetitive defensive verbalizations (NO! STOP! GET BACK! LET ME GO! LEAVE ME ALONE! etc.) to direct the aggressor to stop attacking you.
- Use defensive movements (Escape!)

After all Defenses:

- Follow agency policies and procedures in regard to self-defense.
- Report and Document immediately.

Elbow Block Defense

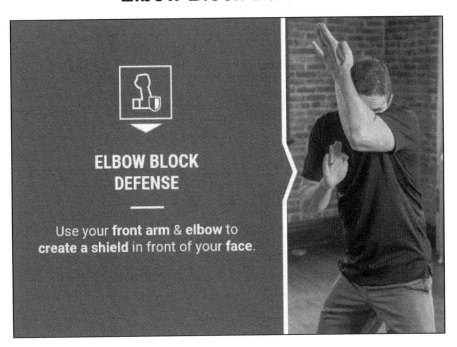

Elbow Block Defense

It is a technique that teaches individuals how to deflect an imminent assault.

Objective—Demonstrate how to properly use a defensive elbow block against a physical assault to your head.

Performance—Elbow Block Defense

1. Assume the bladed stance.
2. Bring your chin down.
3. Bring your front arm up to your face with your elbow directly in front, creating a shield in front of your face.
4. You can slightly rotate your body towards your backside as the assault comes towards you, further deflecting the attack.

During all Defenses:

- Use loud, repetitive defensive verbalizations (NO! STOP! GET BACK! LET ME GO! LEAVE ME ALONE! etc.) to direct the aggressor to stop attacking you.
- Use defensive movements (Escape!)

After all Defenses:

- Follow agency policies and procedures in regard to self-defense.
- Report and Document immediately

Turtle Block Defense

Turtle Block Defense

It is a technique that teaches individuals how to deflect an imminent assault.

Objective—Demonstrate how to properly use a defensive turtle block against a physical assault to your head and torso.

Performance—Turtle Block Defense

1. Assume the bladed stance.
2. Bring your chin down.
3. Bring both arms up in front of your face with your elbows directly in front, creating a shield in front of your body and face.
4. You can slightly rotate your body towards your backside as the assault comes towards you, further deflecting the attack.

During all Defenses:

- Use loud, repetitive defensive verbalizations (NO! STOP! GET BACK! LET ME GO! LEAVE ME ALONE! etc.) to direct the aggressor to stop attacking you.
- Use defensive movements (Escape!)

After all Defenses:

- Follow agency policies and procedures in regard to self-defense.
- Report and Document immediately.

High Block Defense

High Block Defense

It is a technique that teaches individuals how to deflect an imminent assault to their head.

Objective—Demonstrate how to properly use a high defensive block against a physical assault to your head.

Performance—High Block Defense

1. Assume the bladed stance.

2. Bring your chin down.

3. Bring your arm up in front of your face with your palm out.

4. Your hands can be open or closed.

5. You can use your support arm, strong-arm, or both arms to defend against an attack on your head.

During all Defenses:

- Use loud, repetitive defensive verbalizations (NO! STOP! GET BACK! LET ME GO! LEAVE ME ALONE! etc.) to direct the aggressor to stop attacking you.
- Use defensive movements (Escape!)

After all Defenses:

- Follow agency policies and procedures in regard to self-defense.
- Report and Document immediately.

Middle Block Defense

Middle Block Defense

It is a technique that teaches individuals how to deflect an imminent rushing assault or grappling attack towards them.

Objective—Demonstrate how to properly use a defensive middle block against a physical assault coming at you.

Performance—Middle Block Defense

1. Assume the bladed stance.

2. Bring both arms up in front of you (palms out).

3. Push the aggressor away at the shoulders or torso area.

4. Use side-to-side movement after the middle block defense to get into a position of advantage or to continue to defend.

During all Defenses:

- Use loud, repetitive defensive verbalizations (NO! STOP! GET BACK! LET ME GO! LEAVE ME ALONE! etc.) to direct the aggressor to stop attacking you.
- Use defensive movements (Escape!)

After all Defenses:

- Follow agency policies and procedures in regard to self-defense.
- Report and Document immediately.

Outside Block Defense

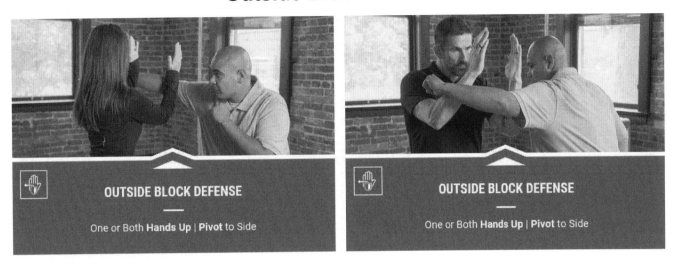

Outside Block Defense

It is a technique that teaches individuals how to deflect an imminent assault to either side of their body.

Objective—Demonstrate how to properly use a defensive outside block against a physical assault coming to either side of your body.

Performance—Outside Block Defense

1. Assume the bladed stance.
2. Bring either your right or left (or both) up arms in front of your body and pivot towards the direction of the attack.
3. Your hands can be open or closed.
4. You can use your support arm, strong-arm, or both arms to defend against an attack on either side of your body.

During all Defenses:

- Use loud, repetitive defensive verbalizations (NO! STOP! GET BACK! LET ME GO! LEAVE ME ALONE! etc.) to direct the aggressor to stop attacking you.
- Use defensive movements (Escape!)

After all Defenses:

- Follow agency policies and procedures in regard to self-defense.
- Report and Document immediately.

Low Block Defense

LOW BLOCK DEFENSE

Right or Left **Arm** or **Hand** | **Sweeping** Motion Away

LOW BLOCK DEFENSE

Double **Open Hand** Catching **Instep** of Aggressor

Low Block Defense

It is a technique that teaches individuals how to deflect an imminent attack to the lower area of the body.

Objective—Demonstrate how to properly use a low defensive block against a physical assault coming to the lower part of your body.

Performance—Low Block Defense

1. Assume the bladed stance.
2. Bring either your right or left (or both) arm down, sweeping in front of your body and moving the attack away.
3. Your hands can be open or closed.
4. You can use your support arm, strong-arm, or both arms to defend against an attack to the lower area of your body.

During all Defenses:

- Use loud, repetitive defensive verbalizations (NO! STOP! GET BACK! LET ME GO! LEAVE ME ALONE! etc.) to direct the aggressor to stop attacking you.
- Use defensive movements (Escape!)

After all Defenses:

- Follow agency policies and procedures in regard to self-defense.
- Report and Document immediately.

Module Three –Personal Defense Skills & Techniques

Personal Defense Techniques Defined

☑ **Personal Defensive Techniques** are used for **Physical Violence** & **Deadly Force** situations

☑ **Deadly Force** is force that is likely or intended to cause **death** or great **bodily harm** to you or another person

☑ Any time **force is used** to defend yourself or others it must be a **last resort**, **reasonable**, & you must be able to articulate **what you did** & **why you did it**

☑ Any use of **Self-Defense** is based on your **policies** & **procedures**

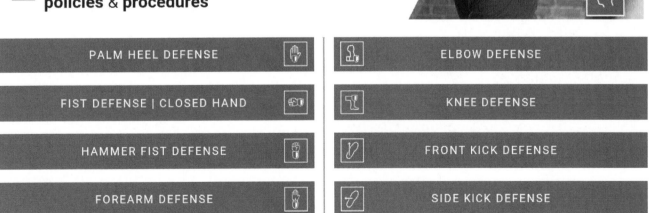

PALM HEEL DEFENSE	ELBOW DEFENSE
FIST DEFENSE | CLOSED HAND	KNEE DEFENSE
HAMMER FIST DEFENSE	FRONT KICK DEFENSE
FOREARM DEFENSE	SIDE KICK DEFENSE

Empower yourself & **your staff** by being able to correctly **defend** against an **imminent assault** from an aggressor.

Palm Heel Defense

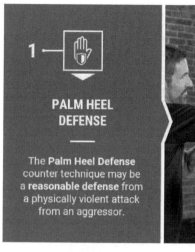

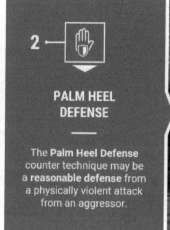

Palm Heel Defense

The palm heel defense counter technique may be a reasonable defense from a physically violent attack from an aggressor. Deadly force is force that is likely or intended to cause death or great bodily harm to you or another person. This defense is for those types of situations. Any time force is used to defend yourself or others. It must be a last resort, reasonable, and you must be able to articulate what you did and why you did it.

Objective—Demonstrate how to correctly use a palm heel defense technique to defend against an attack from an aggressor.

Performance—Palm Heel Defense

1. Assume the bladed stance.
2. Position your strong or support hand with your heel extended outward.
3. Fingers are in a claw position and have nothing to do with the defense.
4. You can pivot your body forward, thrusting your heel into the desired area of impact.

During all Defenses:

▪ Use loud, repetitive defensive verbalizations (NO! STOP! GET BACK! LET ME GO! LEAVE ME ALONE! etc.) to direct the aggressor to stop attacking you.
▪ Use defensive movements (Escape!)

After all Defenses:

▪ Follow agency policies and procedures in regard to self-defense.
▪ Report and Document immediately.

Fist Defense (Closed Hand)

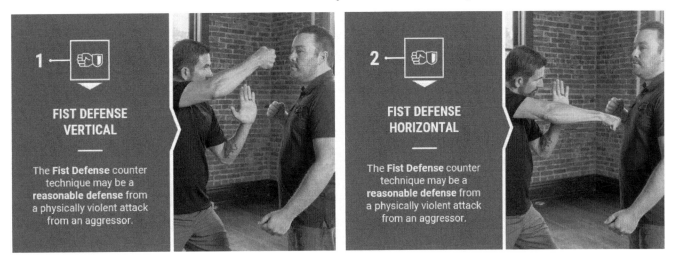

1 — FIST DEFENSE VERTICAL

The **Fist Defense** counter technique may be a **reasonable defense** from a physically violent attack from an aggressor.

2 — FIST DEFENSE HORIZONTAL

The **Fist Defense** counter technique may be a **reasonable defense** from a physically violent attack from an aggressor.

Fist Defense

The fist defense counter technique may be a reasonable defense from a physically violent attack from an aggressor. Deadly force is force that is likely or intended to cause death or great bodily harm to you or another person. This defense is for those types of situations. Any time force is used to defend yourself or others. It must be a last resort, reasonable, and you must be able to articulate what you did and why you did it.

Objective—Demonstrate how to correctly use a fist defense technique to defend against an attack from an aggressor.

Performance—Fist Defense

1. Assume the bladed stance.
2. Position your strong or support hand with your fingers clenched tightly into your palm.
3. Vertical or horizontal fist positions can be used.
4. You can pivot your body forward, thrusting your fist into the desired area of impact.

Caution: Proper fist position is required to avoid injuring yourself.

During all Defenses:

- Use loud, repetitive defensive verbalizations (NO! STOP! GET BACK! LET ME GO! LEAVE ME ALONE! etc.) to direct the aggressor to stop attacking you.
- Use defensive movements (Escape!)

After all Defenses:

- Follow agency policies and procedures in regard to self-defense.
- Report and Document immediately.

Hammer Fist Defense

HAMMER FIST VERTICAL

The **Hammer Fist Defense** counter technique may be a **reasonable defense** from a physically violent attack from an aggressor.

HAMMER FIST DIAGONAL

The **Hammer Fist Defense** counter technique may be a **reasonable defense** from a physically violent attack from an aggressor.

HAMMER FIST HORIZONTAL

The **Hammer Fist Defense** counter technique may be a **reasonable defense** from a physically violent attack from an aggressor.

Hammer Fist Defense

The hammer fist defense counter technique may be a reasonable defense from a physically violent attack from an aggressor. Deadly force is force that is likely or intended to cause death or great bodily harm to you or another person. This defense is for those types of situations. Any time force is used to defend yourself or others. It must be a last resort, reasonable, and you must be able to articulate what you did and why you did it.

Objective—Demonstrate how to correctly use a fist defense technique to defend against an attack from an aggressor.

Performance—Hammer Fist Defense

1. Assume the bladed stance.
2. Position your strong or support hand with your fingers clenched tightly into your palm.
3. Vertical, diagonal, or horizontal hammer fist defenses may be used.
4. You can pivot your body forward, thrusting your fist into the desired area of impact.

Caution: Proper fist position is required to avoid injuring yourself.

During all Defenses:

- Use loud, repetitive defensive verbalizations (NO! STOP! GET BACK! LET ME GO! LEAVE ME ALONE! etc.) to direct the aggressor to stop attacking you.
- Use defensive movements (Escape!)

After all Defenses:

- Follow agency policies and procedures in regard to self-defense.
- Report and Document immediately.

Forearm Defense

FOREARM DEFENSE VERTICAL

The **Forearm Defense** counter technique may be a **reasonable defense** from a physically violent attack from an aggressor.

FOREARM DEFENSE DIAGONAL

The **Forearm Defense** counter technique may be a **reasonable defense** from a physically violent attack from an aggressor.

FOREARM DEFENSE HORIZONTAL

The **Forearm Defense** counter technique may be a **reasonable defense** from a physically violent attack from an aggressor.

Forearm Defense

The forearm defense counter technique may be a reasonable defense from a physically violent attack from an aggressor. Deadly force is force that is likely or intended to cause death or great bodily harm to you or another person. This defense is for those types of situations. Any time force is used to defend yourself or others. It must be a last resort, reasonable, and you must be able to articulate what you did and why you did it.

Objective—Demonstrate how to correctly use a forearm defense technique to defend against an attack from an aggressor.

Performance—Forearm Defense

1. Assume the bladed stance.
2. Position your strong or support hand with your fingers clenched tightly or in an open position.
3. Vertical, diagonal, or horizontal forearm defenses may be used.
4. You can pivot your body forward or backward, thrusting your forearm into the desired area of impact.

During all Defenses:

- Use loud, repetitive defensive verbalizations (NO! STOP! GET BACK! LET ME GO! LEAVE ME ALONE! etc.) to direct the aggressor to stop attacking you.
- Use defensive movements (Escape!)

After all Defenses:

- Follow agency policies and procedures in regard to self-defense.
- Report and Document immediately.

Elbow Defense

ELBOW DEFENSE VERTICAL

The **Elbow Defense** counter technique may be a **reasonable defense** from a physically violent attack from an aggressor.

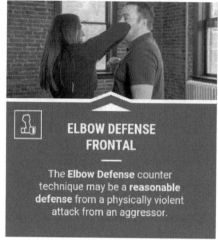

ELBOW DEFENSE FRONTAL

The **Elbow Defense** counter technique may be a **reasonable defense** from a physically violent attack from an aggressor.

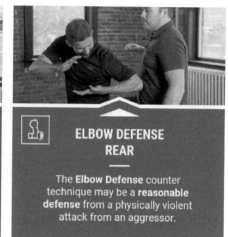

ELBOW DEFENSE REAR

The **Elbow Defense** counter technique may be a **reasonable defense** from a physically violent attack from an aggressor.

Elbow Defense

The elbow defense counter technique may be a reasonable defense from a physically violent attack from an aggressor. Deadly force is force that is likely or intended to cause death or great bodily harm to you or another person. This defense is for those types of situations. Any time force is used to defend yourself or others. It must be a last resort, reasonable, and you must be able to articulate what you did and why you did it.

Objective—Demonstrate how to correctly use an elbow defense technique to defend against an attack from an aggressor.

Performance—Elbow Defense

1. Assume the bladed stance.
2. When using your strong/support hand elbow, you can blade your hand or clenched hand tightly.
3. Vertical, frontal, and rear elbow defenses may be used.
4. You can pivot your body forward or backward, thrusting your elbow into the desired area of impact.

During all Defenses:

- Use loud, repetitive defensive verbalizations (NO! STOP! GET BACK! LET ME GO! LEAVE ME ALONE! etc.) to direct the aggressor to stop attacking you.
- Use defensive movements (Escape!)

After all Defenses:

- Follow agency policies and procedures in regard to self-defense.
- Report and Document immediately.

Knee Defense

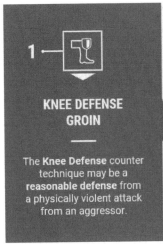   

1 KNEE DEFENSE GROIN

The **Knee Defense** counter technique may be a **reasonable defense** from a physically violent attack from an aggressor.

2 KNEE DEFENSE THIGH

The **Knee Defense** counter technique may be a **reasonable defense** from a physically violent attack from an aggressor.

Knee Defense

The knee defense counter technique may be a reasonable defense from a physically violent attack from an aggressor. Deadly force is force that is likely or intended to cause death or great bodily harm to you or another person. This defense is for those types of situations. Any time force is used to defend yourself or others. It must be a last resort, reasonable, and you must be able to articulate what you did and why you did it.

Objective—Demonstrate how to correctly use a knee defense technique to defend against an attack from an aggressor.

Performance—Knee Defense

1. Assume the bladed stance.
2. Your support or strong knee can be used.
3. Your foot should be pulled back when defending, creating a pointed knee for impact.
4. You can pivot your body forward, thrusting your knee into the desired area of impact.

During all Defenses:

- Use loud, repetitive defensive verbalizations (NO! STOP! GET BACK! LET ME GO! LEAVE ME ALONE! etc.) to direct the aggressor to stop attacking you.
- Use defensive movements (Escape!)

After all Defenses:

- Follow agency policies and procedures in regard to self-defense.
- Report and Document immediately.

Kick Defense

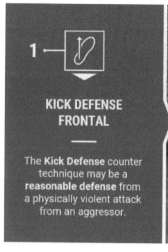   

Kick Defense

The kick defense counter technique may be a reasonable defense from a physically violent attack from an aggressor. Deadly force is force that is likely or intended to cause death or great bodily harm to you or another person. This defense is for those types of situations. Any time force is used to defend yourself or others. It must be a last resort, reasonable, and you must be able to articulate what you did and why you did it.

Objective—Demonstrate how to correctly use a frontal and sidekick defense technique to defend against an attack from an aggressor.

Performance—Frontal and Side Kick Defense

1. Assume the bladed stance.
2. Your support or strong side can be used for frontal and sidekicks.
3. For the frontal kick, your toes should be pulled back.
4. For the sidekick, use the edge of your outer foot.

Caution: Balance may be compromised when deploying a defensive kick.

During all Defenses:

- Use loud, repetitive defensive verbalizations (NO! STOP! GET BACK! LET ME GO! LEAVE ME ALONE! etc.) to direct the aggressor to stop attacking you.
- Use defensive movements (Escape!)

After all Defenses:

- Follow agency policies and procedures in regard to self-defense.
- Report and Document immediately.

Vulnerable Areas of the Body

Knowledge of **Self-Defense Tactics** is very important. Just as important is how and when you would utilize your **Self-Defense Tactics** skills **if** and **when** necessary.

Without this knowledge and understanding, your interventions could be ineffective or expose you to **unnecessary liability risk**.

The "**Vulnerable Areas**" of the body diagram denote **Lower**, **Medium**, and **High-Risk** Target Areas.

An individual **MUST ALWAYS** consider their policies and procedures, as well as State and Federal Laws, when using **force** or **self-defense** interventions.

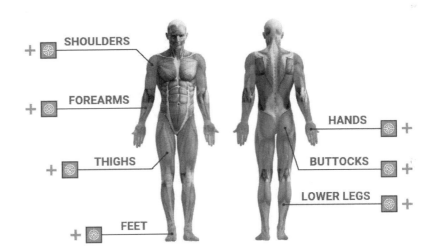

LOW-RISK
TARGET AREAS

Low-Risk Target Areas are for situations where the subject is resisting or attacking **you** or **another person** with physical violence and aggression.

SHOULDERS

FOREARMS

THIGHS

FEET

HANDS

BUTTOCKS

LOWER LEGS

The subject's body would be considered low risk for the application of blocks and restraint techniques (excluding the Head, Neck, Groin, and Spine).

The level of resultant trauma to these areas tends to be minimal or temporary, yet exceptions may occur.

* An individual/agency MUST always consider their policies and procedures, state and federal laws when using any force or self-defense interventions.

Vulnerable Areas of the Body

Knowledge of **Self-Defense Tactics** is very important. Just as important is how and when you would utilize your **Self-Defense Tactics** skills **if** and **when** necessary.

Without this knowledge and understanding, your interventions could be ineffective or expose you to **unnecessary liability risk**.

The "**Vulnerable Areas**" of the body diagram denote **Lower, Medium,** and **High-Risk** Target Areas.

An individual **MUST ALWAYS** consider their policies and procedures, as well as State and Federal Laws, when using **force** or **self-defense** interventions.

MEDIUM-RISK
TARGET AREAS

Medium-Risk Target Areas are for situations where the subject is resisting or attacking **you** or **another person** with physical violence and aggression, or when the force applied to a **Low-Risk Target Area** fails to overcome the subject's resistance or attack.

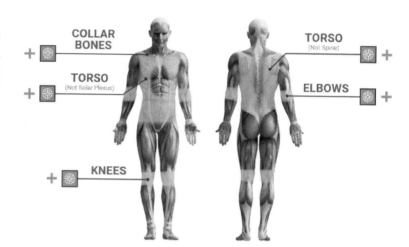

Medium Risk Targets are areas of the human body that include joints and areas that are in close proximity to a High-Risk Target Area. The risk of potential injury is increased.

The level of resultant trauma to these areas tends to be moderate to serious. Injury may last for longer periods of time or may be temporary.

* An individual/agency MUST always consider their policies and procedures, state and federal laws when using any force or self-defense interventions.

Vulnerable Areas of the Body

Knowledge of **Self-Defense Tactics** is very important. Just as important is how and when you would utilize your **Self-Defense Tactics** skills **if** and **when** necessary.

Without this knowledge and understanding, your interventions could be ineffective or expose you to **unnecessary liability risk**.

The "**Vulnerable Areas**" of the body diagram denote **Lower**, **Medium**, and **High-Risk** Target Areas.

An individual **MUST ALWAYS** consider their policies and procedures, as well as State and Federal Laws, when using **force** or **self-defense** interventions.

HIGH-RISK
TARGET AREAS

High-Risk Target Areas are for situations where the subject is using **deadly force** that is likely to cause serious injury or **death** to **you** or **another person**.

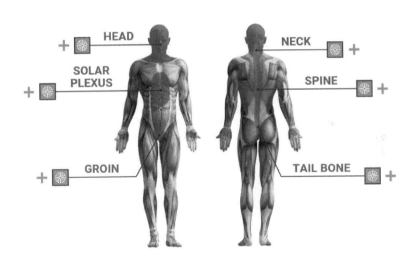

Force-directed to High-Risk Target Areas may cause a greater risk of injury to the subject. Staff must be justified and reasonable in using deadly force against a subject.

The level of resultant trauma to these areas tends to be serious and/or long-lasting. Injury to the subject may include serious bodily injury, unconsciousness, shock, or death.

* An individual/agency MUST always consider their policies and procedures, state and federal laws when using any force or self-defense interventions.

Module Four –Self-Defense Tactics & Techniques

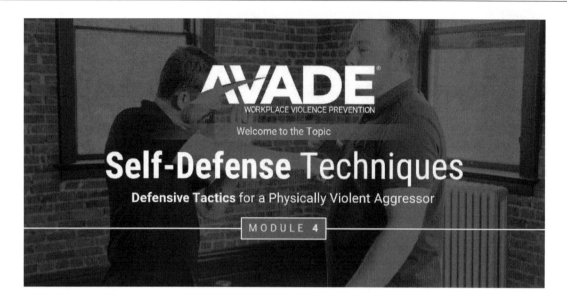

Self-Defense Techniques

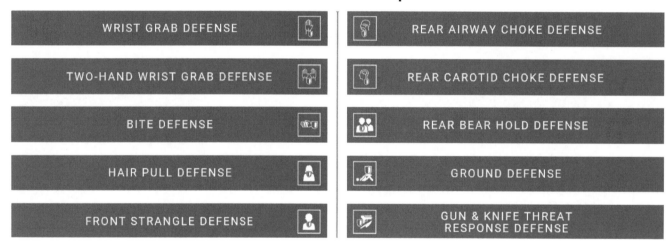

WRIST GRAB DEFENSE	REAR AIRWAY CHOKE DEFENSE
TWO-HAND WRIST GRAB DEFENSE	REAR CAROTID CHOKE DEFENSE
BITE DEFENSE	REAR BEAR HOLD DEFENSE
HAIR PULL DEFENSE	GROUND DEFENSE
FRONT STRANGLE DEFENSE	GUN & KNIFE THREAT RESPONSE DEFENSE

During all Defenses:

- Use loud, repetitive defensive verbalizations (NO! STOP! GET BACK! LET ME GO! LEAVE ME ALONE! etc.) to direct the aggressor to stop attacking you.
- Use defensive movements (Escape!)

After all Defenses:

- Follow agency policies and procedures in regard to self-defense.

- Report and Document immediately.

Special Note: If personal defense techniques are used in these defenses, it MUST be for physical violence or deadly force situations. Any time force is used to defend yourself or others. It must be a last resort, reasonable, and you must be able to articulate what you did, why you did it, and how you did it.

Wrist Grab Defense

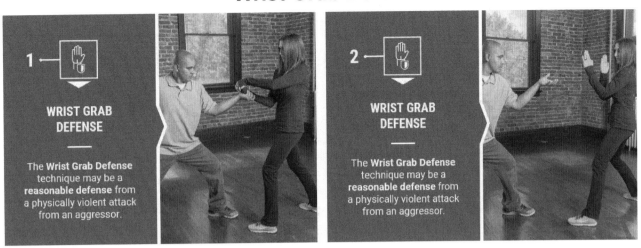

Wrist Grab Defense

It is a technique that teaches individuals how to defend themselves from a one-handed wrist grab assault.

Objective—Demonstrate how to defend against a one-handed wrist grab assault situation.

Performance—Wrist Grab Defense

1. The defender stabilizes after being grabbed by the wrist.

2. Defender pulls elbow into their core (or moves forward to get their elbow into their core).

3. Defender turns palm upward, grabbing their hand with their free hand.

4. Defender then pulls their hand upward, using their core energy to break free of the assault.

5. The defender may need to use a distraction technique or personal defensive technique to break free from the assault.

During All Defenses:

- Use loud, repetitive defensive verbalizations (NO! STOP! GET BACK! LET ME GO! LEAVE ME ALONE! etc.) to direct the aggressor to stop attacking you.
- Use defensive movements (Escape!)

After All Defenses:

- Follow agency policies and procedures in regard to self-defense.
- Report and Document immediately.

Special Note: If personal defense techniques are used in these defenses, it MUST be for physical violence or deadly force situations. Any time force is used to defend yourself or others. It must be a last resort, reasonable, and you must be able to articulate what you did, why you did it, and how you did it.

Two-Hand Wrist Grab Defense

Two-Hand Wrist Grab Defense

It is a technique that teaches individuals how to defend themselves from a two-handed wrist grab assault.

Objective—Demonstrate how to defend against a two-handed wrist grab assault situation.

Performance—Two Hand Wrist Grab Defense

1. The defender stabilizes after being grabbed by the wrists.
2. Defender pulls both elbows into their core (or moves forward to get their elbows into core).
3. Defender turns palms upward while raising both hands upward in a circular outward motion to release the grab.
4. The defender may need to bring their palms back downward in a reverse circular motion to release the grab.
5. The defender may need to use a distraction technique or personal defensive technique to break free from assault.

During All Defenses:

- Use loud, repetitive defensive verbalizations (NO! STOP! GET BACK! LET ME GO! LEAVE ME ALONE! etc.) to direct the aggressor to stop attacking you.
- Use defensive movements (Escape!)

After All Defenses:

- Follow agency policies and procedures in regard to self-defense.
- Report and Document immediately.

Special Note: If personal defense techniques are used in these defenses, it MUST be for physical violence or deadly force situations. Any time force is used to defend yourself or others. It must be a last resort, reasonable, and you must be able to articulate what you did, why you did it, and how you did it.

Bite Defense

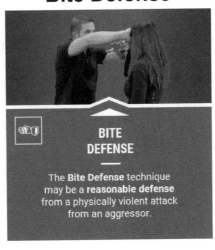

Bite Defense

It is a technique that teaches individuals how to defend themselves from a bite assault.

Objective—Demonstrate how to defend against a bite assault situation.

Caution: The worst thing we can do when we are bitten is to pull away. A bite assault could be considered a deadly force situation.

Performance—Bite Defense

1. Defender stabilizes after being bitten on their arm or hand.
2. The defender distracts the aggressor by covering the aggressor's eyes with their free hand.
3. The defender DOES NOT pull away unless the aggressor opens their mouth.
4. The defender may need to grab the back of the aggressor's head and pull them in as they push the bitten limb/hand into the aggressor's mouth. Push-Pull! "Feed the Bite"
5. The defender may need to use a personal defensive technique to break free from the assault. If the aggressor falls back after being impacted by a personal defensive technique but does not open their mouth: **Move with them**!

During All Defenses:

- Use loud, repetitive defensive verbalizations (NO! STOP! GET BACK! LET ME GO! LEAVE ME ALONE! etc.) to direct the aggressor to stop attacking you.
- Use defensive movements (Escape!)

After All Defenses:

- Follow agency policies and procedures in regard to self-defense.
- Report and Document immediately.

Special Note: If personal defense techniques are used in these defenses, it MUST be for physical violence or deadly force situations. Any time force is used to defend yourself or others. It must be a last resort, reasonable, and you must be able to articulate what you did, why you did it, and how you did it.

Hair Pull Defense

Hair Pull Defense

It is a technique that teaches individuals how to defend themselves from a hair pull assault.

Objective—Demonstrate how to defend against a hair pull.

Caution: The worst thing we can do when our hair is pulled is to pull away. Most hair pulls are done from behind the victim. A hair pull assault could be considered a deadly force situation, as the aggressor may pull the victim down from behind, causing a serious injury due to the fall/whiplash effect.

Performance—Hair Pull Defense

1. The defender stabilizes after their hair has been pulled from behind.
2. Defender immediately interlaces their fingers together behind their head while bringing their chin down.
3. The defender does a slight quarter turn towards the aggressor.
4. The defender initiates a foot stomp onto the instep of the aggressor's foot.

During All Defenses:

- Use loud, repetitive defensive verbalizations (NO! STOP! GET BACK! LET ME GO! LEAVE ME ALONE! etc.) to direct the aggressor to stop attacking you.
- Use defensive movements (Escape!)

After All Defenses:

- Follow agency policies and procedures in regard to self-defense.
- Report and Document immediately.

Special Note: If personal defense techniques are used in these defenses, it MUST be for physical violence or deadly force situations. Any time force is used to defend yourself or others. It must be a last resort, reasonable, and you must be able to articulate what you did, why you did it, and how you did it.

Front Strangle Defense

 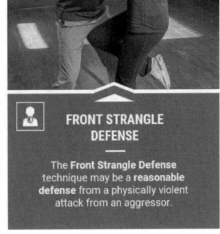 

Front Strangle Defense

It is a technique that teaches individuals how to defend themselves from a frontal strangle assault.

Objective—Demonstrate how to defend against a frontal strangle assault situation.

Note: A front strangle assault is more than likely done from close range unless a person has you up against a wall or pinned to the floor.

Performance—Front Strangle Defense

1. The defender stabilizes after being grabbed around the throat with both hands.
2. The defender can utilize a palm heel defense, knee defense, finger spears to the eyes, foot stomp, or any personal defense technique.
3. Defender may need to use repeated defensive moves to break free from this assault.
4. This assault is potentially life-threatening, and the defender will need to respond immediately to break free from the assault.

During All Defenses:

- Use loud, repetitive defensive verbalizations (NO! STOP! GET BACK! LET ME GO! LEAVE ME ALONE! etc.) to direct the aggressor to stop attacking you.
- Use defensive movements (Escape!)

After All Defenses:

- Follow agency policies and procedures in regard to self-defense.
- Report and Document immediately.

Special Note: If personal defense techniques are used in these defenses, it MUST be for physical violence or deadly force situations. Any time force is used to defend yourself or others. It must be a last resort, reasonable, and you must be able to articulate what you did, why you did it, and how you did it.

Front Strangle Defense (Special Situation)

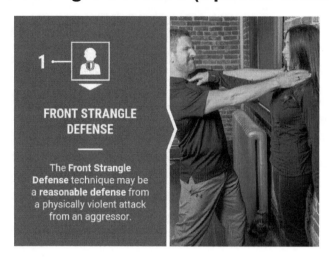

Front Strangle Defense (Special Situation)

It is a technique that teaches individuals how to defend themselves from a frontal strangle assault.

Objective—Demonstrate how to defend against a frontal strangle assault situation.

Note: Typically, a front strangle assault is done from close range unless a person has you up against a wall or pinned to the floor.

Performance—Strangle Defense

1. Defender stabilizes after being grabbed around the throat with both hands, arms extended.
2. The defender can utilize a finger spear technique to the bottom of the throat/top of the rib cage of the attacker.
3. Finger spear is done by placing two fingers together and pushing in and down.
4. Defender may need to turn their body sideways if the attacker's arms are long.
5. Defender may need to use other personal defense techniques.

During All Defenses:

▪ Use loud, repetitive defensive verbalizations (NO! STOP! GET BACK! LET ME GO! LEAVE ME ALONE! etc.) to direct the aggressor to stop attacking you.

▪ Use defensive movements (Escape!)

After All Defenses:

▪ Follow agency policies and procedures in regard to self-defense.

▪ Report and Document immediately.

Special Note: If personal defense techniques are used in these defenses, it MUST be for physical violence or deadly force situations. Any time force is used to defend yourself or others. It must be a last resort, reasonable, and you must be able to articulate what you did, why you did it, and how you did it.

Rear Airway Choke Defense

  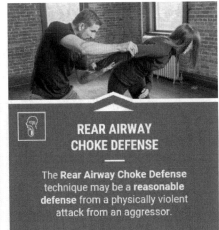

REAR AIRWAY CHOKE DEFENSE

The **Rear Airway Choke Defense** technique may be a **reasonable defense** from a physically violent attack from an aggressor.

REAR AIRWAY CHOKE DEFENSE

The **Rear Airway Choke Defense** technique may be a **reasonable defense** from a physically violent attack from an aggressor.

REAR AIRWAY CHOKE DEFENSE

The **Rear Airway Choke Defense** technique may be a **reasonable defense** from a physically violent attack from an aggressor.

Rear Airway Choke Defense

It is a technique that teaches individuals how to defend themselves from a rear airway choke assault.

Objective—Demonstrate how to defend against a rear airway choke assault situation.
Note: A rear airway choke assault can compromise your ability to breathe and verbalize and render you unconscious. Individuals will need to respond **immediately** to this type of assault.

Performance—Rear Airway Choke Defense

1. The defender stabilizes after being grabbed around the throat from behind.
2. Defender pulls the attacker's arm downward towards their core.
3. After the core is established, the defender will turn their head away from the attackers' elbow and place their palm under the attacker's elbow.
4. The defender will then pivot and push the attackers' elbow into the air to escape the assault.
5. Defender may need to use personal defense techniques to escape the assault.

During All Defenses:

- Use loud, repetitive defensive verbalizations (NO! STOP! GET BACK! LET ME GO! LEAVE ME ALONE! etc.) to direct the aggressor to stop attacking you.
- Use defensive movements (Escape!)

After All Defenses:

- Follow agency policies and procedures in regard to self-defense.
- Report and Document immediately.

Special Note: If personal defense techniques are used in these defenses, it MUST be for physical violence or deadly force situations. Any time force is used to defend yourself or others. It must be a last resort, reasonable, and you must be able to articulate what you did, why you did it, and how you did it.

Rear Carotid Choke Defense

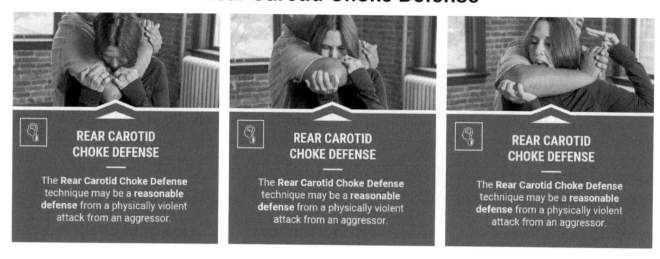

Rear Carotid Choke Defense

It is a technique that teaches individuals how to defend themselves from a rear carotid choke assault.

Objective—Demonstrate how to defend against a rear carotid choke assault situation.
Note: A rear carotid choke assault can compromise your ability to breathe and verbalize and may render you unconscious. Individuals will need to respond **immediately** to this assault.

Performance—Rear Carotid Choke Defense

1. Defender stabilizes and immediately place fingers into their carotid neck areas and pulls downward to their core.
2. Once stabilized, the defender can bring their chin down and push up on the attackers elbow with the same side hand.
3. This position pushes the elbow onto the chin of the defender, allowing defender to breathe.
4. The defender can bite the arm of the attacker and use the hand, not at the elbow, for defense technique techniques. Defense techniques are used to escape.

During All Defenses:

▪ Use loud, repetitive defensive verbalizations (NO! STOP! GET BACK! LET ME GO! LEAVE ME ALONE! etc.) to direct the aggressor to stop attacking you.

▪ Use defensive movements (Escape!)

After All Defenses:

▪ Follow agency policies and procedures in regard to self-defense.

▪ Report and Document immediately.

Special Note: If personal defense techniques are used in these defenses, it MUST be for physical violence or deadly force situations. Any time force is used to defend yourself or others. It must be a last resort, reasonable, and you must be able to articulate what you did, why you did it, and how you did it.

Rear Bear Hold Defense

Rear Bear Hold Defense

It is a technique that teaches individuals how to defend themselves from a rear bear-hold assault.

Objective—Demonstrate how to defend against a rear bear hold assault situation.

Note: A rear bear hold assault can compromise your ability to breathe as well as make you vulnerable to being picked up and thrown down or taken to another location.

Performance—Rear Bear Hold Defense

1. Defender stabilizes, immediately grabs attackers' hands, and bends forward using core.
2. Once bent forward, the defender launches their head back (head butt) into the face of the attacker.
3. The defender will head butt until arms are released.
4. Once arms are released, the defender may elbow or use other personal defense techniques to break free from the assault.
5. Defense techniques are used to escape.

During All Defenses:

- Use loud, repetitive defensive verbalizations (NO! STOP! GET BACK! LET ME GO! LEAVE ME ALONE! etc.) to direct the aggressor to stop attacking you.
- Use defensive movements (Escape!)

After All Defenses:

- Follow agency policies and procedures in regard to self-defense.
- Report and Document immediately.

Special Note: If personal defense techniques are used in these defenses, it MUST be for physical violence or deadly force situations. Any time force is used to defend yourself or others. It must be a last resort, reasonable, and you must be able to articulate what you did, why you did it, and how you did it.

Ground Defenses

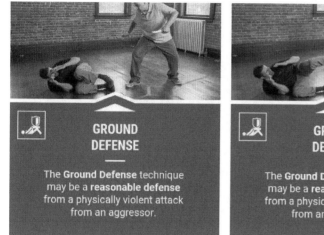

Ground Defenses

It is a technique that teaches individuals how to defend themselves from an attack where they have been thrown, hit, or gone to the ground voluntarily.

Objective—Demonstrate how to defend from a ground assault situation.

Performance—Ground Defenses

1. Defender immediately curls into a fetal position with their dominant side upward (preferably).
2. From this position, the defender is protected and appears submissive.
3. Once the attacker moves in to assault, the defender can launch a sidekick defense just below the knee of the attacker.
4. The defender may need to rotate from one side to another as the attacker moves.
5. Defender should maintain awareness and vigilance when getting up off of the ground. Do not give up your backside! Attacker may have a knife/edged weapon-making this a life-threatening (deadly force) situation for the defender.

During All Defenses:

- Use loud, repetitive defensive verbalizations (NO! STOP! GET BACK! LET ME GO! LEAVE ME ALONE! etc.) to direct the aggressor to stop attacking you.
- Use defensive movements (Escape!)

After All Defenses:

- Follow agency policies and procedures in regard to self-defense.
- Report and Document immediately.

Special Note: If personal defense techniques are used in these defenses, it MUST be for physical violence or deadly force situations. Any time force is used to defend yourself or others. It must be a last resort, reasonable, and you must be able to articulate what you did, why you did it, and how you did it.

Gun Threat Response Defense

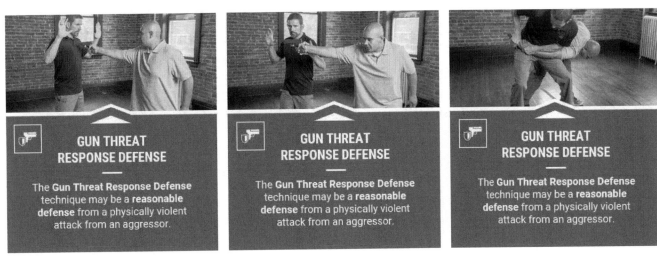

Gun Threat Response Defense

It is a technique that teaches individuals how to defend themselves against a gun threat.

Objective—Demonstrate how to respond/defend from a gun threat.

Note: See the "Active Shooter" response. If possible, ESCAPE immediately!

Performance—Gun Threat Response Defense

1. The defender immediately brings their hands up to a non-threatening position.
2. Defender blocks the hand (same side) holding the gun while turning (blading) their body.
3. Defender then grabs gun with freehand, bringing (pivot) it into the holstered position.
4. The attackers gun muzzle should be pointed upward with the defender's forearm securing the attacker's arm.
5. Defender may need to use personal defense techniques to immobilize the attacker. The attacker may end up on the ground. **Note:** This is a life-threatening (deadly force) situation for the defender.

During All Defenses:

- Use loud, repetitive defensive verbalizations (NO! STOP! GET BACK! LET ME GO! LEAVE ME ALONE! etc.) to direct the aggressor to stop attacking you.
- Use defensive movements (Escape!)

After All Defenses:

- Follow agency policies and procedures in regard to self-defense.
- Report and Document immediately.

Special Note: If personal defense techniques are used in these defenses, it MUST be for physical violence or deadly force situations. Any time force is used to defend yourself or others. It must be a last resort, reasonable, and you must be able to articulate what you did, why you did it, and how you did it.

Knife Threat Response Defense

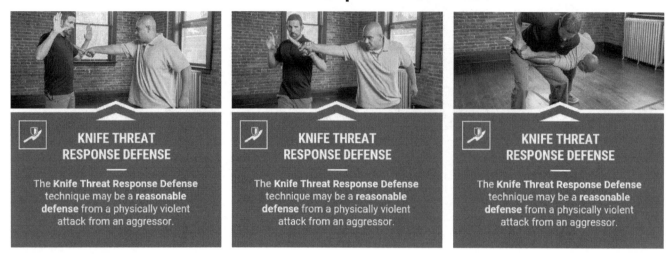

KNIFE THREAT RESPONSE DEFENSE

The **Knife Threat Response Defense** technique may be a **reasonable defense** from a physically violent attack from an aggressor.

KNIFE THREAT RESPONSE DEFENSE

The **Knife Threat Response Defense** technique may be a **reasonable defense** from a physically violent attack from an aggressor.

KNIFE THREAT RESPONSE DEFENSE

The **Knife Threat Response Defense** technique may be a **reasonable defense** from a physically violent attack from an aggressor.

Knife Threat Response Defense

It is a technique that teaches individuals how to defend themselves against a knife threat.

Objective—Demonstrate how to respond/defend from a knife threat.
Note: If possible, ESCAPE immediately!

Performance—Knife Threat Response Defense

1. The defender immediately brings their hands up to a non-threatening position.
2. Defender blocks the hand (same-side), holding the knife while turning (blading) their body.
3. Defender then uses their free hand to grab the attacker's hand, bringing (pivot) it into the holstered position
4. The attacker's knife blade should be pointed upward with the defender's forearm securing the attacker's arm.
5. Defender may need to use personal defense techniques to immobilize the attacker. The attacker may end up on the ground. **Note:** This is a life-threatening (deadly force) situation for the defender.

During All Defenses:

- Use loud, repetitive defensive verbalizations (NO! STOP! GET BACK! LET ME GO! LEAVE ME ALONE! etc.) to direct the aggressor to stop attacking you.
- Use defensive movements (Escape!)

After All Defenses:

- Follow agency policies and procedures in regard to self-defense.
- Report and Document immediately.

Special Note: If personal defense techniques are used in these defenses, it MUST be for physical violence or deadly force situations. Any time force is used to defend yourself or others. It must be a last resort, reasonable, and you must be able to articulate what you did, why you did it, and how you did it.

Module Five –Elements of Self-Defense/Use-of-Force

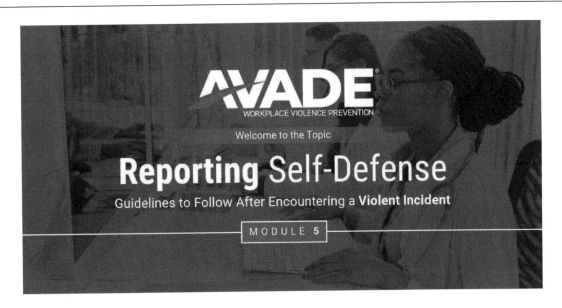

Post-Incident Response

- **Triage (Medical/Hazmat):** Triage is the process of determining the priority of patients' or victims' treatments based on the severity of their condition. Initial first-aid treatment and protocols for hazardous materials and clean-up should be handled immediately.

- **Report to the Police, Security, Risk Management, Human Resources, etc.:** Follow standard operating procedures in reporting incidents.

- **Consider All Involved—staff, guests, visitors**, patients, or anyone who was witness to the incident should be treated accordingly for medical and stress debriefing.

- **Provide for Incident Debriefing:** Debriefing allows those involved with the incident to process the event and reflect on its impact. Depending on the situation, a thorough debriefing may need to take place. Even those not specifically involved in an incident may suffer emotional and psychological trauma.

- **Critical Incident Stress Debriefing (CISD):** is a specific technique designed to assist others in dealing with physical or psychological symptoms that are generally associated with critical incident trauma exposure. Research on the effectiveness of critical incident debriefing techniques has demonstrated that individuals who are provided critical stress debriefing within a 24- to 72-hour window after experiencing the critical incident have lower levels of short- and long-term crisis reactions and psychological trauma.

- **Employee Assistance Programs (EAP):** EAPs are intended to help employees deal with work or personal problems that might adversely impact their work performance, health, and well-being. EAPs generally include assessment, short-term counseling, and referral services for employees and their household members. Employee benefit programs offered by many employers, typically in conjunction with health insurance plans, provide for payment for EAPs.

- **Document Incident to Include Any Follow-Up Investigations:** Post-incident documentation is absolutely critical for reducing liability risk, preventing recurrences, and assisting in follow-up investigations.

- **Initiate Corrective Actions to Prevent Recurrences:** Preventing similar future incidents involves taking proactive corrective actions. Agency management, supervision, security, risk management, employee safety committees, the environment of care committee, etc., should initiate, track, and follow up on corrective actions.

Post-Incident Documentation

- **Who–What–Where–When–Why–How**
The first rule in post-incident documentation is the "who, what, where, when, why, and how" rule of reporting. After writing an incident narrative, double-check to see if you have included the first rule of reporting.

- **Witnesses (Who Was There?)**
Make sure to include anyone who was a witness to the incident. Staff, visitors, guests, and support services (police, fire, EMS, etc.) can be valuable witnesses should an incident be litigated.

- **Narrative Characteristics**
A proper narrative should describe in detail the characteristics of the violent offender/predator.

- **Before, During, and After**
A thorough incident report will describe what happened before, during, and after the incident. Details matter!

- **1st Person vs. 3rd Person**
The account of an incident can be described in the first person or the third person. This can be specific to your agency protocols or the preference of the person documenting the incident.

- **Post-Follow-Up (Track and Trend)**
  Most agencies use electronic documentation, which allows for easy retrieval, tracking, and trending. Using technology assists agencies in following up and initiating proactive corrections.

- **Follow Standard Operating Procedures**
  Whether handwriting incident reports or using electronic documentation and charting, staff should consistently and thoroughly document all incidents relating to violence in the workplace.

Elements of Reporting Force

After any situation involving the defense of yourself or another person, proper documentation and reporting are crucial. The events of the assault or attempted assault should be reported to police/security. Police/security will document the incident and start an investigation. You should also document the account for your personal records. This can protect you in a possible legal situation that could arise out of using force to defend yourself. As you document your account of the incident, make sure to report to police/ security any details you missed during your initial report to them.

What type of force/self-defense/technique was used during the incident?
Be specific in your documentation regarding the type of control, defense, and force that was used during the incident.

How long did the incident and resistance last?
Important to note the length of the resistance, as this is a factor relative to exhaustion and increasing the level of force.

Was any de-escalation used?
Verbal and non-verbal de-escalation techniques should be noted.

Were you in fear of injury (bodily harm) to yourself, others, or the subject?
Fear is a distressing emotion aroused by a perceived threat, impending danger, evil, or pain.

If so, Why?
Fear is a basic survival mechanism occurring in response to a specific stimulus, such as pain or the threat of danger.

Explain thoroughly, and make sure to document completely.
The importance of documentation cannot be over-emphasized. Documentation ensures proper training standards are met, policies and procedures are understood, certification standards are met, liability and risk management are mitigated, and departmental and organizational requirements are maintained.

Special Note
Every person must take into consideration their moral, legal, and ethical beliefs, rights, and understandings when using any type of force to defend themselves or others.

Personal Safety Training Inc. makes no legal declaration, representation, or claim as to what force should be used or not used during a self-defense/assault incident or situation. Each trainee must take into consideration their ability, agency policies and procedures, and state and federal laws.

Civilian Levels of Defense

- **Awareness–Vigilance–Avoidance:** As we learned in modules 1-3, the best defense is to be aware, be vigilant, and avoid conflicts. The base of the chart is the most important aspect of defense.

- **Confident Presence:** Our presence can be a major deterrent to aggressive individuals and predators. Using confident postures, facial expressions, and eye communication show that we are not an easy target.

- **Interpersonal Communications Skills:** When faced with people who are stressed, angry, or intoxicated, your best initial defense is your ability to communicate.
  See Module 4.

- **Escape Options:** When faced with a situation that is escalating and dangerous, you should escape, if possible, to a safe location and alert others.

- **OC Pepper Spray:** Pepper sprays are a non-lethal force option that can distract the predator, giving you time to escape or defend.

- **Personal Defensive Techniques:** Include unarmed defenses using your body, hands, and feet as self-defense techniques for physically violent attacks on you or others.

- **Personal Defense Tools:** Non-lethal items that you can use to defend yourself. Examples: key chains, umbrellas, flashlights, rolled-up newspapers, etc.

- **Deadly Defense:** Defense against what you believe to be a serious injury and/or death by a person(s) using a deadly weapon or violently assaulting you.

Static Air, Blocking, and Impact Practice/Drills

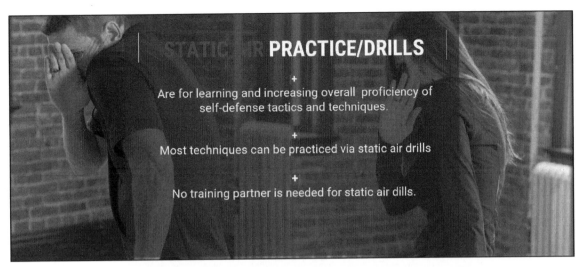

PRACTICE/DRILLS

+ Are for learning and increasing overall proficiency of self-defense tactics and techniques.

+ Most techniques can be practiced via static air drills

+ No training partner is needed for static air dills.

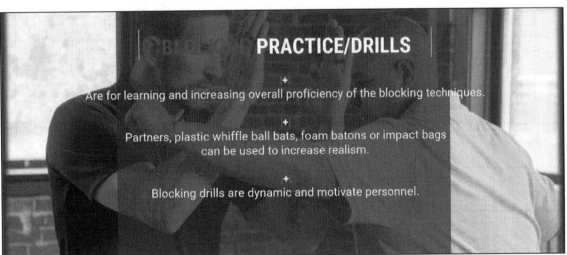

PRACTICE/DRILLS

+ Are for learning and increasing overall proficiency of the blocking techniques.

+ Partners, plastic whiffle ball bats, foam batons or impact bags can be used to increase realism.

+ Blocking drills are dynamic and motivate personnel.

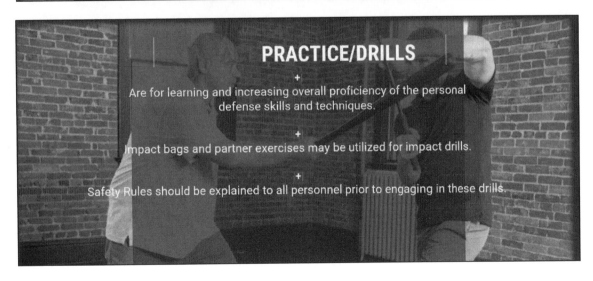

PRACTICE/DRILLS

+ Are for learning and increasing overall proficiency of the personal defense skills and techniques.

+ Impact bags and partner exercises may be utilized for impact drills.

+ Safety Rules should be explained to all personnel prior to engaging in these drills.

Partner, Positioning, and Combination Practice/Drills

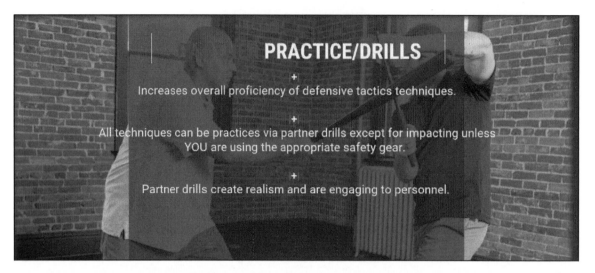

PRACTICE/DRILLS

+
Increases overall proficiency of defensive tactics techniques.

+
All techniques can be practices via partner drills except for impacting unless YOU are using the appropriate safety gear.

+
Partner drills create realism and are engaging to personnel.

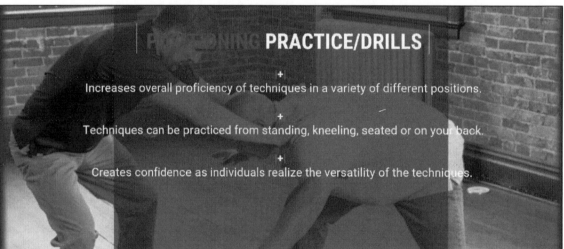

PRACTICE/DRILLS

+
Increases overall proficiency of techniques in a variety of different positions.

+
Techniques can be practiced from standing, kneeling, seated or on your back.

+
Creates confidence as individuals realize the versatility of the techniques.

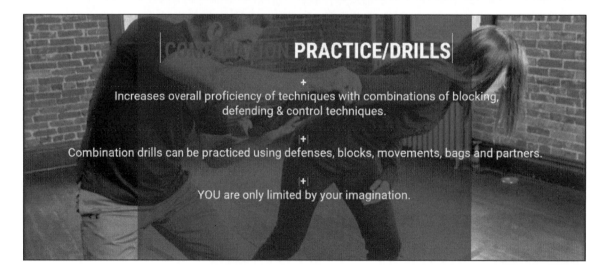

PRACTICE/DRILLS

+
Increases overall proficiency of techniques with combinations of blocking, defending & control techniques.

+
Combination drills can be practiced using defenses, blocks, movements, bags and partners.

+
YOU are only limited by your imagination.

AVADE® Level III

Defensive Control Tactics and Techniques

Introduction to Defensive Control Tactics and Techniques

The goal of this section is to teach defensive control tactics and techniques. Most incidents can be prevented using your awareness, vigilance, and avoidance. However, **there may be times when you need to physically control a subject that is out of control and a risk to themselves or others.**

- After any control tactics and techniques, always follow post-incident responses and documentation procedures.
- Before conducting any physical training, be sure to cover the following safety rules with your class. Safety is the most important rule in physical training.

In today's society, corporations, healthcare, schools, gaming, law enforcement, security, corrections, the military, and protective services agencies realize that defensive control tactics and techniques are essential for protecting themselves and the public they serve. These agencies also understand that mitigating liability begins with proper training and education in defensive control tactics strategies, and techniques.

The AVADE® training program is designed for agencies and staff to reduce the potential of injury and liability risk when lawfully defending themselves or controlling an aggressive individual. The tactics and techniques in this training curriculum are for incidents where the aggressor is physically combative, resistive, and unarmed.

This training manual provides training and education that is designed to empower individuals and to increase awareness, knowledge, skills, and actions regarding the use of force, control and restraint, self-defense, and defending others with defensive control tactics, strategies, and techniques.

This course stresses the importance of knowing your agency's policies and procedures in regard to using force and defending yourself or another person. The **AVADE®** training is intended to give the trainee the basic understanding of self-defense, use of force, control and restraint, reasonable force, and basic legal definitions of force. **Personal Safety Training Inc.** makes no legal declaration, representation, or claim as to what force should be used or not used during self-defense, use of force, or assault incident or situation. Each trainee must take into consideration their ability, agency policies and procedures, and laws in the state and country in which they reside.

Most individuals can learn and develop proficiency in the techniques covered in this training course. The course includes the fundamentals of basic defensive tactics, followed by contact and cover positioning, escort strategies and techniques, control and decentralization, prone and supine restraint, and post-incident response and documentation procedures.

AVADE® FIRST RULE OF TRAINING = SAFETY

▸ AVADE® Training Safety Rules

1 SAFETY & WAIVER AGREEMENT
Each individual trained **MUST** complete the **Student Registration & Recertification Form**. The instructor will advise the student how to fill it out and answer any questions pertaining to it.

2 WEAPONS FREE ENVIRONMENT
NO WEAPONS are allowed anywhere in the training area. Instructor will advise participants in proper procedures in securing weapons and ammunition. Follow agency policy and procedures.

3 REMOVE JEWELRY, ETC.
The following should not be worn during a class which involves hands-on training: all jewelry with sharp edges, pins or raised surfaces, or jewelry that encircles the neck.

4 NO HORSEPLAY RULE
Any participant who displays a disregard for **SAFETY** to anyone in class will be asked to leave the class. Please practice only the technique currently being taught. **DO NOT PRACTICE UNAUTHORIZED TECHNIQUES.**

5 PAT OUT RULE (USED FOR PARTNER TECHNIQUES)
Upon hearing/feeling/seeing the "**PAT**," your partner applying the technique will immediately release the pressure of the technique to reduce discomfort/pain. The technique will be immediately and totally released on instructions from the instructor or when a safety monitor says "**RELEASE**," "**STOP**," or words similar to them.

6 BE A GOOD "DEFENDER" AND A GOOD "AGGRESSOR"
Essentially this means working together with your partner when practicing the techniques. Without cooperation while practicing self-defense or defensive control tactics techniques, time is wasted and injury potential is increased.

7 PRACTICE TECHNIQUES SLOWLY AT FIRST
Gain balance and correctness slowly before practicing for speed. Proceed at the pace directed by your trainer.

8 CHECK EQUIPMENT FOR ADDED SAFETY
The instructor will check **ALL** equipment used during the training to ensure proper function, working order and safety.

9 ADVISE INSTRUCTOR OF ANY PRE-EXISTING INJURIES
Any injury or condition that could be further injured or aggravated should be brought to the **immediate attention** of your instructor, and your partner, prior to participating in any hands-on training.

10 ADVISE INSTRUCTOR OF ANY INJURY DURING CLASS
Any injury, regardless of what it is, **needs to be reported** to the primary instructor.

11 SAFETY IS EVERYONE'S RESPONSIBILITY!
Safety is everyone's responsibility and everyone is empowered to **immediately report** or **YELL OUT** any safety violation.

12 TRAINING HAZARDS
Always keep any items or training equipment and batons off the floor/ground and out of the way when not in use.

13 SAFETY MARKINGS
Colored wrist bands or blue tape marking is a visual aid for pre-existing injury. Use **CAUTION**.

14 LEAVING TRAINING AREA
If you must leave the training area for any reason, please **advise your instructor** prior to doing so.

Education, Prevention, and Mitigation for Violence in the Workplace

© Personal Safety Training Inc. | AVADE® Training

AVADE® Level III Defensive Control Tactics Modules

- DEFENSIVE CONTROL TACTICS FUNDAMENTALS
- CONTACT & COVER POSITIONING
- ESCORT STRATEGIES & TECHNIQUES
- CONTROL & DECENTRALIZATION TECHNIQUES
- ELEMENTS OF REPORTING SELF-DEFENSE & USE-OF-FORCE
- HEALTHCARE RESTRAINT HOLDS & APPLICATIONS

Personal Safety Training Inc. makes no legal declaration, representation or claim as to what force should be used or not used during a self-defense, use of force incident, or assault incident or situation. Each trainee must take into consideration their ability, agency policies and procedures and laws in the state and country in which they reside.

Use-of-Force

A term that describes the right of an individual or authority to settle conflicts or prevent certain actions by applying measures to either:

1. **Dissuade another party from a particular course of action…or**

2. **Physically intervene to stop or control them.**

Use of Force Awareness

- Any of Use of Force must be justified & legally warranted

- Liability Risk: When any force is used, the staff person must take into consideration their ability, agency policies & procedures, & laws in the state and country in which they reside

- Unauthorized or inappropriate Use of Force may expose the staff person/agency to criminal/civil liability

Center for Medicaid Services

☑ **AVADE® Level III** Training aligns with the **Center for Medicaid Services** (CMS) COP § 482.13(e)(2) **Restraint** or **seclusion** may only be used when **less restrictive interventions** have been **determined** to be **ineffective** to **protect** the **patient**, a **staff member**, or **others** from **harm**.

☑ Any **intervention** other than **Verbal De-Escalation** should only be used when it *"is used for the management of violent or self-destructive behavior that jeopardizes the immediate physical safety of the patient, a staff member, or others,"* as defined by **CMS**.

What are YOUR policies and procedures for the use of force and self-defense?

Individuals (staff) MUST have a strong understanding of their agency policies and procedures regarding the use of force and self-defense.

_____
_____
_____
_____
_____
_____
_____
_____
_____
_____
_____
_____
_____
_____
_____
_____

Module One –Self-Defense Fundamentals

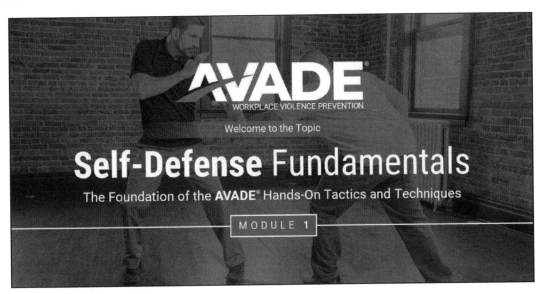

Every tactic and technique requires the use of fundamental laws. If you don't understand the fundamental rules of self-defense, your ability to defend yourself is compromised. A basic understanding and use of these laws will give you an advantage in a situation where you might need to use force to defend yourself or another person.

Fundamentals

Fun·da·men·tal (from the Latin medieval: *fundāmentālis*: late Middle English)
—*Synonyms* 1. Indispensable, primary.
–*adjective* 1. Serving as, or being an essential part of, a foundation or basis; basic; underlying: *fundamental principles; the fundamental structure.*
2. Of, pertaining to, or affecting the foundation or basis: *a fundamental revision.*
3. Being an original or primary source: *a fundamental idea.*
–*noun* 1. A basic principle, rule, law, or the like, that serves as the groundwork of a system; essential part: *to master the fundamentals of a trade.*

Self-Defensive Fundamentals

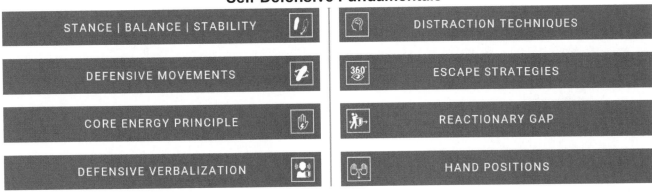

STANCE | BALANCE | STABILITY

DISTRACTION TECHNIQUES

DEFENSIVE MOVEMENTS

ESCAPE STRATEGIES

CORE ENERGY PRINCIPLE

REACTIONARY GAP

DEFENSIVE VERBALIZATION

HAND POSITIONS

Stance | Balance | Stability | Bladed Defensive Stance

The Bladed (defensive) Stance

All techniques in the defense tactics training are performed from the bladed stance.

Objective—Demonstrate how to correctly position your body to protect your vulnerable line and maintain stance, balance, and stability.

Performance—Bladed Stance

Face the clock (diagram on PowerPoint or imagine a clock in front of you) with your feet shoulder-width apart.

1. Step straight back with either left or right foot. Usually, individuals prefer to have their dominant foot to the rear.

2. If you step back with your right foot, turn your feet and body to the one o'clock position.

3. If you step back with your left foot, turn your feet and body to the eleven o'clock position.

4. Keep your weight equal on both feet and your knees slightly bent.

Performance Stability Test (Bladed Stance)

1. Partner exercise (A & B)

2. Partner A places his/her feet together. Partner B gently pushes partner A to the front, back, left side, and right side. Reverse roles.

3. Partner A stands with his/her feet should width apart. Partner B gently pushes partner A to the front, back, left side, and right side. Reverse roles.

4. Partner A now assumes the bladed stance. Partner B gently pushes partner A to the front, back, left side, and right side. Reverse roles.

The Bladed Stance protects your "Vulnerable Line" away from the subject.

ON TARGET TRAINING

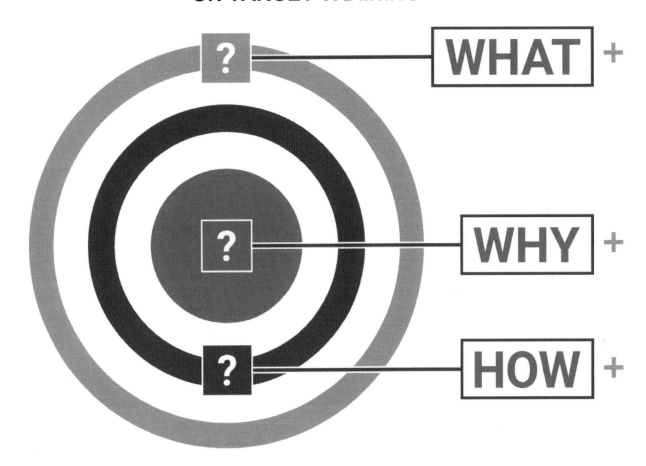

The WHAT describes a technique or tactic.
The first step in teaching a hands-on technique is to explain what the technique is by the name of it. For example, we will be learning about defensive movement, and the first defensive movement technique is forward shuffle.

While the HOW is the manner or method, the technique or tactic is performed.
The second step in teaching a hands-on technique is to explain and demonstrate how to do it. This step should be done a couple of times so that students can see it fully and completely.

And most importantly is the WHY. It's the purpose, reason, intention, justification, or motive of a technique or tactic.
The third step and most important step in teaching hands-on techniques are to explain why the technique is done a certain way and why you should have this technique in your arsenal of defenses. Without this understanding, the student is not bought into believing that the technique is needed or effective.

To really understand a technique or tactic, you must know the WHY (Bullseye).

Defensive Movements: Forward Shuffle

Forward movement is used to engage a subject for control or defense.

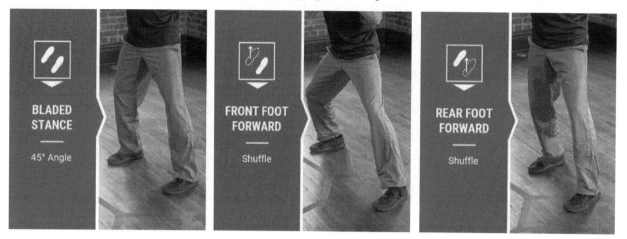

BLADED STANCE — 45° Angle

FRONT FOOT FORWARD — Shuffle

REAR FOOT FORWARD — Shuffle

Forward Shuffle

This Defensive movement involves being able to move forward while maintaining balance and stability. All defensive tactics techniques are enhanced with defensive movement.

Objective—Demonstrate how to move forward correctly.

Performance—Forward Movement

5. Assume the bladed stance.

6. Take a short step forward with your front foot (shuffle).

7. Follow up with a short step forward using your rear foot.

8. Continue forward, using forward shuffling movement.

Caution: If the feet come together, balance and stability are compromised (common mistake).

The rule of defensive movement is: The foot that is closest to the direction you want to go always moves first.

Defensive Movements: Rear Shuffle

Rear movement is used to disengage from an aggressor.

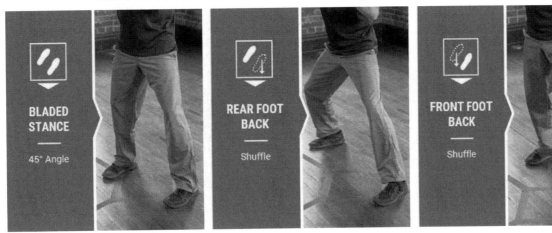

Rear Shuffle

This Defensive movement involves being able to move to the rear (backward) while maintaining balance and stability. All defensive tactics techniques are enhanced with defensive movement.

Objective—Demonstrate how to correctly move to the rear.

Performance—Rear Movement

5. Assume the bladed stance.

6. Take a short step back with the rear foot (shuffle).

7. Follow up with a short step back using your front foot.

8. Continue backward, using the rear shuffling movement.

Caution: If the feet come together, balance and stability are compromised (common mistake).

Caution: Backpedaling is another common mistake.

Caution: Obstacles in your environment.

The rule of defensive movement is: The foot that is closest to the direction you want to go always moves first.

Defensive Movements: Side to Side Shuffle

Side-to-side movement is used to avoid an attack from an aggressor.

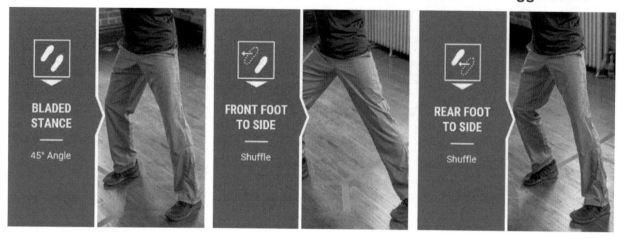

Side to Side Shuffle

This Defensive movement involves being able to move side to side while maintaining balance and stability. All defensive tactics techniques are enhanced with defensive movement.

Objective—Demonstrate how to correctly move side to side

Performance—Side-to-Side Movement

6. Assume the bladed stance.

7. Take a short step to the right using your right foot.

8. Follow up with a short step to the right using your left foot.

9. Take a short step to the left using your left.

10. Follow up with a short step to the left using your right foot.

Caution: If the feet come together, balance and stability are compromised (common mistake).

Caution: Crossing feet up is another common mistake.

Caution: Obstacles in your environment.

The rule of defensive movement is: The foot that is closest to the direction you want to go always moves first.

Defensive Movements: Forward and Rear Pivoting

Pivoting is used to reposition or to enhance your energy when using personal defensive techniques or defensive control tactics

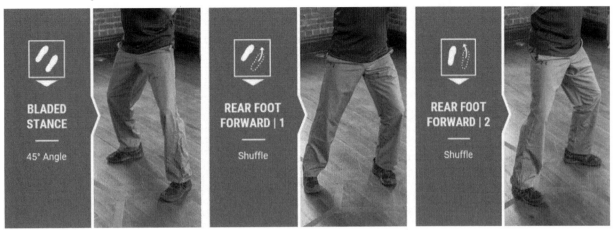

Forward & Rear Pivoting

This Defensive movement involves being able to pivot forward or back while maintaining balance and stability. All defensive tactics techniques are enhanced with defensive movement.

Objective—Demonstrate how to correctly pivot forward and backward.

Performance—Pivoting (forward and back)

6. Assume the bladed stance.

7. Take an arcing step forward with your rear foot (forward pivot).

8. Take an arcing step backward with your front foot (rear pivot).

9. When pivoting forward or backward, always remain balanced and stable.

10. Pivots can be small movements or up to a 360-degree pivot.

Caution: If the feet come together, balance and stability are compromised (common mistake).

Caution: Crossing feet up is another common mistake.

Caution: Obstacles in your environment.

Robot Exercise (The Best Self-Defense Technique!)

Defensive Movement "Robot Exercise"

The robot exercise involves being able to move in a lateral motion (side to side) to avoid an attack that is coming at you from a distance of 4' away or greater.

Objective—Demonstrate how to correctively avoid a forward attack by moving out of the way.

Performance—Robot Exercise.

1. The defender assumes a bladed defensive stance.

2. From 4-6" away, the attacker places hands out directly toward the defender.

3. Attacker moves forward toward the defender, attempting to gently touch either shoulder of the defender.

4. The defender waits for the last moment to move to either side, away from the attack.

5. Using sounds and/or movements will assist the defender in distracting the attacker.

6. Once out of the attack zone, defender can proceed to keep moving away from the attacker.

Caution: Do not move too late!

Caution: Do not move too soon, or the attacker will have time to adjust (reaction time) and follow/track you.

Caution: Crossing feet up is another common mistake.

Caution: Beware of obstacles in your environment.

Core Energy Principle

CORE ENERGY

Energy and **power** are generated and developed from the **core** of the human body, even though a lot of emphasis is placed on the body's extremities.

The **Core Energy Principle** will:

GIVE YOU ADVANTAGE OVER AGGRESSIVE SUBJECTS +

PROVIDE YOU POWER FOR COUNTER BLOCKS +

PROVIDE YOU POWER FOR DEFENSES +

HELP YOU CONTROL & DECENTRALIZE A PHYSICALLY RESISTIVE SUBJECT +

Core Energy: Our central and most essential part of our strength and power is our core energy. Without core energy, we rely on our extremities, which are not as strong as our central core. All defensive tactics techniques utilize this essential principle.

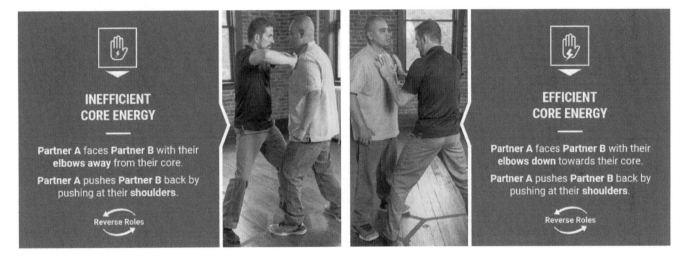

INEFFICIENT CORE ENERGY

Partner A faces **Partner B** with their **elbows away** from their core.

Partner A pushes **Partner B** back by pushing at their **shoulders**.

Reverse Roles

EFFICIENT CORE ENERGY

Partner A faces **Partner B** with their **elbows down** towards their core.

Partner A pushes **Partner B** back by pushing at their **shoulders**.

Reverse Roles

Objective—Demonstrate how to correctly use your core energy.

Performance—Core Energy

5. Partner exercise (A & B)

6. Partner A faces partner B with his/her elbows away from their core.

7. Partner B moves forward toward partner A. Partner A pushes partner B back by pushing at their shoulders. How did it go? Reverse roles.

8. Partner A again faces partner B with his/her elbows down towards their core. Partner B moves forward toward partner A. Partner A pushes partner B back by pushing at their shoulders. How did it go? Reverse roles

Defensive Verbalization

During all Defenses: Use loud, repetitive Defensive Verbalizations

NO!

STOP!

GET BACK!

STOP RESISTING!

BREAK YOUR FALL!

WE'RE GOING DOWN TO THE GROUND!

Defensive Verbalization | Why?
1. Creates Witness
2. Establishes authority
3. Keeps you breathing
4. May be used as a distraction
5. Alerts other of a confrontation
6. Provides direction to the aggressor
7. Mitigates liability risk | You & Agency

The Art of Distraction

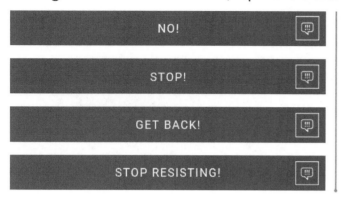    

It is a process by which we buy valuable time to Escape, Defend, or Control.

Sounds (Loud Scream/Yell) - Movements – Psychological - Lights

Distractions affect the senses, which take time for the mind to process the new information. Distractions have been used since ancient times. A valuable advantage!

Sounds: Using a loud scream or yell can cause a momentary delay.
Movements: Using your hands, eyes, and body can distract and cause a momentary delay.
Psychological: Asking a question that is out of the ordinary can cause them a mental delay.
Lights: Flashlights, the sun, emergency lights, etc., can cause a delay.

Escape Strategies

- Escape is the act or instance of breaking free from danger or threat or from being trapped, restrained, confined, or isolated against your will.
- Planning is the cognitive process of thinking about what you will do in the event of something happening.

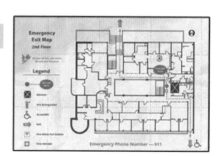

Reactionary Gap

The Reactionary Gap is 4-6 Feet. "Action beats Reaction with-in the Reactionary Gap"
The distance between an individual and an aggressor in which the ability to react is impaired due to the close proximity of the aggressor.

Hand Positions

There are six basic hand positions

Objective—Demonstrate how to correctly use your hands in the open, authority, stop, caution, and directive.

Performance—<u>Open or Authority</u> Hand Positions

4. Assume the bladed stance

5. Position your arms with your elbows down and your palms facing upward (Open).

6. Position your arms with your elbows down and your palms down (Authority).

Performance—<u>Stop or Caution</u> Hand Positions

1. Assume the bladed stance

2. Position your arms with your elbows down and your palms facing outward (Stop).

3. The non-verbal message says, "don't come close to me," or a non-threatening message if you are moving forward (Caution).

Performance—<u>Directive</u> Hand Positions

3. Assume the bladed Stance

4. Position your arms/hands, pointing with your open hand in the direction you want them to go (Directive).

- **Caution:** Do not point when giving, as pointing is perceived as a derogatory gesture.

- **Caution:** Closing your hands into a fist position may send a message of aggression.

Module Two – Contact and Cover Positioning

Contact and Cover (Team Positioning) is the main strategy for the AVADE® Level III Defensive Control Tactics System. Contact and Cover techniques are used by individuals during situations where they are dealing with a subject(s). The purpose of the technique is to deter a situation from getting out of control, and to improve the individual's safety by having other individuals in a constant state of preparation to act in the event that the situation gets out of control.

Contact (Team Leader)

The contact individual is the focal point for the subject as this individual is the primary communicator giving directions to the subject. In many situations, the contact individual(s) will initiate communications.

In the following information, the contact individual will be communicating with the subject, which may act as a distraction, allowing cover individuals (team members) to move in and gain physical control if needed. The contact individual should have a prearranged "cue" (verbal or non-verbal) alerting the cover individuals to initiate physical control.

Cover (Team Members)

The cover individual(s) role is to watch the subject(s) for any attempt to flee or assault the contact individual. The cover individual(s) should be ever vigilant and ready to respond and alert the contact individual of suspicious activity or an imminent attempt to assault the contact individual.

Special Note: Cover individuals should maintain their distance (stay back) until needed. Moving in too soon may cause the subject to feel as though he/she is being cornered.

Contact and Cover should be used for all situations involving subjects and witnesses.

Initial Contact Front (1 Person)

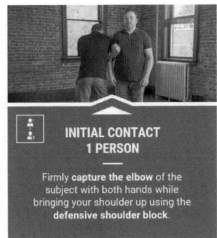

Initial Contact (1 person)

It is a technique that teaches individuals how to safely approach a subject and make initial contact.

Objective—Demonstrate how to safely approach a subject while moving forward with defensive movement to make physical contact.

Note: A two-person Initial Contact is safer as you have controlled both arms of the aggressor.

Note: This technique can be done to the front or behind the subject. It is safer to perform from behind the subject.

Performance—Initial Contact (1 person)

1. Move forward towards the subject at a 45-degree angle.

2. Use defensive movement and keep your hands in a cautious position.

3. Your body should be bladed away (vulnerable line) from the subject. Left side forward on the left side of the subject, and right side forward on the right side of the subject.

4. Firmly capture the elbow of the subject with both hands (thumbs up).

5. Bring your shoulder slightly forward to further protect your vulnerable line if you are in front of the subject. Avoid this if you are behind the subject.

Caution: Armed individuals should keep the gun side back and away from the subject regardless of their approaching side.

Caution: Approaching a subject to the front is more dangerous for the individual than approaching from behind.

Initial Contact Front (2 Person)

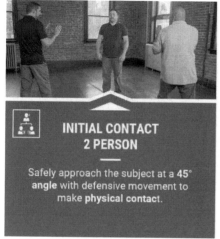

INITIAL CONTACT 2 PERSON

Safely approach the subject at a **45°
angle** with defensive movement to
make **physical contact**.

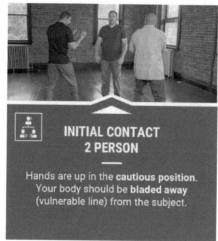

INITIAL CONTACT 2 PERSON

Hands are up in the **cautious position**.
Your body should be **bladed away**
(vulnerable line) from the subject.

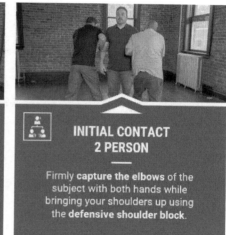

INITIAL CONTACT 2 PERSON

Firmly **capture the elbows** of the
subject with both hands while
bringing your shoulders up using
the **defensive shoulder block**.

Initial Contact (2 person)

It is a technique that teaches individuals how to safely approach a subject and make contact.

Objective—Demonstrate how to safely approach a subject while moving forward with defensive movement to make physical contact.

Note: A two-person Initial Contact is safer as you have controlled both arms of the aggressor

Note: This technique can be done to the front or behind the subject. It is safer to perform from behind the subject.

Performance—Initial Contact (2 person)

1. Move forward towards the subject at a 45-degree angle.

2. Use defensive movement and keep your hands in a cautious position.

3. Your body should be bladed away (vulnerable line) from the subject. Left side forward on left of subject and right side forward on the right side of the subject.

4. Firmly capture the elbow of the subject with both hands (thumbs up).

5. Bring your shoulder slightly forward to further protect your vulnerable line if you are in front of the subject. Avoid this if you are behind the subject.

Caution: Armed individuals should keep the gun side back and away from the subject regardless of their approaching side.

Caution: Approaching a subject to the front is more dangerous for individuals than approaching from behind.

Initial Contact Rear (1 Person)

 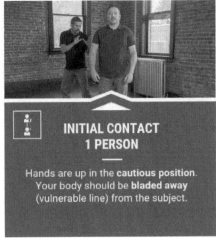 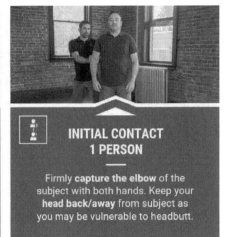

INITIAL CONTACT 1 PERSON	INITIAL CONTACT 1 PERSON	INITIAL CONTACT 1 PERSON
Safely approach the subject at a **45°** **angle** with defensive movement to make **physical contact**.	Hands are up in the **cautious position**. Your body should be **bladed away** (vulnerable line) from the subject.	Firmly **capture the elbow** of the subject with both hands. Keep your **head back/away** from subject as you may be vulnerable to headbutt.

Initial Contact (1 person)

It is a technique that teaches individuals how to safely approach a subject and make initial contact.

Objective—Demonstrate how to safely approach a subject while moving forward with defensive movement to make physical contact.

Note: A two-person Initial Contact is safer as you have controlled both arms of the aggressor.

Note: This technique can be done to the front or behind the subject. It is safer to perform from behind the subject.

Performance—Initial Contact (1 person)

1. Move forward towards the subject at a 45-degree angle.

2. Use defensive movement and keep your hands in a cautious position.

3. Your body can be (but not necessary) bladed away (vulnerable line) from the subject. Left side forward on left of subject and right side forward on the right side of the subject.

4. Firmly capture the elbow of the subject with both hands (thumbs up).

Caution: Armed individuals should keep the gun side back and away from the subject regardless of their approaching side.

Caution: Approaching a subject to the front is more dangerous for the individual than approaching from behind.

Initial Contact Rear (2 Person)

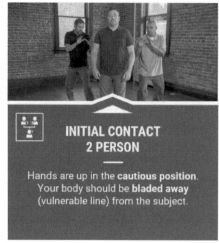

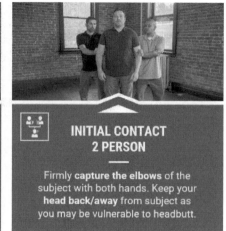

INITIAL CONTACT 2 PERSON

Safely approach the subject at a **45°angle** with defensive movement to make **physical contact**.

INITIAL CONTACT 2 PERSON

Hands are up in the **cautious position**. Your body should be **bladed away** (vulnerable line) from the subject.

INITIAL CONTACT 2 PERSON

Firmly **capture the elbows** of the subject with both hands. Keep your **head back/away** from subject as you may be vulnerable to headbutt.

Initial Contact (2 person)
It is a technique that teaches individuals how to safely approach a subject and make contact.

Objective—Demonstrate how to safely approach a subject while moving forward with defensive movement to make physical contact.

Note: A two-person Initial Contact is safer as you have controlled both arms of the aggressor

Note: This technique can be done to the front or behind the subject. It is safer to perform from behind the subject.

Performance—Initial Contact (1 or 2 person)

1. Move forward towards the subject at a 45-degree angle.

2. Use defensive movement and keep your hands in a cautious position.

3. Your body can be (but not necessary) bladed away (vulnerable line) from the subject. Left side forward on left of subject and right side forward on the right side of the subject.

4. Firmly capture the elbow of the subject with both hands (thumbs up).

Caution: Armed individuals should keep the gun side back and away from the subject regardless of their approaching side.

Caution: Approaching a subject to the front is more dangerous for individuals than approaching from behind.

Contact and Cover Positioning

Contact and Cover (Team Positioning) is the main strategy for the AVADE® Level III Defensive Control Tactics System. Contact and Cover techniques are used by individuals during situations where they are dealing with a subject(s). The purpose of the technique is to deter a situation from getting out of control, and to improve the individual's safety by having other individuals in a constant state of preparation to act in the event that the situation gets out of control.

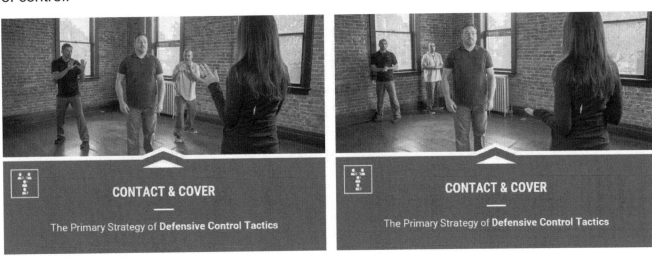

Contact (Team Leader)

The contact individual is the focal point for the subject as this individual is the primary communicator giving directions to the subject. In many situations, the contact individual(s) will initiate communications.

In the pictures, the contact individual is communicating with the subject, which may act as a distraction, allowing cover individuals (team members) to move in and gain physical control if needed. The contact individual should have a prearranged "cue" (verbal or non-verbal) alerting the cover individuals to initiate physical control.

Cover (Team Members)

The cover individual(s) role is to watch the subject(s) for any attempt to flee or assault the contact individual. The cover individual(s) should be ever vigilant and ready to respond and alert the contact individual of suspicious activity or an imminent attempt to assault the contact individual.

Special Note: Cover individuals should maintain their distance (stay back) until needed (see top left picture). Moving in too soon may cause the subject to feel as though he/she is being cornered.

Contact and Cover should be used for all situations involving subjects and witnesses.

Module Three – Escort Strategies and Techniques

Escort (es-kawrt)

Definition of Escort

Noun

1. A group of persons, or a single person, accompanying another or others for protection, guidance, or courtesy.
2. An armed guard, as a body of soldiers or ships.
3. Protection, safeguard, or guidance on a journey.

Verb (used with object)

1. To attend or accompany as an escort.

Strategy (strat-i-jee)

Definition of Strategy

Noun

1. Also strategics. the science or art of combining and employing the means of war in planning and directing large military movements and operations.
2. The use or an instance of using this science or art.
3. A plan, method, or series of maneuvers or stratagems for obtaining a specific goal or result.

Technique (tek-neek)

Definition of Technique

Noun

1. The manner and ability with which an artist, writer, dancer, athlete, or the like employs the technical skills of a particular art or field of endeavor.

Escort Strategies and Techniques (1 Person)

ESCORT TECHNIQUE | 1 PERSON

45° Angle Behind Subject | Distance of **4–6 Feet**

ESCORT TECHNIQUE | 1 PERSON

Use Proper **Verbal & Non-Verbal Communication**

Escort Technique (1 person)

It is a technique that teaches individuals how to safely escort a cooperative subject.

Objective—Demonstrate how to safely escort a cooperative subject using proper distancing, verbal communication, and non-verbal communication.

Performance—Escort Technique (1 person)

1. Maintain a 45-degree angle and distance of (4-6 feet) behind the individual.

2. Direct the subject where you want them to go.

3. Use proper verbal and non-verbal skills.

4. Do not point; use open hand gestures.

5. Maintain Awareness.

Caution: If the subject stops and moves towards you, use verbal and non-verbal communication, and defensive movements.

The A-B-C's of the Escort Technique

A. Maintain a 45-degree angle & proper distance

B. Direct the individual where you want them to go

C. Use your verbal and non-verbal skills

D. Do not point with a finger (use hand)

E. Maintain awareness

Escort Strategies and Techniques (2 Person)

ESCORT TECHNIQUE | 2 PERSON

45° Angle Behind Subject | Distance of **4–6 Feet**

ESCORT TECHNIQUE | 2 PERSON

Use Proper **Verbal** & **Non-Verbal Communication**

Escort Technique (2 person)

It is a technique that teaches individuals how to safely escort a cooperative subject.

Objective—Demonstrate how to safely escort a cooperative subject using proper distancing, verbal communication, and non-verbal communication.

Performance—Escort Technique (2 person)

1. Maintain a 45-degree angle and distance of (4-6 feet) behind the individual.

2. Direct the subject where you want them to go.

3. Use proper verbal and non-verbal skills.

4. Do not point; use open hand gestures.

5. Maintain Awareness.

Caution: If the subject stops and moves towards you, use verbal and non-verbal communication, and defensive movements.

The A-B-C's of the Escort Technique

A. Maintain a 45-degree angle & proper distance

B. Direct the individual where you want them to go

C. Use your verbal and non-verbal skills

D. Do not point with a finger (use hand)

E. Maintain awareness

Hands-On Escort Technique (1 Person)

Hands-On Escort Technique (1 person)

It is a technique that teaches an individual how to escort a subject using light subject control.

Objective—Demonstrate how to safely escort a passive-resistive subject using light subject control with proper hand and body positioning.

Performance—Hands-On Escort (1 person)

1. From the initial contact position.
2. If you are on the right side of the subject, your right-hand slides down and grips the wrist. Same for the left side.
3. Bring the subject's gripped wrist to the side of your body (holstered position).
4. The subject's palm should be facing upward, and above any defensive tools you may be carrying.
5. Maintain a 45-degree angle behind the subject and escort them to the desired location.

Caution: When gripping the appropriate wrist, the web of your hand should be on the ulna side of the subject's wrist. This ensures that their core strength is eliminated due to proper positioning.

Caution: When initiating the hands-on escort and when moving the subject, remember to stay at a 45-degree angle behind the subject.

Hands-On Escort Technique (2 Person)

Hands-On Escort Technique (2 person)

It is a technique that teaches individuals how to escort a subject using light subject control.

Objective—Demonstrate how to safely escort a passive-resistive subject using light subject control with proper hand and body positioning.

Performance—Hands-On Escort (2 person)

1. From the initial contact position.
2. The individual on the right side of the subject will slide their right hand down and grip the wrist. Same for the left side.
3. Bring the subject's gripped wrist to the side of your body (holstered position).
4. The subject's palm should be facing upward, and above any defensive tools you may be carrying.
5. Maintain a 45-degree angle behind the subject and escort them to the desired location.

Caution: When gripping the appropriate wrist, the web of your hand should be on the ulna side of the subject's wrist. This ensures that their core strength is eliminated due to proper positioning.

Caution: When initiating the hands-on escort and when moving the subject, remember to stay at a 45-degree angle behind the subject.

Caution: Both individuals acting with the same timing and control can reduce the possibility of escalation.

Module Four – Control and Decentralization Techniques

Control (Kuhn-trohl))

Definition of Control

Noun

1. The act or power of controlling; regulation; domination or command.

2. The situation of being under the regulation, domination, or command of another.

Verb (used with object)

1. To exercise restraint or direction over; dominate: command.

2. To hold in check; curb:

Decentralize (dee-sen-truh-lahyz))

Definition of Decentralize

Verb

1. To distribute the administrative powers or functions of (a central authority) over a

   less concentrated area.

2. To disperse (something) from an area of concentration.

3. To undergo decentralization.

One Arm Take-Down

One Arm Take-Down (part 1)

It is a technique that teaches an individual how to decentralize a resistive subject using a take-down control technique. This technique is for a subject who displaying violent or self-destructive behavior towards themselves or others.

Objective—Demonstrate how to control a subject using a one-bar take-down for a subject who is actively resisting.

Performance—One Arm Take-Down (part 1)

1. From the hands-on escort position.
2. The individual will place their wrist onto the tricep of the subject (2 -3" above the elbow).
3. The individual will then apply pressure to the tricep while moving forward or pivoting to the rear.
4. Use loud defensive verbalizations (NO, STOP, STOP RESISTING, WERE GOING DOWN, BREAK YOUR FALL, to direct the aggressor to stop resisting you and to direct them down.

Caution: Be aware of your environment and what direction you are moving the resistive subject towards.

CONTINUOUSLY MONITOR THE SUBJECT AND SEEK MEDICAL ATTENTION IF NEEDED.

One Arm Take-Down

ONE ARM
TAKEDOWN
—
Continue to
Decentralize

ONE ARM
TAKEDOWN
—
Subject Breaks
Their Fall

ONE ARM
TAKEDOWN
—
Prone Control
Positioning

One-Arm Take-Down (part 2)

It is a technique that teaches an individual how to decentralize a resistive subject using a take-down control technique. This technique is for a subject who displaying violent or self-destructive behavior towards themselves or others

Objective—Demonstrate how to control a subject using a one-arm take-down for a subject who is actively resisting.

Performance—One-Arm Take-Down (part 2)

5. Continue to use movement and pressure on the tricep to direct the aggressor to the ground.
6. Use loud defensive verbalizations (NO, STOP, STOP RESISTING, WERE GOING DOWN, BREAK YOUR FALL, to direct the aggressor to stop resisting you and direct them down.

Caution: Be aware of your environment and what direction you are moving the resistive subject towards.

Caution: The prone position is a temporary position that may predispose the subject to breathing difficulties.

PRONE CONTROL IS A TEMPORARY POSITION!

CONTINUOUSLY MONITOR THE SUBJECT AND SEEK MEDICAL ATTENTION IF NEEDED.

Prone Control Positions

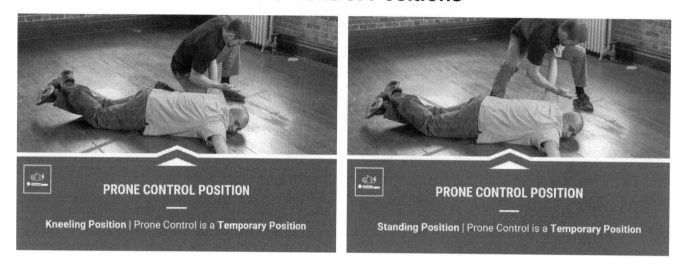

Prone Position Caution

- Individuals in a prone position may have difficulty breathing.

- Monitor individuals and place them on their side, seated position, or get them up as soon as possible.

PRONE CONTROL IS A TEMPORARY POSITION!

Positional asphyxia: Positional asphyxia is a form of asphyxia that occurs when someone's position prevents them from breathing adequately. A small but significant number of people die suddenly and without apparent reason during restraint by police, prison (corrections) officers, and health care staff. Positional asphyxia may be a factor in some of these deaths. Research has suggested that restraining a person in a face-down position is likely to cause greater restriction of breathing than restraining a person face up.

Many law enforcement and health personnel are now taught to avoid restraining people face down or to do so only for a very short period of time.

PRONE CONTROL IS A TEMPORARY POSITION!

CONTINUOUSLY MONITOR THE SUBJECT AND SEEK MEDICAL ATTENTION IF NEEDED.

Standing the Prone Subject

Standing the Prone Subject (part 1)

It is a technique that teaches an individual(s) how to stand a prone controlled subject.

Objective—Demonstrate how to stand a subject who has been placed in a prone controlled position (one or two individuals are needed).

Performance—Standing the Prone Subject (part 1)

1. Once control is established, verbalize to the subject to place their hands in the pushup position.
2. Direct them to push their knees up under them to prepare to stand.
3. Maintain contact with the subject arms and wrists and also prepare to stand up as well.

Caution: Verbalization and constant control is the key to standing a prone controlled subject. Maintain your balance and be prepared to escape if needed.

Standing the Prone Subject

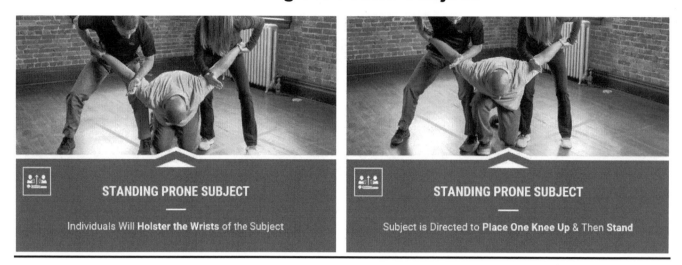

Standing the Prone Subject (part 2)

It is a technique that teaches an individual(s) how to stand a prone controlled subject.

Objective—Demonstrate how to stand a subject who has been placed in a prone controlled position (one or two individuals are needed).

Performance—Standing the Prone Subject (part 2)

4. Bring one of the subject's wrists to the holster position on the side of your body.

5. Once control is established by holstering one wrist, the second person will holster the subject's other wrist.

6. Once both wrists are holstered, have the subject raise one knee.

7. You will need to have the subject raise their torso in order to get them to place one knee in front of them.

8. Ask the subject to then stand up completely. Direct the subject where you want them to go.

Caution: Verbalization and constant control is the key to standing a prone controlled subject. Maintain your balance and be prepared to escape if needed.

Escorting Combative Subject

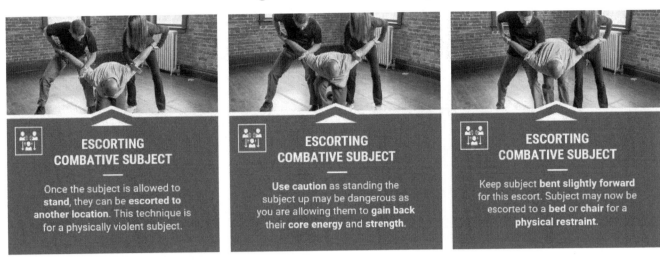

ESCORTING COMBATIVE SUBJECT

Once the subject is allowed to **stand**, they can be **escorted to another location**. This technique is for a physically violent subject.

ESCORTING COMBATIVE SUBJECT

Use caution as standing the subject up may be dangerous as you are allowing them to **gain back** their **core energy** and **strength**.

ESCORTING COMBATIVE SUBJECT

Keep subject **bent slightly forward** for this escort. Subject may now be escorted to a **bed** or **chair** for a **physical restraint**.

Escorting Combative Subject Technique

It is a technique that teaches an individual(s) how to escort a combative/violent subject.

Objective—Demonstrate how to escort a combative/violent subject using the combative subject escort technique (one or two individuals are needed).

Performance—Escorting Combative Subject Technique

1. From the kneeling position have the subject raise one knee.

2. You will need to have the subject raise their torso in order to get them to place one knee in front of them.

3. Ask the subject to then bring their other knee up and stand into a bent over position.

4. From this position (combative escort), you can direct subject to another location for a wall control technique, or to a bed for a supine restraint.

5. Use loud, repetitive defensive verbalizations (NO, STOP, STOP RESISTING, to direct the aggressor to stop resisting you.

Caution: Verbalization and constant control is the key to controlling a combative subject. Maintain your balance and be prepared to escape if needed.

Rear Arm Control Technique

Rear Arm Control Technique (part 1)

It is a technique that teaches an individual how to control a resistive subject from the escort technique. This technique is for a subject who displaying violent or self-destructive behavior towards themselves or others

Objective—Demonstrate how to control a resistive subject using the rear arm control technique from the hands-on escort position (one or two individuals are needed).

Performance—Rear Arm Control Technique (part 1)

1. From the hands-on escort position.

2. The subject becomes resistive by pushing their arm backward.

3. The individual moves with the resistance and repositions him/herself turning 90 degrees towards the aggressor.

4. The individual pulls the resistive subjects' arm into his/her core.

5. Use loud, repetitive defensive verbalizations (NO, STOP, STOP RESISTING, to direct the aggressor to stop resisting you.

Caution: Tuck your head into the shoulder of the aggressor. This will prevent the aggressor from striking you with a rear head butt.

Rear Arm Control Technique

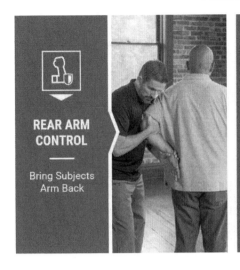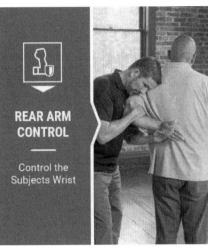

REAR ARM CONTROL

Bring Subjects Arm Back

REAR ARM CONTROL

Control the Subjects Wrist

REAR ARM CONTROL

Tuck Head to Avoid Headbutt

Rear Arm Control Technique (part 2)

It is a technique that teaches an individual how to control a resistive subject from the escort technique. This technique is for a subject who displaying violent or self-destructive behavior towards themselves or others

Objective—Demonstrate how to control a resistive subject using the rear arm control technique from the hands-on escort position (one or two individuals are needed).

Performance—Rear Arm Control Technique (part 2)

6. Continue to control the arm in your core by pulling it into you.

7. Reposition your hand on the wrist; bring your fingertips onto the resistive subject's knuckles.

8. Gently bring the subject's arm upward into their lower back as you bring the subject's fingertips towards you.

9. Use loud, repetitive defensive verbalizations (NO, STOP, STOP RESISTING, to direct the aggressor to stop resisting you.

From the rear arm control, you can:
  ▪ Escort the subject and/or handcuff the subject

Caution: Tuck your head into the shoulder of the resistive subject. This will prevent the subject from striking you with a rear head butt.

Wall Control Technique (Optional)

WALL CONTROL TECHNIQUE

While moving the subject with a hands-on escort the **wall control technique** may be a **reasonable control hold** for physical violence.

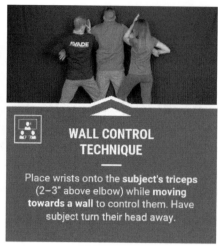

WALL CONTROL TECHNIQUE

Place wrists onto the **subject's triceps** (2–3" above elbow) while **moving towards a wall** to control them. Have subject turn their head away.

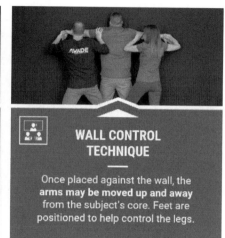

WALL CONTROL TECHNIQUE

Once placed against the wall, the **arms may be moved up and away** from the subject's core. Feet are positioned to help control the legs.

Wall Control Technique

It is a technique that teaches an individual how to decentralize and control a resistive subject and place them against a wall. This technique is for a subject who displaying violent or self-destructive behavior towards themselves or others

Objective—Demonstrate how to control a resistive subject using the wall control technique from the hands-on escort position (two individuals are needed).

Performance—Wall Control Technique

1. From the hands-on escort position.

2. The individuals will place their wrist onto the tricep of the subject (2 -3" above the elbow) while walking the subject towards a wall.

3. Continue to place the individual on the wall (have subject turn their head to the side) and position your feet closest to the subject on the inside of their feet.

4. Bring the subject's arms out to the side and continue to use your wrist or hands on the subject's triceps.

5. Use loud, repetitive defensive verbalizations (NO, STOP, STOP RESISTING, to direct the aggressor to stop resisting you.

Caution: Be aware of your environment and what direction you are moving the resistive subject towards.

Caution: The wall control position is a temporary position that may predispose the subject to breathing difficulties.

CONTINUOUSLY MONITOR THE SUBJECT AND SEEK MEDICAL ATTENTION IF NEEDED.

Child Control Technique (Optional)

Child Control Technique (part 1)

It is a technique that teaches staff how to temporarily control a child who is displaying violent or self-destructive behavior towards themselves or others.

Objective: Demonstrate how to approach, position, and safely control a child in this temporary position until they can regain control.

Performance—Child Control Technique (part 1)

1. Safely approach the child from behind and make initial contact on the child'selbows with your thumbs in an upward position.

2. Once initial contact is established, bring the child's elbows in front of their body.

3. Safely release your inner hand and place it on top of your outer hand, controlling both elbows.

Caution: Keep your head back and away from the child's head as they may toss their headaround and be able to head butt you.

Caution: Do not bend the child forward as this may make it difficult for the child to breathe.

Note: Continue to verbalize to the child while directing them to stop resisting/hurting themselves.

Child Control Technique (Optional)

Child Control Technique (part 2)

It is a technique that teaches staff how to temporarily control a child who is displaying violent or self-destructive behavior towards themselves or others.

Objective: Demonstrate how to approach, position, and safely control a child in this temporary position until they can regain control.

Performance—Child Control Technique (part 2)

4. Your outer hand will slide down to the child's wrist while your inner hand holds both elbows.

5. Your inner hand will now slide down to the remaining wrist of the child.

6. Bring the child's outer elbow under their inner elbow

7. Maintain position, stay aware and prepare to have the child go to a seated position if needed.

Caution: Keep your head back and away from the child's head as they may toss their headaround and be able to head butt you.

Caution: Do not bend the child forward as this may make it difficult for the child to breathe.

Note: Continue to verbalize to the child while directing them to stop resisting/hurting themselves.

Child Control Technique (Optional)

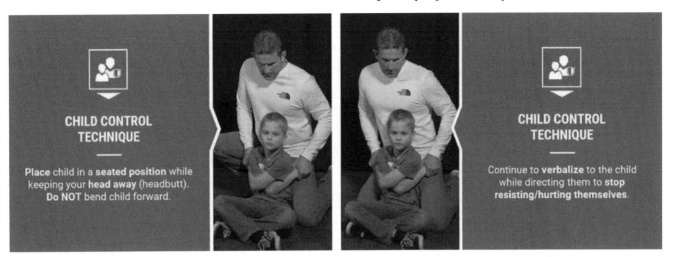

Child Control Technique (part 3)

It is a technique that teaches staff how to temporarily control a child who is displayingviolent or self-destructive behavior towards themselves or others.

Objective: Demonstrate how to position and safely control a child in this temporary position until they can regain control.

Performance—Child Control Technique (part 3)

8. To place the child in a seated position, you will need to drop down to one knee.

9. You will then bring your other knee down.

10. To further secure the child, you may need to bring your knees together to hold the child.

11. Maintain position, stay aware and prepare to disengage once the child has gained

    control.

Caution: Keep your head back and away from the child's head as they may toss their headaround and be able to head butt you.

Caution: Do not bend the child forward as this may make it difficult for the child to breathe.

Caution: Child control techniques are temporary! Disengage immediately once the child regains control.

Note: Continue to verbalize to the child while directing them to stop resisting/hurting themselves.

Module Five –Elements of Self-Defense/Use-of-Force

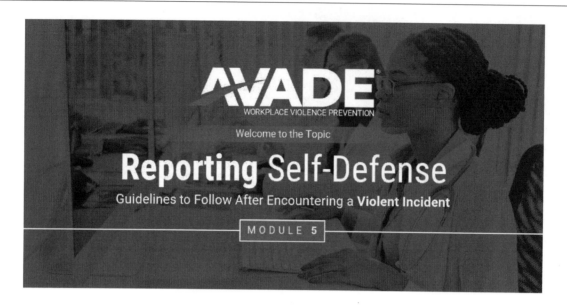

Post-Incident Response

- **Triage (Medical/Hazmat)**: Triage is the process of determining the priority of patients' or victims' treatments based on the severity of their condition. Initial first-aid treatment and protocols for hazardous materials and clean-up should be handled immediately.

- **Report to the Police, Security, Risk Management, Human Resources, etc.:** Follow standard operating procedures in reporting incidents.

- **Consider All Involved—staff, guests, visitors**, patients, or anyone who was witness to the incident should be treated accordingly for medical and stress debriefing.

- **Provide for Incident Debriefing:** Debriefing allows those involved with the incident to process the event and reflect on its impact. Depending on the situation, a thorough debriefing may need to take place. Even those not specifically involved in an incident may suffer emotional and psychological trauma.

- **Critical Incident Stress Debriefing (CISD):** is a specific technique designed to assist others in dealing with physical or psychological symptoms that are generally associated with critical incident trauma exposure. Research on the effectiveness of critical incident debriefing techniques has demonstrated that individuals who are provided critical stress debriefing within a 24- to 72-hour window after experiencing the critical incident have lower levels of short- and long-term crisis reactions and psychological trauma.

- **Employee Assistance Programs (EAP):** EAPs are intended to help employees deal with work or personal problems that might adversely impact their work performance, health, and well-being. EAPs generally include assessment, short-term counseling, and referral services for employees and their household members. Employee benefit programs offered by many employers, typically in conjunction with health insurance plans, provide for payment for EAPs.

- **Document Incident to Include Any Follow-Up Investigations:** Post-incident documentation is absolutely critical for reducing liability risk, preventing recurrences, and assisting in follow-up investigations.

- **Initiate Corrective Actions to Prevent Recurrences:** Preventing similar future incidents involves taking proactive corrective actions. Agency management, supervision, security, risk management, employee safety committees, the environment of care committee, etc., should initiate, track, and follow up on corrective actions.

Post-Incident Documentation

- **Who–What–Where–When–Why–How**
The first rule in post-incident documentation is the "who, what, where, when, why, and how" rule of reporting. After writing an incident narrative, double-check to see if you have included the first rule of reporting.

- **Witnesses (Who Was There?)**
Make sure to include anyone who was a witness to the incident. Staff, visitors, guests, and support services (police, fire, EMS, etc.) can be valuable witnesses should an incident be litigated.

- **Narrative Characteristics**
A proper narrative should describe in detail the characteristics of the violent offender/predator.

- **Before, During, and After**
A thorough incident report will describe what happened before, during, and after the incident. Details matter!

- **1st Person vs. 3rd Person**
The account of an incident can be described in the first person or the third person. This can be specific to your agency protocols or the preference of the person documenting the incident

- **Post-Follow-Up (Track and Trend)**
  Most agencies use electronic documentation, which allows for easy retrieval, tracking, and trending. Using technology assists agencies in following up and initiating proactive corrections.

- **Follow Standard Operating Procedures**
  Whether handwriting incident reports or using electronic documentation and charting, staff should consistently and thoroughly document all incidents relating to violence in the workplace.

Elements of Reporting Force

After any situation involving the defense of yourself or another person, proper documentation and reporting are crucial. The events of the assault or attempted assault should be reported to police/security. Police/security will document the incident and start an investigation. You should also document the account for your personal records. This can protect you in a possible legal situation that could arise out of using force to defend yourself. As you document your account of the incident, make sure to report to police/ security any details you missed during your initial report to them.

What type of force/self-defense/technique was used during the incident?
Be specific in your documentation regarding the type of control, defense, and force that was used during the incident.

How long did the incident and resistance last?
Important to note the length of the resistance, as this is a factor relative to exhaustion and increasing the level of force.

Was any de-escalation used?
Verbal and non-verbal de-escalation techniques should be noted.

Were you in fear of injury (bodily harm) to yourself, others, or the subject?
Fear is a distressing emotion aroused by a perceived threat, impending danger, evil, or pain.

If so, Why?
Fear is a basic survival mechanism occurring in response to a specific stimulus, such as pain or the threat of danger.

Explain thoroughly, and make sure to document completely.
The importance of documentation cannot be over-emphasized. Documentation ensures proper training standards are met, policies and procedures are understood, certification standards are met, liability and risk management are mitigated, and departmental and organizational requirements are maintained.

Special Note

Every person must take into consideration their moral, legal, and ethical beliefs, rights, and understandings when using any type of force to defend themselves or others.

Personal Safety Training Inc. makes no legal declaration, representation, or claim as to what force should be used or not used during a self-defense/assault incident or situation. Each trainee must take into consideration their ability, agency policies and procedures, and state and federal laws.

Civilian Levels of Defense

- **Awareness–Vigilance–Avoidance:** As we learned in modules 1-3, the best defense is to be aware, be vigilant, and avoid conflicts. The base of the chart is the most important aspect of defense.

- **Confident Presence:** Our presence can be a major deterrent to aggressive individuals and predators. Using confident postures, facial expressions, and eye communication show that we are not an easy target.

- **Interpersonal Communications Skills:** When faced with people who are stressed, angry, or intoxicated, your best initial defense is your ability to communicate.
  See Module 4.

- **Escape Options:** When faced with a situation that is escalating and dangerous, you should escape, if possible, to a safe location and alert others.

- **OC Pepper Spray:** Pepper sprays are a non-lethal force option that can distract the predator, giving you time to escape or defend.

- **Personal Defensive Techniques:** Include unarmed defenses using your body, hands, and feet as self-defense techniques for physically violent attacks on you or others.

- **Personal Defense Tools:** Non-lethal items that you can use to defend yourself. Examples: key chains, umbrellas, flashlights, rolled-up newspapers, etc.

- **Deadly Defense:** Defense against what you believe to be a serious injury and/or death by a person(s) using a deadly weapon or violently assaulting you.

Aggressive Subject and Staff Factors

Many factors may affect your selection of an appropriate level of use-of-force or self-defense. These factors should be articulated in your post-incident documentation.

Examples may include:

Age: In dealing with an aggressive subject who is agile, younger, faster, stronger, and has more stamina, an older staff person may have to use more force/control/defense. In contrast, a younger staff person would use less control/force/defense on an older person.

Size: In dealing with a larger aggressive subject, a smaller staff person may need to use more force/control/defense during the incident. A larger staff person would obviously, use less force/control/defense on an aggressive subject who is smaller.

Skill Level: Based on their skill level, it may be more difficult to control or defend against a subject who is skilled in mixed martial arts or an expert in karate. A staff person who is skilled in defensive tactics may only need to use a minimum of force (with proper technique) to control/defend against the subject. A staff person without current training and experience may need to use more force/defense to control or defend against the subject.

Relative Strength: The different body compositions of males and females may be a factor in controlling a member of the opposite gender. Females typically have less torso strength than their male counterparts. A male staff person may have to use less force to control a female subject, whereas a female staff person may need to use more force to control a male subject.

Multiple Aggressors: A staff person who is being physically attacked by multiple aggressors is at a disadvantage. Even a highly skilled staff person involved in defensive tactics is likely to be harmed in a situation such as this. In order to survive multiple aggressor attacks, higher levels of force may be necessary.

Every person must take into consideration their moral, legal, and ethical beliefs and rights and understandings when using any type of force to defend themselves or others. Personal Safety Training Inc. makes no legal declaration, representation or claim as to what force should be used or not used during a self-defense/assault incident or situation. Each individual must take into consideration their ability, agency policies and procedures and laws in their state and/or country.

Module Six –Healthcare Restraint Holds/Applications

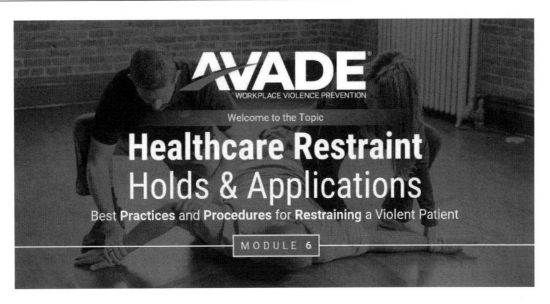

Use of Restraints

✓ Using **restraints** to **control violence** is **acceptable** in certain cases, but **clinical policy** & **procedures** must be **rigidly adhered to**

✓ **Restraint** use is very **controversial** & not always **understood** by staff. Acceptability of **restraint** use should be carefully **identified** & **approved** by **medical staff**

✓ Agencies should seek to **reduce** the use of physical **restraints** & therapeutic **holds** through **risk assessment** & **early intervention** with **less restrictive** measures

✓ **AVADE® Level III** Training aligns with the **Center for Medicaid Services** (CMS) COP § 482.13(e)(2) **Restraint** or **seclusion** may only be used when **less restrictive interventions** have been **determined** to be **ineffective** to **protect** the **patient**, a **staff member**, or **others** from **harm**.

✓ Any **intervention** other than **Verbal De-Escalation** should only be used when it *"is used for the management of violent or self-destructive behavior that jeopardizes the immediate physical safety of the patient, a staff member, or others,"* as defined by **CMS**.

Supine Holding Position

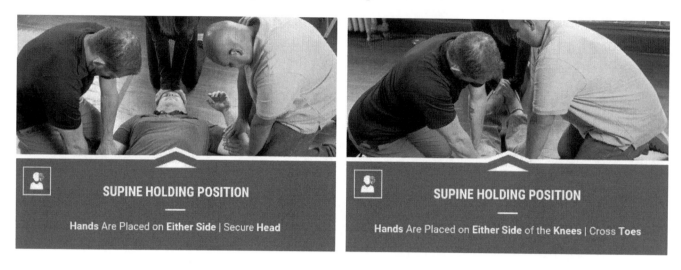

SUPINE HOLDING POSITION
—
Hands Are Placed on **Either Side** | Secure **Head**

SUPINE HOLDING POSITION
—
Hands Are Placed on **Either Side** of the **Knees** | Cross **Toes**

Supine Healthcare Restraint

The above pictures depict a 4pt healthcare holding position for a behavioral/violent person restraint application. This technique is for a subject who displaying violent or self-destructive behavior towards themselves or others

Objective—Demonstrate how to hold and apply healthcare restraints to a combative/violent individual.

Performance—Supine Restraint Hold/Application

1. Once staff (2 persons) have placed an individual on the bed, they (+ 2 other staff) will hold patient down on either side of the elbow and knee. Not on joint!

2. A 5th staff person can then apply restraints to the ankles and wrists.

3. Keeping one arm raised above the head reduces the individual's ability to use their core strength and resist.

4. A 6th person may be needed to control the individual's head (do not turn their head).

5. A 7th staff person may be needed to control the individual's feet until restraints can be applied (pigeon toe position).

Note: Restraints can be removed for a 3pt, 2pt, or even 1pt restraint. Follow your SOP's.

Always:

- Follow agency policies and procedures in regard to restraint and seclusion.
- Report and Document immediately.

Supine Restraint Position

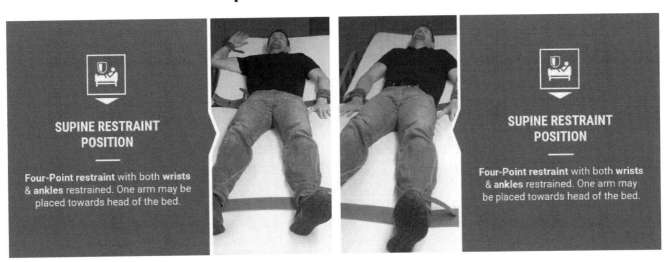

Supine Healthcare Restraint

The above pictures depict a 4pt healthcare restraint for a behavioral/violent person restraint application. This technique is for a subject who displaying violent or self-destructive behavior towards themselves or others

Objective—Demonstrate how to hold and apply healthcare restraints to a combative/violent individual.

Performance—Supine Restraint Hold/Application

1. Once staff (2 persons) have placed an individual on the bed, they (+ 2 other staff) will hold patient down on either side of the elbow and knee. Not on joint!

2. A 5th staff person can then apply restraints to the ankles and wrists.

3. Keeping one arm raised above the head reduces the individual's ability to use their core strength and resist.

4. A 6th person may be needed to control the individual's head (do not turn their head).

5. A 7th staff person may be needed to control the individual's feet until restraints can be applied (pigeon toe position).

Note: Restraints can be removed for a 3pt, 2pt, or even 1pt restraint. Follow your SOP's.

Always:

- Follow agency policies and procedures in regard to restraint and seclusion.
- Report and Document immediately.

Risk Factors for Restraints

1. **Patients who smoke**

2. **Positional Asphyxiation**

3. **Patients with deformities**

4. **Lack of continuous monitoring**

5. **Improper restraining Techniques**

6. **Incomplete medical assessment**

7. **Improper restraints, room, and beds**

8. **Insufficient staff orientation and training**

9. **Supine position may predispose them to aspiration**

10. **Prone may predispose them to suffocation**

Strategies for Reducing Risk

- Reduce the use of physical restraints and holds through risk assessments and early interventions.

- Clarification of restraint use in clinical protocols.

- See alternatives to restraint use (de-escalation techniques).

- Enhance staff orientation/education regarding alternatives and proper application.

- Develop structured procedures and competencies for consistent application of restraints.

- Develop safety guidelines and continuous observation of those restrained.

- The "one-hour" rule.

- Utilize patient, quiet rooms/seclusion rooms.

- Revise the staffing model.

- Increase awareness of medical/surgical vs. behavioral restraints.

- Comply with JCAHO and State/Federal Standards

- If the patient is restrained in the supine position, ensure that the patient's head is free to rotate and, when possible, that the head of the bed is elevated to minimize the risk of aspiration.

Strategies for Reducing Risk

- If the patient must be controlled in the prone position, ensure that the airway is unobstructed at all times (do not cover or bury the patient's face). Ensure that the patient can expand their lungs to properly breathe (do not put any pressure on their back).
  - Special caution is required for children, elderly patients, and very obese patients.

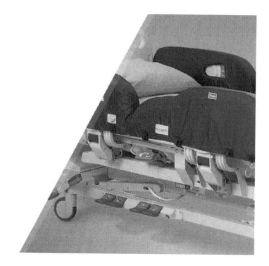

- Never place a towel, bag, or other covers over a patient's face.

- Do not restrain a patient in a bed with unprotected split side rails.

- Do not use certain types of restraints, such as high vests and waist restraints.

- Ensure the patient is properly searched and free of weapons and smoking materials.
  - This would also include limiting access from friends and family
  - Policy and Procedures should be adhered to for all Healthcare Restraint Applications/Holds.

Chemical Restraints (Emergency Medications)

A **chemical restraint** is a form of medical restraint in which a drug is used to restrict the freedom of movement of a patient, or in some cases, to sedate a patient. These are used in emergency, acute, and psychiatric settings to control aggressive patients who are interfering with their care or who are otherwise harmful to themselves or others.

Drugs that are often used as chemical restraints include benzodiazepines (such as Lorazepam (Ativan), Midazolam (Versed), or Diazepam (Valium). Haloperidol (Haldol) is a drug chemically unrelated to benzodiazepines and is also popular for chemical restraint, without the potentially dangerous side effects of benzodiazepine drugs.

Any use of chemical restraints must be authorized and administered by a licensed clinician or doctor.

Positional Asphyxia

Positional asphyxia is a form of asphyxia that occurs when someone's position prevents them from breathing adequately. A small but significant number of people die suddenly and without apparent reason during restraint by police, prison (corrections) officers, and health care staff. Positional asphyxia may be a factor in some of these deaths.

- Positional asphyxia is a potential danger of some physical restraint techniques.
- People may die from positional asphyxia by simply getting themselves into a breathing-restricted position they cannot get out of, either through carelessness or as a consequence of another accident.

Research has suggested that restraining a person in a face-down position is likely to cause greater restriction of breathing than restraining a person face up. Many law enforcement and health personnel are now taught to avoid restraining people face down or to do so only for a very short period of time.

Risk factors that may increase the chance of death include Obesity, Prior Cardiac or Respiratory Problems, Alcohol Intoxication, Illicit drugs such as cocaine, and Excited Delirium "Bizarre or Frenzied Behavior" (mental disease including psychosis and schizophrenia and/or drug intoxication).

Excited Delirium

Excited delirium is a controversial term used to explain the deaths of individuals in police custody, in which the person being arrested or restrained shows some combination of agitation, violent or bizarre behavior, insensitivity to pain, elevated body temperature, or increased strength. It has been listed as a cause of death by some medical examiners.

- The term has no formal medical recognition and is not recognized in the Diagnostic and Statistical Manual of Mental Disorders. There may also be a controversial link between "excited delirium" deaths and the use of Tasers to subdue agitated people.

- Almost all subjects who have died during restraint have engaged in extreme levels of physical resistance against the restraint for a prolonged period of time.

- Other issues in the way the subject is restrained can also increase the risk of death; for example, kneeling or otherwise placing weight on the subject and particularly any type of restraint hold around the subject's neck.

About the Author

David Fowler is the founder and president of (PSTI) Personal Safety Training Incorporated and AVADE® Training, located in Coeur d' Alene, ID. He is responsible for the overall management and operations of PSTI and AVADE®, which offers seminars, training, consulting, and protective details. Since 1990, David has been involved in security operations, training, and protective details.

He is the author of the SOCS® (Security Oriented Customer Service) program and training manual, as well as the AVADE® Personal Safety Training and Workplace Violence Prevention programs and training manuals. He is also the author of the book *Be Safe Not Sorry - The art and science of keeping YOU and your family safe from crime and violence*. David has worked with thousands of individuals and hundreds of agencies and corporations throughout the United States and Canada. His presentations have included international, national, and local seminars. David's thorough understanding of safety and security and martial science adds an exciting and interesting approach to his style of presentation.

David is a certified master instructor in several nationally recognized training programs such as Workplace Violence Prevention (AVADE®), Pepper Spray Defense™, Handcuffing Tactics™, Security Oriented Customer Service (SOCS®), Defensive Tactics System™ (DTS™), Defense Baton™, Security Incident Reporting System™ (SIRS™) and AVADE® Personal Safety Training. David has certified and trained thousands of individuals in these programs and others throughout the United States and abroad.

He is a graduate of (ESI) Executive Security International's Advanced Executive Protection Program and the Protective Intelligence and Investigations program. He is also a member of ASIS (American Society for Industrial Security), The International Law Enforcement Educators & Trainers Association (ILEETA), and the International Association of Healthcare Safety & Security (IAHSS).

David brings insight, experience, and a passion for empowering people and organizations utilizing the training programs and protective services that he offers here in the United States and in other countries. He is considered by many to be the most dynamic and motivational speaker and trainer in the security and personal safety industry.

David is happily married to the love of his life, Genelle Fowler. They live in Coeur d' Alene, ID, and have five children and two grandchildren. David and Genelle have committed their lives to serving others through the mission of safety. Both David and Genelle travel extensively, providing training and consulting to corporations throughout North America.

Appendix I

Bibliography, Reference Guide, and Recommended Reading

Adams, Terry, and Rob. *Seminar Production Business: Your Step by Step Guide to Success.* Entrepreneur Press, Canada 2003.

Albrecht, Steve. *Surviving Street Patrol: The Officer's Guide to Safe and Effective Policing.* Paladin Press, Boulder, CO 2001.

Amdur, Ellis. *Dueling with O-sensei: Grappling with the Myth of the Warrior Sage.* Edgework, Seattle, WA 2000.

Andersen, Peter A. *The Complete Idiot's Guide to Body Language.* Alpha Books, Indianapolis, IN 2004.

Andrews, Andy. *The Travelers Gift: Seven Decisions that Determine Personal Success.* Nelsen Books, Nashville, Tennessee, 2002.

Arapakis, Maria. *Soft Power: How to Speak Up, Set Limits, and Say No Without Losing Your Lover, Your Job, or Your Friends.* Warner Books Inc., NY, NY, 1990.

Artwhohl, Alexis & Christensen, Loren. *Deadly Force Encounters: What Cops need to know to mentally and physically prepare for and survive a gunfight.* Paladin Press, Boulder, CO 1997.

ASIS International. *Security Management Magazine.* www.securitymanagment.com, 2006-2016.

Branca, Andrew. The Law of SELF-DEFENSE: The indispensable Guide for the Armed Citizen. Law of Self Defense, Maynard, MA 2016

Brown, Tom. *Survival Guides: Americas Bestselling Wilderness Series.* Berkley Books, New York, 1984.

Byrnes, John D. *Before Conflict: Preventing Aggressive Behavior.* Scarecrow Press, Lanham, Maryland and Oxford 2002.

Canfield, Jack, and Switzer, Janet. *The Success Principles: How to Get from Where You Are to Where You Want to Be.* Harper Collins Publishers, NY, NY 2005.

Canfield, Jack and Bunch, Jim. *The Ultimate Life Workshop: 7 Strategies for Creating the Ultimate Life*. Live Workshop - February 2008.

Carnegie, Dale. *Golden Book*. www.dalecarnegie.com

Carnegie, Dale. *How to Win Friends & Influence People*. Pocket Books, NY, NY 1936.

Chodron, Thubten. *Working With Anger*. Snow Lion Publication, Ithaca, NY 2001.

Christenson, Loren. *DEFENSIVE TACTICS: Modern Arrest & Control Techniques for Today's Police Warrior*. Turtle Press, Washington, DC 2008

Christenson, Loren. *Fighting in the Clinch: Vicious Strikes, Street Wrestling, and Gouges for Real Fights*. Paladin Press, Boulder, CO 2009

Christensen, Loren. *The Way Alone: Your Path to Excellence in the Martial Arts*. Paladin Press, Boulder, CO 1987.

Christensen, Loren. *Warriors: On Living with Courage, Discipline, and Honor*. Paladin Press, Boulder, CO 2004.

Covey, Stephen R. *The 7 Habits of Highly Effective People: Powerful Lessons in Personal Change*. Fireside, NY, NY 1989.

Covey, Stephen R. *The 8th Habit: From Effectiveness to Greatness*. Better Life Media, DVD and CD, 2004.

Day Laura, *Practical Intuition*. Villard Books, NY, NY 1996

DeBecker, Gavin. *The Gift of Fear*. Dell Publishing, NY, NY 1997.

DeBecker, Gavin. *Fear Less: Real Truth about Risk, Safety, and Security in a Time of Terrorism*. Little Brown and Company, Boston, NY, London 2002.

DeBecker, Gavin & Taylor, Tom & Marquart, Jeff. *Just 2 Seconds: Using Time and Space to Defeat Assassins*. The Gavin DeBecker Center for the Study and Reduction of Violence, a not-for-profit foundation, Studio City, CA 2008.

DeBecker, Gavin. *Protecting the Gift: Keeping Children and Teenagers Safe (and Parents Sane)*. A Dell Trade Paperback, NY, NY 1999.

Deshimaru, Taisen. *The Zen Way to the Martial Arts: A Japanese Master Reveals the Secrets of the Samurai*. Penguin Compass. NY, NY, 1982.

DeMasco, Steve. *The Shaolin Way: 10 Modern Secrets of Survival from a Shaolin Kung Fu Grandmaster.* Harper, NY, NY 2006.

Divine, Mark. *The WAY of the SEAL: Think Like an Elite Warrior to Lead and Succeed.* Readers Digest, White Plains, NY 2013

Dyer, Wayne. *The Power of Intention; Learning to Co-Create your world your way.* Hay House, CA, 2004.

Eckman, Paul. *Emotions Revealed: Recognizing Faces and Feelings to Improve Communication and Emotional Life*: Henry Holt & Company, NY, NY, 2007.

Eckman, Paul. *Telling Lies.* WW. Norton Company, NY, and London. 1991.

Eggerichs, Emerson. *Love & Respect: The Love She Most Desires and The respect he Desperately Needs.* Gale Cengage Learning. US 2010

Fowler, David. *Be Safe Not Sorry, the Art and Science of keeping YOU and your family Safe from Crime and Violence.* Personal Safety Training, Inc. Coeur d Alene, ID 2011.

Fowler, David. *Violence In The Workplace: Education, Prevention & Mitigation.* Personal Safety Training, Inc. Coeur d Alene, ID 2012.

Fowler, David. *To Serve and Protect: Providing SERVICE while maintaining SAFETY in the Workplace.* Personal Safety Training, Inc. Coeur d Alene, ID 2015

Fowler, David. SURVIVE an Active Shooter: Awareness, Preparedness, and Response for EXTREME VIOLENCE. Personal Safety Training, Inc. Coeur d Alene, ID 2019

Funakoshi, Gichin. *Karate-Do My Way of Life.* Kodansha International, Tokyo, NY. London, 1975.

Funakoshi, Gichin. The Twenty Guiding Principles of Karate. Kodansha International, Tokyo, NY. London, 2012

Gallo, Carmine. *Inspire Your Audience: 7 Keys to Influential Presentations*. Paper. Communication Skills Coach – Author of Fire Them Up!

Gallups, Carl. Be Though Prepared: Equipping the Church for Persecution and Times of Trouble. WND Books. 2015

Gardner, Daniel. *The Science of Fear: How the Culture of Fear MANIPULATES YOUR BRAIN*. Penguin Books Ltd, Strand, London 2009

Garner, Bryan. *Black's Law Dictionary: Seventh Edition*. West Group, St. Paul, MN, 1999.

Gawain, Shakti. *Creative Visualization*. New World Library, Novato, CA, 2002.

Gawain, Shakti. *Developing Intuition: Practical Guide for Daily Life*. New World Library, Novato, CA, 2000.

Gilligan, James. *VIOLENCE: Reflections on a National Epidemic*. Vintage Books, NY 1996

Gladwell, Malcolm. *Blink*. Little, Brown & Company, NY 2005.

Glennon, Jim. *Arresting Communication: Essential Interaction Skills for Law Enforcement*. LifeLine Training & Caliber Press, Elmhurst, IL 2010.

Goleman, Daniel. *Emotional Intelligence*. Bantam Books, NY, NY 2005.

Gray, John. *Beyond Mars and Venus*. Better Life Media, DVD and CD, 2004.

Gregory, Hamilton. *Public Speaking for College and Career: Fifth Edition*. McGraw-Hill, Boston, 1999.

Gross, Linden. *Surviving A Stalker: Everything you need to know to keep yourself safe. Marlowe and Company,* NY, NY, 2000.

Grossman, Dave & Christensen, Loren. *On Combat: The Psychology of Deadly Conflict in War and Peace*. PPCT Research, IL, 2004.

Grossman, Dave & DeGaetano, Gloria. *Stop Teaching our Kids to Kill: A call to action against TV, Movie & Video Game Violence*. Crown Publishers, NY, NY 1999.

Harrell, Keith. *Attitude is Everything: 10 Life-Changing Steps to Turning Attitude Into Action*. Harper Collins Publishing, NY, NY 1999.

Hawkins, David R, MD. *Power vs. Force: The Hidden Determinants of Human Behavior*. Veritas, Sedona, AZ, 2004.

Headley, Steve. *Assault Prevention Workshop*. Assault Prevention Workshops, LLC, 2009.

Hyams, Joe. *Zen in the Martial Arts*. Bantam Books, Toronto, NY, London, Sydney, Auckland, 1982.

IAHSS. *Basic Training Manual and Study Guide for Healthcare Security Officers*. Lombard, IL, 1995.

IAHSS. *Journal of Healthcare Protection Management*. Bayside, NY 2008-2016.

Jo-Ellan Dimitrius, Ph.D., and Mark Mazzarella. *Reading People: How to Understand People and Predict their Behavior-Anytime, Anyplace*. Ballantine Books, NY, NY 1999.

Kane, Lawrence A. *Surviving Armed Assaults*. YMAA Publication Center, Boston, MA, 2006.

Kinnaird, Brian. *Use of Force: Expert Guidance for Decisive Force Response*. Looseleaf Law Publications, Flushing, NY 2003.

Krebs & Henry & Gabriele. *When Violence Erupts: A Survival Guide for Emergency Responders*. The C.V. Mosby Company, St. Louis, Baltimore, Philadelphia, Toronto, 1990.

Lamnier, Sandra. Workplace Violence: Before, During, and After. ASIS International 2003

Larkin, Tim, and Ranck-Buhr, Chris. *How to Survive The Most Critical 5 Seconds of Your Life.* The TFT Group. Sequim, WA 2008

Larkin, Tim. When Violence is the Answer: Learning how to do what it takes when your life is at stake. Little, Brown and Company, NY, NY 2017

Lawler, Jennifer. *Dojo Wisdom: 100 Simple Ways to Become a Stronger, Calmer, more Courageous Person*. Penguin Compass, NY, NY 2003.

Leaf, Caroline. *Switch on your Brain: The Key to Peak Happiness, Thinking, and Health*. Baker Books, Grand Rapids, MI 2013

Lee, Bruce. *Tao of Jeet Kune Do*. Ohara Publications, Santa Clarita, CA 1975.

Lee, Johnny. *Addressing Domestic Violence in the Workplace*. HRD Press, Inc. Amherst, MA 2005

Lee, Linda. *The Bruce Lee Story*. Ohara Publications, Santa Clarita, CA 1989.

Lion, John, MD. *Evaluation and Management of the Violent Patient: Guidelines in the Hospital and Institution*. Charles C. Thomas Publisher, Springfield, IL 1972.

Little, John. *The Warrior Within: The philosophies of Bruce Lee to better understand the world around you and achieve a rewarding life*. Contemporary Books, Chicago, IL 1996.

Loehr, James, and Migdwo, Jeffrey. Breathe In Breathe Out: Inhale Energy and Exhale Stress By Guiding and Controlling Your Breathing. Time-Life Books, Alexandria, VI 1986

Lorenz, Conrad. *On Aggression*. MJF Book. NY1963

Machowicz, Richard J. *Unleash The Warrior Within: Develop the Focus, Discipline, Confidence, and Courage You Need to Achieve Unlimited Goals.* Marlowe & Company, NY, 2002.

Mackay, Harvey. "Harvey Mackay's Column This Week." Weekly e-mail publication, www.harveymackay.com

MacYoung, Marc "Animal." *Ending Violence Quickly: How Bouncers, Bodyguards, and Other Security Professionals Handle Ugly Situations.* Paladin Press, Boulder, CO 1993.

Maggio, Rosalie. *How to Say It: Choice Words, Phrases, Sentences, and Paragraphs for Every Situation.* Prentice-Hall Press, NY, NY 2001.

Maltz, Maxwell, MD. *Psycho-Cybernetics: A New Way to Get More Living Out Of Life.* Essandress, NY, NY 1960.

Marcinko, Richard. *The Rogue Warriors Strategy For Success*. Pocket Books, NY, NY 1997.

Mason, Tom & Chandley Mark. *Managing Violence and Aggression: A Manual for Nurses and Health Care Workers.* Churchill Livingstone, Edinburgh, 1999.

McGrew, James. *Think Safe: Practical Measures to Increase Security at Home, at Work, and Throughout Life.* Cameo Publications, Hilton Head Island, SC, 2004.

McTaggart, Lynne. *The Intention Experiment: Using Your Thoughts to Change Your Life and the World.* Free Press, NY, NY 2007.

Medina, John. *Brain Rules: 12 Principles for Surviving and Thriving at Work, Home, and School.* Pear Press, Seattle, WA 2008.

Miller, Rory. *FACING VIOLENCE: Preparing for the Unexpected-Ethically, Emotionally, Physically, Without Going to Prison.* YMAA Publication Center, Wolfeboro, NH 2011

Miller, Rory. *Training For Sudden Violence. 72 Practical Drills*. Publication Center, Wolfeboro, NH 2016

Murphy, Joseph, Dr. *The Power of Your Subconscious Mind*. Bantam Books, NY, Toronto, London, Sidney, Auckland 2000.

Musashi, Miyamoto. Translated by Thomas Cleary. *The Book of Five Rings*. Shambala, Boston, and London 2003.

Norris, Chuck. *The Secret Power Within: Zen Solutions to Real Problems*. Broadway Books, NY 1996.

Norris, Chuck. *Winning Tournament Karate*. Ohara Publications, Burbank, CA 1975.

Nowicki, Ed. *Total Survival*. Performance Dimensions, Powers Lake, MI 1993.

Omartian, Stormie. *PRAYER WARRIOR: The Power of Praying Your Wat to Victory*. Harvest House Publishers, Eugene, OR 2013

Ouellette, Roland W. *Management of Aggressive Behavior*. Performance Dimension Publishing, Powers Lake, WI 1993.

Palumbo, Dennis. *The Secrets of Hakkoryu Jujutsu: Shodan Tactics*. Paladin Press Boulder, CO 1987.

Parker, S.L. *212, the extra degree*. The Walk the Talk Co. 2005 www.walkthetalk.com.

Patire, Tom. *Tom Patire's Personal Protection Handbook*. Three Rivers Press, NY 2003.

Peale, Norman Vincent. *Six Attitudes for Winners*. Tyndale House Publishers, Inc. Wheaton, Il, 1989.

Peale, Norman Vincent. *The Power of Positive Thinking*. Ballantine Books, NY, NY 1956.

Pease, Allan, and Barbara. *The Definitive Book of Body Language*. Bantam Dell. NY, NY, 2004.

Perkins, John & Ridenhour, Al & Kovsky Matt. *Attack Proof: The Ultimate Guide to Personal Protection*. Human Kinetics, Champaign, IL, 2000.

Pietsch, William. *HUMAN BE-ING: How to have a creative relationship instead of a power struggle*. Lawrence Hill & Company Publishers Inc, NY, NY 1974

PPCT Management Systems, Inc. *Defensive Tactics Instructor Manual.* PPCT 2005.

Purpura, Philip. *The Security Handbook: Second Edition.* Butterworth Heinemann, Boston, 2003.

Rail, Robert R. *The Unspoken Dialogue: Understanding Body Language and Controlling Interviews and Negotiations.* Varro Press, Kansas City 2001.

Ralston, Peter. *Cheng Hsin: The Principles of Effortless Power.* North Atlantic Books, Berkeley, CA 1989.

Ratey, John J. *Spark: The Revolutionary New Science of Exercise and the Brain.* Little, Brown and Co., NY, NY 2008.

Rawls, Neal. *BE ALERT BE AWARE HAVE A PLAN: The complete guide to protecting yourself, your home, your family.* Globe Pequot Press, Guilford, CT

Rodale Inc. *Men's Health Today, 2007.* Rodale Inc. US 2007.

Sandford, John, and Paula. *The Transformation of the Inner Man.* Bridge Publishing Inc. S. Plainfield, NJ 1982

Strong, Sanford. *Strong on Defense: Survival Rules to Protect You and Your Family from Crime.* Pocket Books, NY, NY 1996.

Sjodin, Terri. New Sales Speak: *The 9 Biggest Sales Presentation Mistakes and How to Avoid Them.* Better Life Media. DVD and CD 2004.

Soo, Chee, *The Chinese Art of T'ai Chi Ch'uan: The Taoist way to mental and physical health.* The Aquarian Press, Wellingborough, Northamptonshire 1984.

Staley, Charles. *The Science of Martial Arts Training.* Multi-Media Books, Burbank, CA 1999.

Tarani, Steve. Prefense The 90% Advantage: Preventing Bad Things from Happening to Good People. Tarani, US, 2014

The Evidence Bible, NKJV, Bridge-Logos Publishers- © 2011 by Ray Comfort. Alachua, FL.

The Results Driven Manager. *Dealing with Difficult People.* Harvard Business School Publishing Corp, Boston, MA 2005.

Theriault, Jean Yves. *Full Contact Karate.* Contemporary Books Inc., Chicago, 1983.

The World's Greatest Treasury of Health Secrets. Bottom Line Publications, Stamford, CT 2006.

Thompson, George. *Verbal Judo.* Quill William Morrow, NY 1993.

Tsunetomo, Yamamoto. *Hagakure: The Book of the Samurai.* Kodansha International, Tokyo, NY, London 1979.

Turner, James T. *Violence in the Medical Care Setting.* Aspen Systems Corporation, Rockville, MD 1984.

Tzu, Sun. *The Art of War.* Samuel Griffith Interpretation, Oxford University Press, 1993.

Ueshiba, Kisshomaru. *The Spirit of Aikido.* Kodansha International, Tokyo, NY, London, 1987.

Van Horne, Patrick, and Riley, Jason. *LEFT of BANG: How the Marine Corps' Combat Hunter Program Can Save Your Life.* Black Irish Entertainment LLC, NY and Los Angeles, 2014

US Dept. of Justice. *Workplace Violence: Issues in Response.* Critical Incident Response Group, National Center for the Analysis of Violent Crime, FBI Academy, Quantico, Virginia 2001.

Wallace, Bill. *The Ultimate Kick: The Wallace Method to Winning Karate.* Unique Publications, Burbank, CA, 1987.

Wagner, Pellegrini, Kanarek, Ryan, Janich, McCann. The Ultimate Guide to Reality-Based Self-Defense. Black Belt Books, South Korea 2010

Webster, Noah. *Webster's Dictionary.* Modern Promotions/Publishers, NY, NY 1984.

Willis, Brian. *W.I.N. 2: Insights Into Training and Leading Warriors.* Warrior Spirit Books, Calgary, Alberta, Canada 2009.

Websites and Weblinks

http://www.AVADEtraining.com

http://www.personalsafetytraining.com

http://www.socstraining.com
http://www.tribalsecuritytraining.com

http://www.wpvprevention.com

http://www.aaets.org/article54.htm

http://en.wikipedia.org/wiki/Excited_delirium

http://en.wikipedia.org/wiki/Chemical_restraint

http://en.wikipedia.org/wiki/Positional_asphyxia
http://www.aele.org/law/2008ALL12/chicago.pdf

http://www.hospitalmedicine.org/AM/Template.cfm?Section=Reference_Material&Template=
/CM/ContentDisplay.cfm&ContentID=17070

Workplace Violence: http://cms.nursingworld.org/workplaceviolence

http://helpguide.org/mental/eq4_emotion_communicates.htm

http://hawaii.gov/ag/cpja/quicklinks/workplace_violence/WVfull.pdf

http://www.ena.org/media/PressReleases/Pages/WorkPlaceViolence.aspx

http://www.jointcommission.org/SentinelEvents/SentinelEventAlert/sea_40.htm

http://www.dli.mn.gov/Wsc/PDF/WorkplaceViolencePreventionGuide.pdf

http://www.cbs.state.or.us/external/osha/pdf/workshops/702w.pdf

http://blog.awareity.com/2010/03/04/identifying-red-flags-warning-signs-and-indicators/

http://www.co.midland.tx.us/edp/pdf_files/Misc/Workplace%20-%20Violence.pdf

http://sk.sagepub.com/reference/crimepunishment/n419.xml

http://www.cdc.gov/violenceprevention/pdf/nisvs-fact-sheet-2014.pdf

http://changingminds.org/techniques/body/parts_body_language/eyes_body_language.htm

http://www.phoenixhouse.org/prevention/signs-and-symptoms-of-substance-abuse/

AVADE® WPV PREVENTION
NOTEPAD

AVADE® WPV PREVENTION
NOTEPAD

Education, Prevention, and Mitigation for *Violence in the Workplace*

© Personal Safety Training Inc. | AVADE® Training

AVADE® TRAINING COURSES
FOR YOU & YOUR AGENCY

> ## Personal Safety Training Inc. | AVADE® Training Programs

The only way to deal with conflict and avoid violence of any type is through *awareness, vigilance, avoidance, defensive training, and escape planning*.

David Fowler, President of Personal Safety Training Inc., specializes in nationally recognized training programs that *empower individuals, increase confidence, and promote pro-active preventative solutions*.

OSHA, Labor & Industries, Joint Commission, State WPV Laws, and the Department of Health all recognize that programs like PSTI's are *excellent preventive measures to reduce crime, violence, and aggression in the workplace*.

Personal Safety Training Inc. is committed to providing the finest level of training and service to you and your employees. Whether you are an individual or represent an agency, we have the Basic and Instructor Course Certifications that you need.

> ## PSTI | AVADE® Offers Multiple Training Options for Your Organization:

☑ **On-Site Training (We will come to you!)**
No need to send staff away for training. PSTI will come to your place of business and train your staff.

☑ **Train-the-Trainer (Instructor Seminars)**
The most cost-effective way to implement PSTI Training courses for your organization. We can come to you for instructor courses or you can send staff to one of our upcoming seminars.

☑ **Combo Classes**
Combination classes are where Basic Training and Instructor Training are combined during on-site training. It is a great way to introduce PSTI Training with our initial instruction and then continue on with your own instructors.

☑ **E-Learning**
Are you looking for a training solution to integrate a Workplace Violence Prevention Program in order to meet compliance standards for both State and Federal guidelines? The AVADE® E-Learning programs offer a great solution to give your staff an introductory yet comprehensive training program that can be completed as needed.

☑ **Course Duration Options**
PSTI offers multiple options and course durations from introductory to advanced training. Course lengths range from: 2-hr. Introductory Courses, 1/2 Day Training Sessions, 1-Day Classes, 2-Day Classes, and Train the Trainer (Instructor Classes)

CONTACT US TODAY!
Personal Safety Training Inc. | AVADE® Training
P.O. Box 2957 Coeur d'Alene, ID 83816
Phone: 208-664-5551 | Fax: 208-664-5556 | Email: info@personalsafetytraining.com
personalsafetytraining.com | avadetraining.com

Education, Prevention, and Mitigation for *Violence in the Workplace*

© Personal Safety Training Inc. | AVADE® Training

AVADE® TRAINING COURSES
FOR YOU & YOUR AGENCY

> **Training Courses**

AVADE® Training Courses

☑ **AVADE® Workplace Violence Prevention | avadetraining.com**
The AVADE® WPV Training is offered as a Basic and Instructor level course for private corporations, healthcare, security, and agencies wanting to educate, prevent, and mitigate the risk of violence to their employees.

☑ **AVADE® De-Escalation | avadedeescalation.com**
When individuals are in crisis, you are either escalting or de-escalating them. The AVADE® De-Escalation Training is designed to educate, prevent, and mitigate the risk of escalation, aggression, and violence in the workplace.

☑ **AVADE® Active Shooter | avadeactiveshooter.com**
The AVADE® Active Shooter Training is designed to increase awareness, preparedness, and response to extreme violence. The philosophy of education, prevention, and mitigation is the cornerstone of this training program.

☑ **AVADE® Home Health Care | avadehomehealthcare.com**
The AVADE® Home Health Care Training program is designed to educate, prevent, and mitigate aggression and violence for workers in the Home Health Care and Hospice industry.

☑ **AVADE® DTS™ (Defensive Tactics System) | dts-training.com**
The AVADE® DTS™ Training program covers basic defensive tactics, control techniques, and defensive interventions. This course includes stance, movement, escort techniques, takedowns, defensive blocking, active defense skills, weapon retention, handcuffing, post-incident response and documentation, and more.

☑ **AVADE® HDTS™ (Healthcare Defensive Tactics System) | hdts-training.com**
The AVADE® HDTS™ Training program for healthcare covers basic defensive tactics, control techniques, and defensive interventions. This course includes stance, movement, escort techniques, takedowns, team intervention, defensive blocking, active defense skills, weapon retention, patient restraint techniques, handcuffing, post-incident response and documentation, and more.

☑ **AVADE® Handcuffing Tactics™ | handcuffingtactics.com**
Training in the use of plastic, chain, or hinged handcuffs. standing, kneeling, and prone handcuffing techniques are covered. In this training course you will also learn defensive tactics fundamentals, proper positioning, nomenclature, risk factors, and post-incident response and documentation.

☑ **AVADE® Defense Baton™ | defensebaton.com**
Training in the use of an expandable bat, straight stick, or riot control baton. Techniques and topics in this training include: vulnerable areas of the body, stance, movement, blocks, control holds, counter techniques, draws, and retention techniques.

☑ **AVADE® Pepper Spray Defense™ | pepperspraydefense-training.com**
Tactical and practical concepts of when and how to use pepper spray in a variety of environmental situations. Aerosol pepper is a great less-than-lethal control and defense option for agencies that encounter violence and aggression.

Education, Prevention, and Mitigation for *Violence in the Workplace*

AVADE® TRAINING COURSES
FOR YOU & YOUR AGENCY

☑ **AVADE® SIRS™ (Safety Incident Reporting System) | sirs-training.com**
The AVADE® SIRS™ Training program teaches staff how to effectively and intelligenty write safety incident reports. Documentation of safety incidents is absolutely cirtical to your agency's ability to track and trend, reduce liability, and share vital information. If you're like most agencies, you know that proper, structured, effective, and reliable reports save time, money, and allow you to track incidents and reduce liability risk.

SOCS® Training Course

☑ **SOCS® (Safety Oriented Customer Service) | socstraining.com**
SOCS® Training teaches staff how to identify and provide great customer service while maintaining safety in the workplace. The core concept of the training is to be able to provide excellent service without having to think about it. Creating habits, skills and taking action, for exceptional customer service is the goal of the SOCS® Training program.

Safety Training Books

☑ **AVADE® Personal Safety Training**
Buy the ultimate book and training on how to keep you and your family safe. This training guide is designed to increase your overall safety in all environments. The curriculum is based on David Fowler's book, Be Safe Not Sorry-The Art and Science of Keeping You and Your Family Safe From Crime and Violence.

☑ **AVADE® Violence in the Workplace (Versions I, II, & III)**
Purchase the book on how to be safe in the workplace. This text is based on the AVADE® Training program. Can't come to a class, at least get the book! The knowledge contained in these pages will teach you awareness, vigilance, avoidance, defensive interventions, and escape strategies for your place of business.

▸ AVADE® Training Programs Serves Multiple Industries

Industries: Healthcare | Corporate | Security | Gaming | Churches

HEALTHCARE

CORPORATE

SECURITY

GAMING

CHURCHES

Education, Prevention, and Mitigation for *Violence in the Workplace*

© Personal Safety Training Inc. | AVADE® Training

AVADE® TRAINING COURSES
FOR YOU & YOUR AGENCY

▶ PSTI Training Products

Training Products: Instructor Manuals | Student Guides | Training Weapons

CORPORATE BASIC
DAVID FOWLER

CORPORATE ADVANCED
DAVID FOWLER

HEALTHCARE BASIC
DAVID FOWLER

HEALTHCARE ADVANCED
DAVID FOWLER

DE-ESCALATION
DAVID FOWLER

ACTIVE SHOOTER TRAINING
DAVID FOWLER

DEFENSIVE TACTICS SYSTEM
DAVID FOWLER

HEALTHCARE DEFENSIVE TACTICS SYSTEM
DAVID FOWLER

HANDCUFFING TACTICS
DAVID FOWLER

DEFENSE BATON
DAVID FOWLER

PEPPER SPRAY DEFENSE
DAVID FOWLER

SAFETY INCIDENT REPORTING SYSTEM
DAVID FOWLER

VISIT **PERSONALSAFETYTRAINING.COM** OR
CONTACT US AT **1-866-773-7763** TO LEARN MORE!

Education, Prevention, and Mitigation for *Violence in the Workplace*

© Personal Safety Training Inc. | AVADE® Training

NOTES

Made in the USA
Middletown, DE
28 May 2023

31516012R10150